The Master Musicians Series

DVOŘÁK

SERIES EDITED BY

SIR JACK WESTRUP,
M.A., Hon. D.Mus.(Oxon.), F.R.C.O.

THE MASTER MUSICIANS SERIES

DVOŘÁK

by

ALEC ROBERTSON

With eight pages of plates
and music examples in the text

LONDON
J. M. DENT AND SONS LTD

FOR MY FRIEND
IAN WESTMACOTT

SBN: 460 03116 3

FOREWORD

SINCE this book was begun two others on the same subject have appeared: *Anton Dvořák*, by Paul Stefan, and *Antonín Dvořák*, edited by Viktor Fischl. The first of these is an amplification, for the American public, of the Stefan-Šourek volume published in Germany. Shockingly translated, full of misprints and minor inaccuracies, old-fashioned in its critical method, it is yet useful as a work of reference, as all Dvořák's compositions are alluded to in chronological order. The other book, a symposium by various writers, contains two chapters to which I owe a special debt: Gerald Abraham's brilliant essay on Dvořák's musical personality, and Julius Harrison's authoritative discussion of Dvořák's orchestra and his symphonic expression. Frank Howes's chapter on 'The National and Folk Elements' is also of great interest.

This little book cannot pretend to such scholarship. It is meant to be a popular and, I trust, readable account of Dvořák's life and a critical coverage of his whole output. To achieve this last aim has, in these days, called for the skill of a detective.

I have to thank Mr. B. de Nevers of Messrs. Lengnick and Mr. R. H. Gibson of Messrs. Chester, both publishers of Dvořák's music, for their kindness in letting me examine little-known works, and I must also thank Mr. Harry Weil for help with the earlier chapters of the book, and Dr. Joseph Löwenbach for much assistance.

LONDON,   A. R.
    September 1943.

I SHOULD like to express my gratitude to Dr. John Clapham for his valuable help in enabling me to make the majority of the corrections in this revised edition. It had not been possible to include the knowledge I have since gained of the early four symphonies, all of which are now published and recorded.

    1964.   A. R.

v

CONTENTS

CONTENTS

ILLUSTRATIONS

CHAPTER I

As a nation we cannot be said to excel in geography. We have been, perhaps we still are, indefensibly vague as to the whereabouts of the different parts of the British Empire. We think, many of us, of the journey from Australia to New Zealand almost as if it were the pleasant crossing from Southsea to the Isle of Wight. And we wonder much at the exasperated corrections of our cousins from those dominions.

If, then, our minds are in some confusion about the British Empire, it is small wonder that Dvořák's Bohemia suggests, to those of us who have not been fortunate enough to visit it, and to whom maps are a bore, a transferable region, Chelsea, it may be, or Montparnasse; and bohemianism a code of manners—or lack of them—best exhibited in Puccini's most popular opera rather than in Smetana's *Bartered Bride*.

If this book were about one of the contemplative composers such geographical and social vagueness would not greatly matter, but in the case of an avowedly nationalist composer such as Dvořák, and one, moreover, whose sources of inspiration were primarily visual and aural, rather than intellectual, it is important to have some understanding and some mental picture of his country.

It will not, fortunately for the author, be necessary to give a summary of the history of a country situated in that part of the Continent ominously known as 'the Cockpit of Europe'; but those who do wish to read about it may like to know of Dr. Kamil Krofta's excellent *Short History of Czechoslovakia*, in which the Professor of History at the Charles University of Prague assembles his tangled mass of facts in a masterly manner.

I have selected from his book, and other sources, such facts as can really be regarded, I hope, as sketching in a sufficient background for the central figure of this study. That background is made up of assorted 'shots' of history, something of musical conditions about a century before and up to Dvořák's birth, and a word about the

I

beginnings of the Nationalist movement, with special reference to the great Czech painter, Josef Mánes, whose ideals are closely allied to those of Smetana and Dvořák.

The ancient kingdom of Bohemia was the most powerful and glorious in Europe for many centuries, and its position, with frontiers continually enlarging or contracting, shows clearly enough why its history has been so troubled. North-west, west and south, it had Germanic peoples for neighbours; north-east there were the Poles; east there were the Slovaks (in the part called North Hungary until 1918). From these surrounding peoples, from, as we should say to-day, Germany, Austria, Poland and Hungary, came constant infiltration and encroachment, hostile or friendly, and in the midst of them the Czechs stubbornly and optimistically struggled, as they always have done, to keep their national identity, to follow out their national aspirations, to secure freedom.

Needless to say the most enthusiastic 'tourists' into Bohemia were the Germans. There is a familiar sound about German merchants settling, like a swarm of ants, round Prague Castle between 1061 and 1092. And during the same period German monks poured into the Cistercian and Premonstratensian monasteries of the country, German clergy became bishops, German *Hochgeborene* married into court circles.

It would be foolish to deny that these 'tourists' conferred many benefits on Bohemia in the matters of art, industry and agriculture, but, of course, they only did so at the price of retarding Czech progress and self-determination.

One monarch, Charles IV, son of John of Luxemburg, who reigned from 1346 to 1378, stands out in the long line of foreign rulers as having paid real regard to the internal welfare of his kingdom. Under this emperor of Germany and founder of the Austro-Hungarian empire Bohemia achieved its greatest glory. Prague had, for some time, the only university in central Europe (founded in 1348), and Czech painting and literature, as well as the plastic arts, went forward at this time with real independence. As Sir Henry Hadow says in his study of Dvořák:

Up to the Thirty Years War Bohemia maintained an honourable place in the forefront of European civilization. She was printing books when hardly any of her neighbours could read them; she inaugurated one of the greatest religious movements of the Middle Ages; her university took rank with Paris and Oxford; her teaching was accepted by scholars from every corner of Christendom.

But this happy state of affairs did not survive under Charles's successor Václav, and it vanished in the Hussite period, when Bohemia was plunged into the midst of religious dissensions.

It is clear from the respect now paid to the memory of John Huss [1] by both Catholic and Protestant Czechs that he is regarded much more as a national hero than as a religious reformer. He was, Dr. Krofta tells us:

the leading Czech professor at the university, the author of large and important religious works in both Czech and Latin, and a reformer of Czech orthography, who greatly improved the Czech literary language and cultivated the popular Czech hymn.

As a practising Catholic Dvořák could hardly approve of Huss's dispute with Rome, and his followers' insistence on Communion in both kinds—which was the rallying point of the dispute—but as a tribute to a man who, to the point of martyrdom, 'contributed largely to a powerful growth of the Czech national sentiment and consciousness' he could and did, with a clear conscience, project a dramatic trilogy on the subject of Huss, though he composed only the prelude to it, the *Hussite Overture*.

It would be both tedious to the reader and irrelevant to sort out here the ramifications of the Hussite movement, but in leaving it one must record a word of admiration for the south Bohemian peasant, the great Hussite Petr Chelčický (died *circa* 1460). He demanded the abolition not only of all church but of all secular institutions inconsistent with the law of God. Not much would have been left then, or now! This fiery individual would undoubtedly have included the constantly encroaching Germans in his manifesto as

[1] John Huss (*c.* 1373–1415), a precursor of Martin Luther, and an admirer of Wycliffe, preached against ecclesiastical greed and forged miracles, and disputed the primacy of Peter. He was, after trial, handed over to the secular arm and burnt at the stake.

thoroughly ungodly and, more than all, the house of Hapsburg, which, with the accession of Ferdinand I (1526–64), was now to hold power in Bohemia for almost four centuries.

Another most important historical event, commemorated by Dvořák in a choral work, *The Heirs of the White Mountain*, was the failure of the Czech revolt against the Hapsburg dynasty at the battle of the White Mountain (8th November 1620). This victory over the Czechs gained by Ferdinand II (1620–37) led to the worst kind of religious intolerance. 'Better a desert,' he said, 'than a land full of heretics.' He proved as bad as his word. Those who were unwilling to become Catholics were to be forcibly persuaded or banished, but—and this, as we shall see, was of the greatest importance to the national music—the peasants were bound to the land and were not allowed to emigrate.

The German tongue was now theoretically put on equal terms with the Czech language, but in fact German soon became, and for long remained, exclusively the official tongue. (As late as the first half of the nineteenth century J. Dobrovský, the great founder of Slavonic studies, was writing, ironically enough, in German.)

In spite of all national losses the saving factor for the future of Czech music was that the country people remained obstinately Czech, and thus kept in their hands a torch from which Smetana and, after him, Dvořák, would light fires that the whole civilized world could see. And, again, in spite of the extinction of speci-fically Czech intellectual and artistic life, the period after the battle of the White Mountain witnessed a flowering of Italianate baroque art—which was not without influence on Dvořák—and, according to Dr. Krofta, there was also 'the expansion and improvement of music, ecclesiastic and secular.'

We must now look at musical conditions in eighteenth-century Bohemia, the century which proved to be the period of national awakening. Burney, in the journal of his continental travels, writing in 1772, gives a revealing glimpse of the inherent musicality of the Czechs, whom he calls 'the most musical people of Germany or, perhaps, of all Europe.' He notes that in every large town but Prague, and in all the villages, children of both sexes are taught music in the schools. At Čáslav, south of Kolín, he observed children,

from six to eleven, being taught the violin, oboe and bassoon, while
little boys were industriously practising on four clavichords owned
by the schoolmaster. This was, in what we should call to-day the
primary schools, a remarkable state of affairs even though the music
these infants were 'industriously practising' was, presumably, mainly
of foreign origin. (It is a pity that Burney did not enlighten us on
this point.)

The good doctor is puzzled at the lack of any great musicians
amidst this musical plenty and decides, quite justly, that with no
encouragement to pursue the art in riper years the Czechs 'seldom
advanced further than to qualify themselves for the street or servitude.'
(This argument was doubtless much used by Dvořák *père* to Dvořák
fils when the latter proposed to forsake butchery for music.)

The itinerant Bohemian musician, who made his most recent
operatic appearance in Weinberger's *Švanda the Bagpiper,* has received
praise not only from Burney, but from Spontini, Wagner and Berlioz.
In his person is summed up the innately musical nature of the
Czechs. Burney, supping at an inn at Prague, was serenaded with
'very delightful minuets and polonaises' played on harp, violin and
horn—a somewhat odd instrumental combination. Spontini's ears
were agreeably assailed, at six o'clock in the evening, by delicious
and ravishing sounds, the mellow and tuneful melodies of Mozart,
Haydn, Beethoven, Gluck, Cherubini, Méhul, Weber, Spohr, etc.
(an abundant repertory!), that a small number of obscure and humble
Bohemian artists—artists for three summer months, artisans and
workers in their villages for the rest of the year—played on the promenade with, as he relates,

a rare exactitude of instinct, of intonation, of rhythm, of movement,
of intention, and of justness in light and shade, in short, with a sentiment
calculated to make me feel, not only astonishment, but the sweetest sen-
sations! . . . here is the true art of nature, and the pure nature of art, which
once upon a time produced the truly great masters.[1]

Wagner, in his *Visit to Beethoven*, records a similar impression.
This time it was a small travelling orchestra he encountered, made
up of a violin, bass, clarinet, two horns, a harpist and two female

[1] *Smetana*, by Julian Tiersot.

singers with excellent voices. The repertory consisted of dances and ballads—were these true folksongs?—and, amongst other things, the Beethoven Septet. Berlioz agrees with Burney that the Bohemians are, in general, the best musicians in Europe and finds a love of music in all classes of society.

There was the 'street' for these wandering musicians, or there was service in the families of the nobility. These families, amongst whom were such well-known names as Černín, Lobkowitz and Schwarzenberg, saw to it that their servants could wield a violin or blow a flute as well as dust or cook; and so they were able to form and maintain orchestras, with notable economy, in their town houses or on their country estates.

Those musicians, however, who objected to combining musical and domestic science, and who were averse to the wandering life of the *Musikant*, had no choice but to go abroad to develop their often considerable talents and to earn their living.

Edward Holmes—whose delightful *Ramble among the Musicians of Germany by a Musical Professor* deserves to be reprinted—writing in 1828, noted, after a heartfelt tribute to the iced beer of Prague, that the Bohemians acquired a greater skill in instrumental music than any other class of Germans (!) 'from their firmness of purpose and desire for the best.' It was these qualities that secured their artistic future in exile. Gluck, who had been compelled to lead the life of a *Musikant* in the villages round Prague in order to pay for his studies, had remarked on the same thing when a pupil of the famous Franciscan father, Bohuslav Černohorsky. And Gluck, who seems to have been of pure Bohemian extraction, is a good example of a first-rate talent escaping from impossible conditions. He became completely cosmopolitan, and is reported to have said: 'I wish to abolish the idiotic distinction between the music of one nation and another,' a remark which would deeply have angered Smetana.

Those Bohemian musicians who sought their fortune abroad proved themselves well able to hold their own with most of their contemporaries. Mysliveček (1737–81), composer of Italian operas, nicknamed for greater ease 'il Boemo divino' by the impressionable Neapolitans, in Naples; Gassmann, court composer to Joseph I, in Vienna; and Jan Zach, the only one 'to reflect something of Czech nationalism' in his music, all did good work, the last two especially in chamber music; and a concert of Mozart's Czech predecessors and contemporaries given at the Prague Conservatory in the autumn of 1926 brought to light at least one fine work, a cello Concerto by Vranický.

Rosa Newmarch, from whose account of Czechoslovakian chamber music I have drawn these facts, tells us that the music for this concert came from the Lobkowitz library at Roudnice, 'which is rich in forgotten eighteenth-century music.' It was this family that owned the village where Dvořák was born and the castle dominating it.

A famous Czech name in musical history is that of Johann Wenzel Anton Stamitz (1717–57), founder of the Mannheim school of symphonic composition; and in the realm of virtuosi there is the celebrated pianist and composer, Dussek (1761–1812), who wandered about all over Europe, but seldom visited his own country. In Prague the great pianist and teacher—and the much less great com-poser—Tomášek (1774–1850), upon whom Beethoven's playing made an unforgettable impression, was an outstanding figure. He was, like so many other Czech musicians, attached to a noble house-hold, that of Count Bucquor von Longueval, but his house became a centre of musical life in Prague.

The most significant figure, for the future of Czech as opposed to Bohemian music, was Škroup (1801–62). This man was a lawyer by profession and an amateur singer and conductor in his spare time. By sheer industry he worked himself up to professional status, becoming conductor of the State Theatre Opera House in 1827, the first Czech to hold a post filled not many years before by Weber.

The success of a German opera based on *The Swiss Family,* but given in the Czech language, led the promoters of the scheme to commission a wholly Czech opera from Škroup. This opera, called *The Tinker,* was produced with enormous success in 1826. Its chief claim to fame is the fact of its being the first native opera ever staged in Bohemia, for the music itself is said to be 'bright, fluent and un-inspired,' with only a superficial use of the folk element. It may have been nationalistic rather than national, but still, there it was, a rather feeble infant which survived to hand on the succession, forty years later, to Smetana's *Brandenburgers in Bohemia.*

Anything of an epic character was quite outside Škroup's range, and the heroic theme of Libuša, which he attempted, had to wait for Smetana's great opera on the subject. But Škroup did provide the Czechs with many folksongs, including a patriotic hymn, *Where is my Fatherland?* which became famous.

At the start of the nineteenth century, which I have just anticipated, the outlook for a truly national art of any kind seemed very poor. There were, for reasons we have seen, no masters, no commissions. German influences seemed to have obliterated the links with the glorious past, and no one yet seriously thought of searching for those links in the country places that lay all round them. There was only provincial dilettantism; all interest in the history of art had faded, and such production as there was had become mere hack-work.

Then to art and music and literature came the powerful intellectual and spiritual movement known as Romanticism, which was to put flesh and blood on the skeleton of Czech creative art.

The effect of it in Prague has been well described by Antonín Matějček in his chapter on painting in *Modern and Contemporary Czech Art*:

At Prague itself the tide of Romanticism was beginning to sweep through the whole realm of thought, and emotion and the lofty ideas of race and nationality which had already provoked fiery outbursts in Czech literature were gradually finding expression in the arts as well.

By 1848, even if it witnessed political collapse, the Nationalist idea was in full swing throughout every domain of intellectual life. In short, the stage was set for the appearance of a powerful personality, firmly resolved to dispel all the doubts and hesitations that hampered Czech art, revealing new sources of poetic inspiration, bringing art once more into touch with the race and nation, and furnishing to those who came after him a potent example of artistic courage and sincerity.

The allusion is to the great Czech painter, Josef Mánes; but it might almost equally serve as one to Smetana (1824–84), who in that very year of revolutions, 1848, had left the service of Count Thun to devote himself to the cause of national freedom.

In the Thun country estates of north-east Bohemia Smetana had seen with delight the varied landscapes and rural customs which he afterwards so lovingly painted in *Má Vlast* and elsewhere.

DVOŘÁK'S BIRTHPLACE AT NELAHOZEVES

Again, what Matějček writes of the essentials of Mánes's art might as well be written of Smetana:

He was the first modern Czech to seek the well-springs of emotion in immediate reality, to counter the lifeless convention of his day with an ardent, almost religious fidelity to man and nature, to substitute the creative impulse for the arid labour of academic permutations and combinations.

Thus Mánes and Smetana turned romantic art in Bohemia away from German sources of inspiration, and the painter Adolf Kosárek and Dvořák in their turn carried on the good work. Might not this description of Kosárek's art be written of Dvořák's maturity?

He now felt convinced that, impressionable as he was, his eye would find something to delight it at every step he took, and that he had merely to look around him, in the Bohemian countryside, in order to possess all the material that a Czech landscape painter could require, an inexhaustible storehouse of subjects for his brush.

When some degree of liberty came to the Czechs with the Imperial Diploma of 1861, Czech music found Smetana, returned now from his Swedish exile at Götaborg,[1] where he had been teaching in the Harmoniska Sellskapet, ready to give it a strength and purpose it had not yet come near attaining; to give it, in fact, powerful national significance. Mánes, in his painting, turned his back on outworn classicism and demoded religious motifs, while literature was in the hands of a number of brilliant poets and prose writers such as Vrch-lický—librettist on more than one occasion for Dvořák. Complete political liberty might yet be half a century distant, but artistic self-determination was about to be realized, and it was in the hands of the right men.

[1] Smetana's championship of national freedom, expressed in a *March for the Students' Legion* and a *Solemn Overture,* brought him under suspicion, and after trying to make a success of a private music school in Prague in the years after leaving the service of Count Thun, he went abroad where he could work without obstruction.

CHAPTER II

THE EARLY YEARS

ANTONÍN LEOPOLD [1] DVOŘÁK was born on 8th September 1841,
the feast day of the Nativity of the Blessed Virgin, in the small village
of Nelahozeves (known as Mühlhausen in the Hapsburg régime) in
Bohemia, which lies on the banks of the river Vltava (Moldau),
about forty-five miles north of Prague.

There are several idyllic descriptions of this village, which seems
to have been an unusually quiet and peaceful spot. Perhaps the
most charming of these descriptions is the one given by Sir Henry
Hadow in his *Studies in Modern Music*: [2]

> The clean well-kept cottages sun themselves upon a slope of the low
> hills, or nestle among the trees by the river bank: a tiny street comes trickling
> along the shallow dale like a tributary: at its mouth a great square castle
> rises on a spur of jutting sandstone, and seems to dominate the very land-
> scape by feudal right. Behind are uplands of corn and pasture and orchard
> where you may idle for half a summer's afternoon, watching the play of
> light tremulous among the leaves, the smoke curling lazily from the cluster
> of red roofs, and below them the brown turbid river and the long timber
> rafts floating down them to the Elbe.

The castle belonged to Prince Lobkowitz, a usually absentee but
kindly landlord in whose service Anna Zdeněk, Dvořák's mother,
had worked before her marriage. His father, František, kept the
village inn, a white-walled, red-roofed, solid-looking and quite
unpicturesque building where, doubtless, the beer was as good as
Edward Holmes had found it in Prague. Antonín's father, it is said,
came of good and ancient stock. The important point is rather that
the stock was good than that it was old. Pan Dvořák's social position
was also good, not only by reason of his having married a daughter
of one of the prince's stewards, and thus given the inn a flavour of

---

[1] Presumably the name given to Dvořák at confirmation, according to
custom. It does not appear in his baptismal certificate.

[2] Second Series, 1897.

the 'big house,' but because of his being also the village butcher and
an attractive and popular person into the bargain. To be 'a handsome active youngster of twenty-seven, vigorous, alert, clean-limbed,'
to dispense beer and meat, and, since he was a good singer, violin
and zither player, also music, is to recommend yourself very strongly
to your fellow men as a person worth knowing.

Antonín was thus born into very pleasant company and surroundings. The Bohemian villages seem to have retained their native
brightness and gaiety even in the worst times of political oppression,
and the inhabitants had a natural optimism which made them see
the silver lining rather than the cloud. In the course of time four
more sons and three daughters followed on the birth of Antonín,
a cause of rejoicing to this pious Catholic couple, if a matter of some
financial anxiety; and undoubtedly, as on this occasion, a cause of
great satisfaction to Dvořák's customers.

No doubt as Antonín grew up he became accustomed to hearing
political discussions proceeding in the inn, just as they do in any
public-house in the world. Rumours of what was going on in
Prague to secure national freedom must have penetrated to Nelahozeves, but Antonín was never interested in politics, and peasants
themselves—sensible folk—are more interested in crops than in
politicians.

The swarthy black-haired boy, by no means so ill-favoured—to
judge by a photograph taken, without beard, when he was twenty-
seven—as his later hirsute portraits display him, had certainly plenty
of colour and gaiety in his life.

Catholic countries, especially in rural districts, interpret the word
'feast' literally; and the church gives them ample opportunity to do
so. After singing, on Sundays and the greater feasts, in the choir,
at mass, music which, for the most part, cheerfully forgot such a
thing as Gregorian chant had ever existed and indulged, voice and
organ, in plenty of baroque decoration (Pius X's *Motu proprio* had
not yet gone forth and would make small difference when it did)—
after a reasonably swift period of religious observance young Dvořák
would be free with the rest to enjoy himself in secular pursuits.
There were the tempting stalls and—above all—there was the dance.
Furiants and polkas in gaily coloured costumes on the village green

with, perhaps, one of those famed bands of wandering musicians from Prague or some nearby town to accompany the revels. The Czechs are tireless dancers, and it has been noted that with a repertory of forty or more dances they cheerfully keep it up from after church on a Sunday or feast-day till early the following morning.[1]

Antonín, like the rest of the youth in his village, must have become saturated with folk-music of one kind or another, and in course of time these early impressions all bore fruit in his music, when he had learnt to look inwards instead of outwards; into, that is, his own country instead of over its frontiers.

When he was eight years old Antonín went to the village school for the two compulsory years' teaching and found there one of those schoolmaster-village-organists whom many a musician has had reason to call blessed. It was the pride of the village that Josef Spitz could play on any instrument; and doubtless he could play a little on any that came his way. From him young Dvořák learnt the violin, which he soon played well enough to sit beside his father at the second desk when the village band went into action.

As well as listening with delight to the wandering musicians who passed through the village, making the inn their natural headquarters, Antonín was no doubt often called upon to exhibit his talent to the 'locals' under the proud eye of his father.

Unfortunately any interesting facts that might have been handed down about his early training were lost when the old schoolhouse was burnt down in 1885. We do not know, therefore, exactly how far Dvořák had progressed in the years between going to school and leaving Nelahozeves, towards the end of 1853, for Zlonice. His father sent him to this small town, some four hours' journey west from the village, in order to learn German. The hand of the Hapsburgs still lay heavy over Bohemia, and no one who could not speak the official tongue could hope to succeed in business. At Zlonice Antonín stayed with his maternal uncle Zdeněk, who was childless and able to shoulder the burden of his nephew's education. It is

---

[1] Dvořák told Herman Klein that in Bohemia every child must learn music and, if possible, sing in church. After church the people revel in music and dancing, and sometimes until early morning.

reasonable to assume that Antonín had absorbed most of what the amiable Spitz could teach him and was now ready to extend his studies. He found the right man in Antonín Liehmann, headmaster of the school at Zlonice, teacher of German and local organist. Dvořák began to emulate Spitz's multiple accomplishment, for he now learnt from Liehmann the organ, piano and viola, as well as continuing with the violin and studying harmony, figured bass and modulation. Liehmann taught in the families of the local big-wigs and had an orchestra of his own for which he composed many pieces 'betraying the influence of the classics and of Bohemian folk-music.' A large number of these are in existence, and Dvořák must often have played them.

Besides being a good teacher Liehmann was also a disciplinarian, and trained his pointer not only upon the notes on the blackboard, but also upon the head of any pupil who misread them. Dvořák does not seem to have resented this if he ever suffered from it, and always remembered gratefully the man who had a firm belief in his talents. (Liehmann was the model for Benda, the lovable schoolmaster-organist in Dvořák's opera *The Jacobin*.) His services to Dvořák are not the only claim Liehmann has on our gratitude. He coined a delightful word for extemporization, 'brambulieren,' which exactly describes—though he may not have intended it to be taken quite like this—the average organist's 'weary and ill-at-ease' ramblings over the keys when an interval has to be filled in.

With Antonín German evidently came a poor second to music, for when, in 1855, the Dvořák family moved from Nelahozeves to Zlonice, at the instance of Uncle Zdeněk, who thought they might do better in his home-town, Antonín was soon sent off to the Sudeten-German Česká Kamenice (Böhmisch-Kamnitz), where he could concentrate, without distractions, on the necessary language.

Financial reasons also entered into this decision. Pan Dvořák, on the advice of his brother-in-law, had taken over the Big Inn, an establishment in the house of a disgruntled peasant, Novotný. This individual appears to have resented another's undertaking what he had not the means to do himself, and started luring 'the week-day customers to another beerhouse and the country visitors to another village.' He must have had remarkable determination.

The end of it, anyway, was bankruptcy for the elder Dvořák, and
it was all he could do to finish off Antonín's education in German.
He made an *au pair* arrangement with a miller called Ohm, at
Česká Kamenice, and received his son in exchange for Antonín.

But Antonín was not without consolation, for Hancke, the choirmaster of St. Jacob's Church at this place, noted his unusual talent
and even found in him an able understudy.

When a year had passed and Antonín was home again Liehmann
once more took him in charge, but urged upon his father that he
should be sent to Prague—upon which Antonín's eyes were as
eagerly set as any pilgrim's on Rome—in order to enjoy the far wider
opportunities for musical education which the capital city offered.
But Pan Dvořák was firm in his refusal. He simply could not afford
it, even if the prospects had been favourable. 'It is impossible,' he
told Antonín, 'you must be a butcher, and succeed to your grandfather's trade.'

This utterance has, of course, brought forth many sympathetic
and well-meaning references to Keats. There may be some analogy
between a dissecting-chamber and a slaughter-house, but there is a
difference between Keats, a stranger in grimy London, and Dvořák
at home in the possibly grimy (it lay in a coal district) but far more
pleasant places of Zlonice. He could not have liked the trade to
which he was now apprenticed, and in any case he knew very well
that his real trade was music, but at any rate he was able to go on
working with Liehmann. That excellent man never lost sight of the
goal he desired for his best pupil and urged it upon the elder Dvořák
at every opportunity.

Dvořák was fast maturing as a musician. Lessons in harmony
had produced some compositions, said to be marches and dances
for Liehmann's orchestra, and put away because they were too
difficult. He now sat at the first violin desk, or, which he preferred,
with the violas (the viola became, in fact, his favourite instrument).
And he was as competent to take his teacher's place on the organ
bench as he had been to wield the conductor's baton at St. Jacob's.

The story goes that about this time, 1856, young Dvořák thought
to break down his father's opposition to a musical career for his
eldest son, if he showed his ability in composition as well as in per-

14

formance. The simple are impressed by notes on paper produced by their offspring far more than by those of others that they play on instruments. Antonín as a composer would be sure to win the admiration of his family and the consent of his father. He secretly wrote a polka, the story goes, issued out the parts, but failed to have a general rehearsal. As he was unaware that the trumpet is a trans/ posing instrument, the result, played to papa Dvořák and the rest, proved more curious than beautiful. No mention of this story is made by Stefan or Hoffmeister, both of whom base themselves on Šourek, and it is exceedingly difficult to believe it is true. It first appeared in English in Hadow's *Studies in Modern Music*.

Liehmann's training had given his pupil a sound technical foundation, and Dvořák was in his orchestra. It is hardly credible that he should have been so incurious as not to have made some inquiries into the technique of writing for the orchestra when he is known to have composed 'difficult' marches and dances. It is still more unlikely that he should have allowed the town band to sight/ read his polka when so much hung in the balance. We may con/ clude, therefore, that this amusing little story is apocryphal.

In any case when Antonín's uncle, seeing the boy was really set on being a musician, promised to help him, the father set aside his very natural opposition—for the prospects were poor indeed, and meat offered a far more secure future than music—and gave consent.

The most obvious course was for Antonín to qualify as an organist, and it was decided—in consultation with Liehmann—that the lad should go to the Organ School in Prague, an institution founded in 1830 by the Association for the Improvement of Church Music in Bohemia, and presided over, at this time, by a German, Karl Pitsch. And so in the autumn of 1857 Dvořák and Antonín set forth in a hay cart with a peasant called Veselý, for Prague, some forty/five miles distant.

On arrival they stayed in Huss Street at the Bee Inn.

CHAPTER III

THE boy of sixteen who came to study in the organ school was, to name his own heroes, no Schubert in composition, no Beethoven as an executant. He possessed a talent which might have seemed quite considerable in Zlonice but which, in open competition at Prague, appeared nothing very remarkable. His credentials were the reports of three schoolmasters (only one of whom had detected great potentialities in him), some ability on the violin, viola and organ, and a bundle of unperformed manuscripts. But to these moderate achievements was added abounding energy and immense determination. There was no need to instruct Dvořák that genius is the art of taking pains.

The Organ School—which in 1890 was absorbed into the Prague Conservatory of Music—has been called the nursery of Czech composers, in spite of its German direction. (The Conservatory, at this time, catered mainly for executants.) It was housed in the northern wing of a onetime Jesuit house in Bartholomew and Convict Street, and in the southern wing lived Professor Josef Zvonař, who was the chief representative of Czech interests in the school.

Antonín himself lodged at first with his cousin, Paní Plevá, who had married a tailor of that name, in a house next to the German Technical High School, now known as Dominikánská Ulice 238. He does not seem to have been happy here. Perhaps the Plevýs looked down, as people of the same class who have 'bettered' themselves are apt to do, on the clumsy and silent peasant lad billeted on them, who wasted his time studying music.

Dvořák's teachers were Josef Foerster [1] as organ master, František Blažek as teacher of theory and Josef Zvonař (singing). He was therefore entirely in the hands of his countrymen, for these professors

---

[1] 'Who took an active part in the reformation of liturgical music in Bohemia, and reawakened a taste for the works of Palestrina and for Gregorian music.'—GROVE.

were all Czechs. In the second year of his studies the German director, Pitsch, died suddenly, and was succeeded by a Czech, Josef Krejčí, who now became Dvořák's principal teacher. This man, while a good musician, was 'narrow-minded and pedantic, suspicious by nature.' Worst of all he was something of a quisling: for in his view only what was German was good, and he had no sympathy at all with nationalist aspirations.

Dvořák does not seem to have learnt enough German at Česká Kamenice to explain himself easily to this irritable gentleman, and found himself in a thoroughly unsympathetic atmosphere. The Society of St. Cecilia provided a much more congenial environment. To quote his fellow pupil Urban:

After the evening lecture at the Organ School we went every week to the Cecilia Society, which gave two concerts a year at Žofín.[1] These concerts, at which orchestral and vocal works were given, were famous. Dvořák played viola in the Cecilia orchestra, and sat at the same desk as Adolf Čech, who afterwards became conductor at the National Theatre.

The conductor of this society was Antonín Apt, a clever amateur musician, whose sympathies lay with contemporary music, Wagner and Schumann, rather than with the classics which were the staple fare at the Organ School.

Any musical diet that included Wagner was dangerous fare for impressionable youngsters. By day Dvořák might keep respectable company with the classics under Krejčí's watchful eye: by night he disported himself with the siren Wagner and, like most other young men, lost his heart to that heady music. It took him ten or more years to shake off the spell completely enough to absorb what he wanted of Wagner without being absorbed by him. And in later years he confessed openly to an abiding love for Wagner's music, a confession that it would have been dangerous to make before.

These evening draughts of Wagner, the richly coloured orchestration that went like wine to the head, may have helped Dvořák to forget the rather bleak present with which he was faced. The allowance from his uncle had ceased, and that meant that his studies

[1] 'A summer concert hall in Prague, built on one of the islets of the river Vltava, "Sophia's Island." '—HOFFMEISTER.

would also have to cease. It also meant finding quarters where he could lodge free of charge. These he found with his father's sister, Josefa Dušík, who lived in Charles Square; and he had a good friend in Karel Bendl, the son of a prosperous innkeeper, who was able to offer him the hospitality of a piano and a collection of scores. Dvořák passed second out of a class of twelve at the end of his second year at the Organ School (from which fact alone history records the name of the first prize-winner, one Siegmund Glanz, a German youth). His report declared that he had 'a good but on the whole merely practical talent. Practical knowledge and skill seem to be his chief aim. In theory he is weak.'

The director can scarcely have suspected how right this report, intended to be adverse, would prove to be. Dvořák's weakness in theory amounted to little more than his use of false relations and consecutive fifths, which one would like to think he employed deliberately to annoy his painstaking teachers; and without practical knowledge and skill he would not have become, as he did, so great a master of orchestration. We can, however, allow that contrapuntal writing was never one of his strong points.

Dvořák's leaving certificate announced that he was admirably fitted to fulfil the duties of organist and choirmaster. But he had other plans and joined, instead, as viola player an orchestra conducted by Karel Komsák, which was very popular in the Prague restaurants, and became eventually the nucleus of the Czech National Opera orchestra. The salary he received from this organization did not do much to ameliorate his poverty. He had no piano, he could ill afford to buy music paper, still less musical scores, and there is a story of his being unable to take advantage of an opportunity to hear Weber's *Freischütz* for lack of a few pennies.

The Komsák band entertained its patrons only with 'popular overtures and the usual pot-pourris.' To hear great orchestral music Dvořák had to gate-crash behind the timpani of a friendly player. He might well have reflected bitterly on the legend that every Bohemian child is born with a silver spoon on its right hand and a violin on its left. If it stretches out for the spoon it will grow up a rich man or a thief (or both!), if the fiddle, a musician. If Dvořák had been given to speculation—which he was not—it might have seemed to him then that he had stretched out the wrong hand. But already the clouds were lifting, and brighter days lay ahead.

In 1860 Italy's victories over Austria brought about a larger degree of political freedom, which had immediate repercussions on the artistic life of the Czech nation. Bohemia was ready for her second spring. Smetana returned from exile to enter the lists on behalf of modern and national music as against Italian opera and the star system. Mánes was revitalizing painting, a number of poets and prose-writers literature. The German Provincial Theatre was now challenged by the erection of the Provisional Theatre in 1862, from funds raised by public subscription.

It is Smetana's activities that particularly concern us here. He helped to found the Umělecká Beseda (Society of Arts), he conducted the fine Hlahol Choral Society and, above all, he saw that the best platform for propagating the national idea in music was the opera, which appealed both to eye and ear.

Smetana became conductor of the Czech National Theatre orchestra (Dvořák, as a member of the Komsák concert-band, was already a violist in this orchestra), and had now to provide it with a repertory of native works. This meant, more or less, starting from scratch and making sure of which way to go. In one of his early orchestral works, *The Camp of Wallenstein,* he had not even quoted a folk-tune where its use was clearly indicated, and he did not propose to work on such easy lines now. The art of the people had its own place, and that was in the lives of the people. Smetana held that the national character was manifested not in outward show, but in the thought and substance of a work. No national art could be built on the mere imitation of folk-melodies. As Nejedlý said: 'The essence of his Czech spirit was thought, not playing with notes.'

His first opera, an affair of mixed styles founded on a libretto akin to *Boris Godunov,* was written in 1863, but produced only in 1866. By that time he had found his true style: for in the intervening years he wrote the opera that has brought him world-wide fame, *The Bartered Bride.* The citizens of Prague, to whom music was as catching as measles, had adopted the airs of *Figaro* as popular songs; here, in the Mozartian manner, they were given as popular airs by one of their own countrymen, and they took them to their hearts.

While all these exciting events were in progress Dvořák was endeavouring to live on his thirty-five shillings a month (and what he could pick up by teaching), and puzzling over exactly which path he should tread. Always silent and reserved, he neither asked for nor received advice, and the extent of his ambition to succeed as a composer, which was firm and deep-rooted, would probably have surprised his few friends.

The need for a piano became urgent—for to use, when convenient, your friend's piano is not the same thing—and he moved once more to the rooms of a fellow member of the orchestra, Moric Anger, in Havlíček Square. This Schubert-like establishment consisted of, in addition to Anger, a medical student, Karel Čech, afterwards an operatic singer, two other students and a tourists' guide. These five kept an ancient spinet[1] company in a bedroom, and Dvořák had to make do with it as best he could.

And so, with every hard-saved penny going on music paper, which his determined and industrious pen rapidly filled in every spare moment, sat this unregarded student, 'poring over Beethoven in hopes to discover the secret of that magic style,' and with the music of the Venusberg ever ringing in his ears. Which path was he to take? The way laid down by the Organ School, the well-trod, safe paths of the established forms on which Smetana appeared to have turned his back, or the exciting nonconformity of the newly trodden ways? Whatever answer would eventually be given he had first to learn by writing, and in the twelve hidden years of training and self-discipline peculiar to himself he wrote copiously.

[1] So the biographers say, but it was doubtless a square piano, so often inaccurately called 'spinet,' which is a harpsichord.

CHAPTER IV

HIDDEN YEARS

THE recorded utterances of a man so reticent and uncommunicative as Dvořák are worth close attention, and so when he grimly declared that in his early days in Prague he always had enough paper to make a fire we can be sure that he was speaking the truth. Furthermore we can be glad that the slaughter of the innocents which, in common with Brahms, he undertook from time to time, gave him some needed warmth.

It is exceedingly doubtful whether either of these composers destroyed anything valuable to posterity—or indeed whether any composer has ever done so. Any really good ideas that went to warm Dvořák's hands were probably, consciously or otherwise, used up in later compositions. (There is evidence that he was averse to wasting material which he felt to be good. For example, the tenth song from *The Cypresses* appears in an aria in the first version of *King and Collier*: and when that version was discarded it pops up in the equally unsuccessful opera *Wanda*. What became of it after that I do not know!)

There are, in any case, quite enough of Dvořák's early compositions to make it possible to follow the general direction of his mind during this formative period.

The twelve years that elapsed between the time he left the Organ School in 1859, at the age of eighteen, and his emergence before the public as a composer in 1871, were occupied with copious writing in classical forms.

Dvořák, as his report had said, was weak in theory and strong in practice. And his practice was to study his models, pre-eminently Beethoven, and then to write and, having written destroy. This composer 'by the grace of God,' as Hans Richter called him, was a follower rather of Pelagius than of Augustine, and 'If I ought, I can' might well have been his motto. He knew he ought to be a composer, and so a composer he could be. He was quite sincere in saying that he 'studied with the birds, flowers, trees, God and myself,' but he knew that the last was the most important. He had the sense not to submit to a public keyed up for works by Czech composers anything that he felt was unlikely to make the right impression. It was, no doubt, this, as well as modesty, which held him back for so long, and it is significant of his belief in his powers that he should consider at once composing in the largest forms.

There were two main roads he might have taken. One led to opera, or rather, as it was now being called, music-drama: a much more intriguing title. Wagner had blazed this trail, and the public, fed, so far as national opera went, on pretty works on which folk-tunes were stuck like ornaments on an iced cake, were now in a mood to accept, or rather to demand, opera on a more ambitious scale. The national honour, as well as the National Opera House, required it. It must have been clear to Dvořák that Smetana was travelling fast down this main road. It would be difficult, if not improper, to try to catch him up.

The other main road, to which a conservative son of the soil might expect to be attracted, and which the Organ School had done its best to make him follow loyally, was that of the classic forms—symphony and chamber music. And this was the one he proposed to take.

Smetana, it was understood, was to give the people a national opera in a National Opera House; Dvořák's chance lay down the other road: he would give the people symphonies and chamber music which, if not wholly national—he never could be that—would at least be the work of a Czech composer, and would, he might dream in optimistic moments, help to put Bohemia on the European musical map.

The national note is absent from Dvořák's Opus 1, a string Quintet in A minor (with two violas) dated 6th June 1861, but there is some faint sounding of it in the A major string Quartet written in March 1862. Between 1863 and 1865, 1866 and 1869, Dvořák's burnings were on so large a scale that he must rarely have been cold. The Symphony in C minor called *The Bells of Zlonice,* composed in February and March 1865, and not discovered until 1923, was probably intended for inclusion in this holocaust, since much of its material reappears in the *Silhouettes* for piano of 1879.

During his stay in the Anger establishment Dvořák wrote one work he was not only unwilling to destroy, but which he always regarded with great affection. This was a cycle of songs called *The Cypresses*, composed, Hoffmeister says, 'to somewhat tearful and effeminate verses by the Moravian lyrical poet, Gustav Pfleger'. Dvořák published four of these songs in 1882 as his Op. 2 and arranged twelve of the original cycle for string quartet under the title *Evening Songs* in 1887 (ten of these were published in 1921).

The reason for this tenderness lay, of course, in the region of the heart, although Dvořák, ever reticent, dedicated the songs, not to the object of his passion, but to his friend, Karel Bendl. The young lady in question, Anna Čermáková, was, needless to say, a pupil, one of the daughters of a goldsmith. Dvořák—like Mozart in the case of the Weber family—fell in love first of all with one daughter, but married another. His first love was Josefa: but as she gave him no encouragement he kept his heart in the family and proposed to Anna. She was a good contralto singer and became a far more useful wife to Dvořák than ever poor Constanze was to Mozart.

A second Symphony in B flat major and a cello Concerto in A major also belong to this period. Probably Dvořák meant to destroy both of them. He himself stated that he 'tore up and burnt' two overtures for orchestra, a string Quartet in B minor, a Mass in B major,[1] a clarinet Quintet in B flat minor and a quantity of incidental music composed for the National Theatre.

The benevolent spirits of Mozart, Beethoven and Schubert haunted the majority of these works, but in the B flat major Symphony Wagner pushes them aside; and with him comes the first sign of a diffuseness which, all the rest of his life, lay in wait for Dvořák as for Wagner and for Schubert.

Shortly after the completion of the B flat major Symphony Dvořák found that an ancient spinet and a bedroom so over-populated were no longer tolerable, and returned to his Aunt Dušík's house, where, greatly daring, he expended two of the twenty gulden he was earning in the orchestra on the hire of a piano belonging to his tailor.

He was now fairly well 'written in' as a composer, though known

[1] V. J. Novotný thinks another Mass in F minor was also included.

as such only to a very few friends, and he was in close contact with Smetana, under whose conductorship he regularly played at the Provisional Theatre.

It is typical of Dvořák's wisdom or self-distrust—perhaps a combination of both—that he kept his surviving musical children from the public gaze; nor were many of them permitted to appear, so it seems, even before his friends. The unburnt remained hidden.

Possibly he was waiting to see what would be the fate of the opera Smetana had ready for production in 1863, *The Brandenburgers in Bohemia*. The usual delays attended this work, and when it was produced, three years later, it disclosed to the discerning a style not yet fully formed but, as we have seen, clearly not content to be merely national.

While waiting for production Smetana composed the opera which conquered both Bohemia and its frontiers, *The Bartered Bride*. This time his librettest, Sabina, who had provided the book for his first opera, could work on familiar territory, the village life both he and Smetana knew and loved, and though there is no Mussorgskyan realism in the opera it does give a live and faithful picture of one side of the Czech nature, its natural optimism and joyousness. This was the best possible thing, also, for export.

Dvořák, of course, was present in the orchestral pit at the rehearsals and performance of these and other operas by Czech composers,[1] and, whatever resolutions he had made, he caught opera as adults catch measles, badly; and he never got rid of the infection. Moric Anger, Hoffmeister tells us, 'remembered that Dvořák at that time (1868) gladly and frequently accompanied him to the German Theatre, where Wagner's operas interested him immensely. He also listened spellbound to Liszt playing his Wagner transcriptions.' The end of it was that he determined to get to work on an opera of his own.

Now reticence is all very well, but if Dvořák had opened his mouth a little more frequently he would surely have been advised by Smetana, or one of his professional colleagues, not to use for a libretto a turgid story about a struggle between Danes and Britons (synonyms for

[1] Such as Šebor's operas *The Templars in Moravia*, *Drahomira* and *Hussite Bride* and Bendl's *Lejla*.

DVOŘÁK AND HIS WIFE ANNA

Hapsburgs and Czechs), ending in 'an apotheosis of British freedom.' This story, by Theodor Körner, he found in an old German almanac, where he should have left it. *Alfred the Great,* a 'Heroic Opera in Three Acts,' duly completed, suffered the fate of Dvořák's other early compositions; but amongst the posthumous works was found a *Tragic Overture,* published by Simrock in 1912 as *Dramatic Overture,* which was, in fact, the overture to *Alfred.* Dvořák had got an opera off his mind, but not Wagner off his back. He had doubtless noted the ever-conservative public's reaction to Smetana's third opera, *Dalibor,* which, taking a hint from Liszt, was entirely monothematic. Charges of Wagnerism were freely levelled at the composer, who had been expected to bring forward, like a rabbit out of a hat, another *Bartered Bride.*

Wagner was all very well in the German Provincial Theatre, but in the National Theatre only Czech music must be heard. Dvořák, however, ignored this and, aligning himself with the progressives, gave himself up to the enchantments of Wagner as freely as an opium smoker to his pipe. Two string Quartets, Opp. 9 and 10, in D major and E minor, composed in 1870, are said to be thoroughly Wagnerian in spirit, and sound more like stage than chamber music. After this pair of works the opera bug again attacked Dvořák and, with the resounding success of *The Bartered Bride* before him—and the potent bait of *The Mastersingers,* which had its first performance in Prague at the German Provincial Theatre in 1871—he finished a comic opera in three acts to a libretto by Bernhard Guldener. This time he was ready to face the public, and the fact that this unknown member of the National Theatre orchestra had written and submitted an opera to the management appeared in a musical periodical dated June 1871. It was the first time his name had appeared in print. The overture was played by the Czech Philharmonic Orchestra, conducted by Smetana, with success, but the National Opera management, like such bodies everywhere, was in no hurry to produce it.

It may have been the great success of Dvořák's *Hymnus* that decided the authorities eventually to take the opera seriously. This cantata is based on a poem by Vítězslav Hálek, *The Heirs of the White Mountain,* which summons the Czech people, defeated at the battle of the White Mountain in 1620, and thereafter oppressed, to love their native land ever more fervently. It is really a call to self-determination, and Dvořák's music sounds the patriotic note in no uncertain way. The first performance, on 9th March 1873, took place at the Novoměstský Theatre, when the Hlahol Choral Society was conducted by Dvořák's old friend, Karel Bendl. The work was triumphantly successful, and one of Dvořák's critics, Procházka, who had been severe about the few small works so far heard at concerts, allowed that the work had unity and truth, and was indeed worthy of the new epoch.

Dvořák had completed the *Hymnus* on 3rd July 1872. In September came a pianoforte Quintet in its composer's favourite key of A major, upon which Procházka fell with relish. This work, which shows Dvořák putting his musical house in order, is castigated for its 'lack of formal polish,' and the composer's attention is drawn to classical models. The use of the national dance idiom in the scherzo was thought to be vulgar. Heads were gravely shaken, even in more progressive quarters, over the 'excessive modernity' of the two song cycles that appeared later in this fruitful year. One was a setting of four Serbian songs translated into Czech for Dvořák. They have no musical reference to their country of origin. The other consisted of six songs from the famous Králodvorský Manu-script,[1] one of which, *The Lark,* printed as a supplement to the musical periodical *Dalibor* in 1873, was Dvořák's first published composition. Three *Nocturnes* for orchestra, the third of which, given at a concert of the Prague Philharmonic Orchestra on the Žofín Island, where Dvořák made first acquaintance with Wagner, had a great success with critics and public, but were committed to the flames by this relentless critic, and the same fate seems to have overtaken a violin sonata, last performed in 1875.

Self-distrust went hand in hand with determination in Dvořák. He seems to have been exceedingly susceptible to unfavourable

[1] 'This famous manuscript, around which controversy raged for over a century, was discovered by Hanka in 1817, at Königinhof (Králové Dvůr) in the north-east of Bohemia. Its authenticity was challenged at once, particularly by the German scholars. In later years several Czechs, in-cluding Thomas Masaryk . . . have helped to explode the illusion of its veracity.'—HOFFMEISTER, page 16. Another manuscript appeared in 1818.

critical verdicts. Thus, though his third Symphony, in E flat major, begun in April and finished in June 1873, was a great favourite with its composer, and thought well of by Smetana, who conducted it at one of the Philharmonic concerts on 30th March 1874, because of a bad press—complaining not of its Wagnerian accents, but of its lack of form—Dvořák would not have the Symphony given again during his life. It won him, as we shall see, the Austrian State Prize the following year.

The tale of Dvořák's miscarriages is long, and now he added to it a string Quartet in F minor (originally Op. 9), which seems to have been intended to fulfil the same biographical function as Smetana's first 'Z mého života' ('From my Life') Quartet. It is a record of his past troubles and a greeting to better prospects, in which Anna Čermáková was to have a large share.

Unfortunately a new chamber music organization which had now come into existence in Prague, with Antonín Bennevic as leader, Deutsch as second violin, Vojtěch Hřímalý as viola and Smetana as pianist, did not regard either this Quartet or the one in A minor, originally Op. 12, that followed it, with any favour, and the two works remained in manuscript. A theme from the F minor Quartet was used as the jumping-off point of the Romance for violin and orchestra, Op. 11, published in 1879—another instance of Dvořák's unwilling ness to lose sight of a good idea.

The outstanding success of the *Hymnus* may have helped to over come the steady opposition Anna Čermáková's parents had shown all these years to her marriage with Dvořák. The long-delayed ceremony took place on 17th November 1873 at St. Peter's Church, Prague, and after three months at his 'in-laws' Dvořák at last found a home of his own, 'modest but cosy,' at No. 14 Rybnická.

Dvořák took this opportunity to give up his orchestral work, and drew on his early training by taking a post as organist at the church of St. Adalbert, where his salary was the princely sum of ten gulden a month.

Perhaps Anna had a hand in this decision, for she provided just the qualities that Dvořák lacked, being energetic and practical in the affairs of daily life. An organist, even the not very good one her husband proved to be, gets a better social position and more pupils than an orchestral viola player; and quiet evenings are good for creative work.

Dvořák needed them. Ill fortune dogged his opera *King and Collier,* which must have had the most chequered career of any opera ever written.[1] It had been, as we have seen, accepted for production by the management of the Provisional Theatre in 1871 and the overture had been successfully performed under Smetana. When the management did turn their attention to production of the opera rehearsals lasted for four weeks and ended, so the story goes, with the following pronouncement from Smetana: 'It is a serious work, full of ideas imbued with genius—but I don't believe it can be performed.' One can be sure that any other Czech composers with operas in their desks handed this verdict on with interest. Dvořák, sensitive and stubborn, withdrew the opera and it dropped out of sight. It merely stimulated his inclination to arson.

But now, between April and August 1874, and after the completion of his Symphony in D minor (originally Op. 13), he decided, urged on by the success that had come in full measure to *The Bartered Bride,* though not yet to *Dalibor* or *Libuša,* to provide the opera, bar by bar, with entirely new music. Not one bar of the original work remains and it was lost until 1916, when a member of the German Provincial Theatre bought the score, without any idea as to what it was, at Nuremberg. The second act, which was missing, turned up in the archives of the National Theatre in 1928, together with the complete parts, and the opera was given in its original form in 1929.

The new opera—for such in fact it was—was not given its new overture until November 1874, when it went into rehearsal. This time no voice was heard to speak of impossible difficulties, but many rumours went round of the beauties of the work and the first night, 24th November 1874, proved a brilliant success. Procházka, recovered from the A major Quintet, wrote in the musical journal *Dalibor*:

There is no need to be anxious about Dvořák's future. The composer,

---

[1] The nearest parallel is Rimsky-Korsakov, who entirely rewrote his *Maid of Pskov,* and then, finding the new work unsatisfactory, revised and rescored the original version.

after long groping, has found the right path to the temple of independent Slavonic art . . . in future Dvořák will liberate his work more and more from exotic influences, and with the triumphant future of Slavonic music the enthusiasm of this artist will place him in the ranks of those whose names will stand out in letters of gold in our annals.

This prophecy came true, but not quite in the way Procházka pictured it.

Dvořák's opera suffered the not unusual fate of apparently success-ful operatic first nights. It was sunk now not by too difficult or Wagnerian music, but by its poor libretto—a fact which had escaped Dvořák's attention. Novotný, who had worked over Smetana's *Dalibor* libretto with success, performed a major operation on Dvořák's, and the composer obligingly provided entirely new music for the amended third act without, however, concealing a mixture of styles. This version obtained eight performances over four of the original version. Then the opera was dropped out of the repertory until 1914.

The remaining works of 1874 were a Rhapsody in A minor and a Quartet, in the same key, which Dvořák, at this time, much favoured; also a comic opera in one act, *Tvrdé Palice* (*The Pig-headed Peasants*), to an excellent libretto by Dr. Josef Štolba. The opera, completed on Christmas Eve 1874, was not produced until seven years later, on 2nd October 1881, and was then so badly staged that it was, in spite of success, withdrawn until 'decent and worthy' scenery and costumes could be procured for it.

(Bernard Shaw says that hell is full of 'musical amateurs, music is the brandy of the damned.' There should also be an especial place there for operatic managements, sung to endlessly by aged prima donnas!)

The Quartet, his sixth, and all as yet unperformed, was Dvořák's first chamber-music work to appear in print—in 1875—and, being a melancholy and severely classic work, not the most suitable to re-commend him to the public. This Quartet, composed twelve days after the Lisztian Rhapsody, is like the confession of a bad conscience.

CHAPTER V

ENTRY OF BRAHMS

THE inauguration in 1863 of a State grant for 'young, poor and talented painters, sculptors and musicians, in the Austrian half of the Empire' is one of the things that can be put to the credit side of the Hapsburg account. The Austrian Commission for the State Music Prize sat, of course, in Vienna; and as Bohemia still belonged to the Hapsburg Monarchy it was open to any Czech to submit his works for the prize. Spurred on by his friends and, doubtless, by his admirable wife, Dvořák sent in his E flat major Symphony, and some other works,[1] and learnt that to youth and poverty he added, in the eyes of the Commission, sufficient talent to merit an award of 400 gold florins (about £32 10s.). It was by far the largest sum he had ever earned, and he continued to receive the award, with each new batch of works he sent in, for several years in succession. Dvořák was, of course, a mere name to the members of the Commission, but they must have seemed like gods to him. Amongst them was Eduard Hanslick, the famous critic of the *Neue freie Presse,* in which his fulminations against Wagner appeared. Hanslick was a native of Prague and did not care for the Czechs, but in his judgment of Dvořák's neo-Wagnerian Symphony (No. 2) he showed himself fair-minded and discerning. At least, he may have argued to himself, it was a symphony and not one of the new-fangled tone-poems or music dramas so favoured by the rising generation. The young man had a regard for classical form and was evidently familiar with the Viennese classical school. That alone earned him a good mark. And for their perception of a true creative instinct in Dvořák we can award a good mark to the other members, who included Johann Herbeck, conductor of the Vienna State Opera, and Johannes Brahms.

Brahms had been forced, not altogether unwillingly, into a strong anti-Wagnerian position. He knew, as Dvořák did not yet fully

---

[1] No two accounts agree as to what these were.

30

know, that the road trodden by Wagner and Liszt could never be his road, and even in Dvořák's youthful works he saw a nature in many ways complementary to his own. There is something rather touching in the regard the town-bred and now famous composer, who had begun his career with a flourish of trumpets on the note B, had for the country-born and almost unknown Czech, eight years his junior. Both were, in their own ways, reserved. One was a North German Protestant, the other a Bohemian Catholic. One was a confirmed and lonely bachelor, the other a happily married man (with, in the event, a large family). Brahms composed with mind and heart, Dvořák with heart and mind. Both of them shared a deep-seated sensuousness, with this great difference: Brahms was ashamed of it, Dvořák, in his direct peasant way, revelled in it. Brahms cherished his toy soldiers; Dvořák loved trains—real ones.

The influence Brahms exercised over his young friend was considerable, and for the most part admirable, though it is fortunate that he did not persuade Dvořák to come and live in Vienna for regularly prescribed inoculations against Wagnerism. The result of losing touch with his own soil might have been to turn him into a pale shadow of his master.

Brahms's name will often recur in this chronicle, and though he antagonized many of his best friends there never seems to have been any real disagreement between him and Dvořák. (It is true, and very odd, that when Dvořák received an honorary doctorate at Cambridge in 1891 he showed a notable lack of interest in his great benefactor, and was enthusiastic only about Verdi's music. Perhaps some Brahmsian criticism had momentarily upset him.)

Dvořák's lucky star was in the ascendant, for he won another prize with his newly composed string Quintet in G major, completed, after a short holiday, in March 1875. This work serves as a good example of the muddle that arose over his opus numbers. It appeared as Op. 77, which was unfair to him and disconcerting for the critics, when the true facts were established.

A Serenade in E major for strings, Op. 22, a piano Trio in B flat major, Op. 21, and a piano Quartet in D major, Op. 23, followed on the G major Quintet, all written between May and June. It was the *Moravian Duets*, however, that were to bring wide fame to Dvořák,

but before considering these it will be easiest to deal with the events
before their appearance.

Five days after finishing the piano Quartet Dvořák turned again
to the orchestra and began the Symphony in F major, Op. 76, which
was confusingly placed as the third of the five symphonies published in
his lifetime. This fifth Symphony, his first major work, was revised
in 1877, and dedicated to Hans von Bülow, who accepted the honour
in a characteristically warm-hearted letter addressed to the composer:

MOST HONOURED MASTER,

A dedication from you, next to Brahms the most God-gifted composer
of the present day, is a higher decoration than any 'Grand Cross' from the
hands of any ruler. With most heartfelt thanks, I accept this honour.

With most sincere esteem,

Your devoted admirer,

HANS BÜLOW.

Dvořák was also at work, from June to December of 1875, on a
new tragic opera, *Vanda,* which was saddled with an impossible
libretto, in five gloomy acts, by Messrs. Zakrejs and Beneš-Šumavský.
These two gentlemen appear to have been pretentious bunglers of the
worst kind, and the opera was doomed before the rise of the curtain.
Once again a little expert advice would have saved Dvořák from
accepting a farrago of nonsense which had not even the merit of being
concerned with Czech history, for the subject was Polish. It is
possible that he had knowledge of Smetana's as yet unperformed
Libuša (composed in 1872) and, with his usual mixture of modesty
and distrust, thought it best to go to Poland for the heroic Slavonic
opera he felt impelled to write.

Dvořák had only reached the end of the first act of this ill-starred
opera when his eldest daughter died, after a brief illness, and very
naturally this tragic event cast a shadow over the first compositions
of the following year, 1876. These were a pianoforte Trio in G
minor,[1] completed on 20th January, the string Quartet in E minor
(published as Op. 80!), begun on that date and completed two weeks
later, and his setting of *Stabat Mater.*

[1] The same form and key chosen by Smetana for a memorial work when
his daughter died.

This fine work, dedicated to the Union of Musical Artists, his real memorial to his daughter, was sketched out between 19th February and 7th May of this year, and not finally completed until 13th November 1877. *Stabat Mater*, as Stefan says, 'is the first oratorio of modern Czechish music,' and it was destined to bring him world-wide fame, especially in England. The first performance at Prague was delayed until 23rd December 1880, the London performance taking place three years later.

We must turn back now to the origin of the *Moravian Duets*, which enchanted Brahms, and led to his writing a letter to the publisher Simrock that was of the utmost consequence to Dvořák. Early in 1875 he had turned again, after three years' abstinence, to song-writing, using for this purpose four poems from Sušil's collection of Moravian national songs. At this time Dvořák was teaching the piano in the house of a Prague wholesaler, Johann Neff, and the songs, scored for soprano and tenor, were dedicated to this man's wife, Marie.

Delighted with the music Mme Neff prevailed on Dvořák to set more of the poems, and a second cycle of five songs was composed beween 17th May and 21st May 1876, a third cycle of ten songs between 26th June and 17th July of the same year. These songs were set for soprano and contralto, which the composer considered more effective than the original lay-out. Thirteen of the songs were privately published in Prague, with assistance from the Neffs, at Christmas 1876, and had an immediate and deserved success. Dvořák sent them to the Austrian State Commission when applying for the grant in 1877, and Simrock shortly afterwards received the following enthusiastic letter:

DEAR SIMROCK,

Through the opportunity which the State Scholarship has afforded me, I have for several years now been rejoicing over the works by Anton Dvořák (pr. Dworshak) of Prague. This year he sends me amongst others a book of ten duets for two sopranos [*sic*] with pianoforte, which seem to me to be very pretty and practical for publication. He appears to have had this book printed at his own expense. The title and unfortunately also the words are Bohemian only. I induced him to send the songs to you. When you play them through you will be as pleased as I am, and as a publisher, be especially pleased with the piquancy of them. Very likely many of the words have already been translated by (the lately deceased) Wenzig. Otherwise, perhaps Dr. Siegfried Kapper of Prague would be the best one to do them. Dvořák has written every possible thing, operas (Bohemian), symphonies, quartets and pianoforte pieces. Anyway he is a very talented man. Almost poor! And I ask you to consider this! That the duets are good will be evident to you, and they would be 'a good article.' The address is: Prague, Kornthorgasse No. 10, ii.

Best wishes,

Yours,

J. Br.

When the songs under the title of *Airs from Moravia* (*Klänge aus Mähren*) eventually appeared in 1878, the German musical world took notice of this new composer for the first time. Rarely heard now, they are just the sort of music to draw easy tears from the sentimental German public.

Several partsongs for mixed voices and male choir and some small works for piano, a piano Concerto in G minor in four movements and a fine *Theme and Variations* for piano—a great advance on the earlier piano writing—all belong to this period.

In 1877 Dvořák moved to No. 12 Žitná Street (Kornthorgasse), finding the enthusiastic pianists in the Rybnická too much for his peace of mind. He had felt confident enough to give up his organist's post and devote himself to composition, and he was sufficiently important now for his new landlord to ensure that he should not be disturbed by other people's music, while the inconvenience of his new quarters was compensated for by the absence of competing pianos. The noises of his own family did not worry him at all. His study, with a piano, a desk and a picture of Beethoven, was in general use as a parlour; and his favourite spot for work was the kitchen, amid the usual domestic clatter. Like Mozart and Schubert he could compose amidst noise of an indefinite kind; it was noise of a definite pitch from which he had to escape. As Hoffmeister says, the piano, in his concerto, took its revenge, and it is only in recent years that the work, in a new version made for Rudolf Firkušný, has had any success.

Still plodding after Smetana, whose comic opera *Hubička* (*The*

Kiss) had come out with great success in 1876, Dvořák turned to opera in the first part of 1877 and, after the tragic and futile *Wanda* subject, he set a poor libretto by J. O. Veselý, *Šelma Sedlák* (*The Peasant a Rogue*). This was a kind of anaemic *Marriage of Figaro*, but Dvořák's music, although it may be regarded as a homage to Mozart, is sparkling and rich in melody. The reception, at the Provisional Theatre at the first performance on 27th January 1878, was very favourable, and Vienna, as well as Dresden, showed interest. Dvořák's luck was out again, however, as the first performance in Vienna on 19th November 1885 coincided with political strife between Austrians and Czechs, and both cast and management were lukewarm.

Hugo Wolf, aware of Brahms's friendship with the composer, spat out some critical venom. He speaks of the orchestration as 'revolting, brutal and trite,' and remarks that it is bad enough to come across Dvořák's music on the concert platform. 'There may be people who are serious enough to find this opera comic, just as there are people comical enough to take Brahms's symphonies seriously.' Such ill-regulated criticism does not increase one's respect for Wolf.

Dvořák had a work in his desk which might have shown Wolf what a master of orchestration he had already become. This was the *Symphonic Variations for Large Orchestra*, composed in September 1877 and first performed in Prague that year. Ten years later Dvořák sent the score to the great conductor, Hans Richter, and received the following reply:

I gladly avail myself of this opportunity of coming into touch with a composer by the grace of God. In any case I had been thinking that before my London scheme was quite fixed I would ask if you had anything for me. Now, your Symphonic Variations have come as a brilliant addition to my programme.

The work was played at one of the Richter concerts in May 1887, and the conductor declared that he could not remember any novelty having a comparable success. Brahms said the same thing when Richter conducted the work at a concert of the Vienna Philharmonic Society in December of the same year.

With the string Quartet in D minor, Op. 34, composed in

December 1877 as a token of gratitude for Brahms's interest in his work, Dvořák passes from his formative first period to that of his richest creative activity. It may be well briefly to look back upon the chief points in his career since, at the age of sixteen, he arrived in a hay-cart at Prague, up to the present moment when he was to walk a larger stage. Dvořák's extreme reticence in speech and with pen lays his biographers open to charges of over-simplification and a forced inter-pretation of such clues as there are. The clues exist and each writer has to follow them as best he can and provide the solution that appears to him the most likely.

Elgar once said that there was plenty of music in the air: you had only to reach out your hands and pluck it down; but one must be able to distinguish between inspiration and note-spinning. Dvořák perhaps surrendered rather too easily to the ideas with which he bubbled over, but he was eventually able to control and canalize them. This he achieved in his own individual way. He was like a man with a large sum of money to invest who will not consult a broker or even a friend, but anxiously follows rumours and hints, and reads the financial news and places his money more by instinct than reason. Gradually he learns his way about the markets and eventually lands on a good thing. After that he never looks back, except for a moderate failure here and there, for nothing succeeds like success.

Dvořák had, at the age of thirty-six, eight string quartets, five operas, a big choral work and five symphonies, amidst a great deal else on a fairly large scale, to show for his twenty years of creative work; but, so far, of the compositions performed only the smaller works seemed likely to continue proving a success. *Stabat Mater*, the F major Symphony and the two operas were as yet unperformed. The chamber music, which will be discussed in detail later in this book, affords the best view of his changes of direction and of the way his mind was working. National flavouring, in the form of a polka, a *furiant* and so forth, is added early and with increasingly sure touch. He also uses the *dumka*, which comes from South Russia, and he set a Polish story in the unsuccessful opera *Wanda*. Dvořák, to continue the analogy above, was not going to invest solely in Czech securities, though he saw the wisdom of placing a good deal of his resources there. He was fond of the word Slavonic, and seems to have realized that an exclusive nationalism is merely an exaggerated form of provincialism. He invested something, then, in all the Slav countries and, since he now had the eyes of Vienna on him, a great deal in that quarter. The more or less successful fusion of all these elements, added to a remarkable artistic personality, was to make him the great figure he now became.

From 1877 onward Brahms was a very important influence in his life: important both socially, for he held the key to the larger musical world Dvořák was soon to enter, and musically, because of his logical habit of thought and his great constructive powers. Most important of all, his friendship gave Dvořák that confidence in himself which had been lacking and which no wife, however loving, could wholly supply.

Dvořák had now a true friend in one of the greatest composers of the day; he had, through this friend, a publisher; and he was about to make that publisher's fortune, as well as his own fame.

CHAPTER VI

SUCCESS never spoiled Dvořák. What he had been, a simple, rather obstinate, God-fearing man, he remained. Happiness for him lay in his family circle and, for the most part, in pleasures that money cannot buy.

The Franz-Josef (Wilson) railway station was near his house in Žitná Street and thither he repaired daily, for his early morning walk, to study with absorbed interest the engines in the yards. He made a particular point of noting the opus numbers of the locomotives and —which cannot have been so easy—the names of their drivers. In later years when he was teaching at the Conservatoire he would send one of his pupils down to the yards to find out which engine was going to take out an express train on that day. His favourite pupil and future son-in-law, Josef Suk, got into trouble for returning with the number not of the engine but of the coal-tender. 'So that,' remarked Dvořák to his daughter, with ironic humour, 'is the kind of man you want to marry.'

At other times he took a stroll in the Charles Square Park, where he could listen to the birds singing: a sound more congenial to him, perhaps, than that of the human voice.

His domestic happiness and the encouraging prospects before him are reflected in the cheerful Serenade in D minor, Op. 44 (1878), for wind and string bass, which, for the first time, uses in its Minuet another national dance form, the *sousedská*. It was dedicated, on publication a year later, to Louis Ehlert.

Dvořák now turned his attention to a commission recently received from Simrock. That astute publisher, with the success of Dvořák's *Moravian Duets* in mind and pocket, had suggested that Dvořák should write something in the same sort of vein as Brahms's *Hungarian Dances*. As what was Slav was evidently popular, let them be called *Slavonic Dances*. This idea naturally appealed to Dvořák, and on 18th March 1878 he composed the first of these dances, seven more following in rapid succession. Although he wrote them, like Brahms's *Hungarian Dances,* for piano duet at first, Dvořák saw the wisdom of orchestrating them at the same time.

This first set of *Slavonic Dances,* Op. 46, was published by Simrock in August 1878, the composer receiving 300 marks for them and the publisher a fortune. It is satisfactory to record that for the second set Dvořák's price went up to 3,000 marks.

These dances, enthusiastically praised by the German critic Louis Ehlert in the *Berliner Nationalzeitung,* who rightly spoke of their 'heavenly naturalness,' rapidly made their way round the world in their orchestral dress, and had to submit to many arrangements. In the process the order became confused; but that is so usual with Dvořák as to be hardly worth mentioning!

Dvořák dedicated the *Three Slavonic Rhapsodies,* which followed on the dances, to Louis Ehlert in gratitude for his enthusiastic review. These works also attained immediate popularity.

By this time the unsuccessful were talking darkly of Dvořák's 'writing to order,' which, of course, was precisely what they longed themselves to be doing, if only some publisher would give them the chance. Dvořák, however, saw no reason to refuse orders, but he turned out next a miniature suite, *Maličkosti (Bagatelles),* for two violins, cello and harmonium, designed to be played at the house of a friend who possessed a harmonium. This is real home music, and it reflects the composer's own happy circumstances.

On 14th May 1878 he began his string Sextet in A major, the first of his chamber-music works to cross the frontiers of his country and even to be heard abroad before it was performed in Bohemia. The Joachim Quartet gave the first public performance in Joachim's house at which Dvořák, marvelling and very shy, mingled with the great.

On 17th November of this year he made his bow as a conductor at a concert of his own works consisting of the first and second *Slavonic Rhapsodies,* the Serenade for wind instruments, two *Furiants* for piano played by Slavkovský and the newly composed *Three Modern Greek Songs,* Op. 50, sung by Lev, a baritone from the National Theatre.

At the end of 1878 Dvořák paid his first visit to Brahms, composing

his *Five Choruses for Male Voices*, Op. 27, in the train. (The manuscript is headed: 'Composed 12th December, on the way from
Prague to Vienna.') He wanted personally to give Brahms the score
of the D minor Quartet dedicated to him, and to thank him for his
kindness and interest.[1] The meeting proved more successful than
the older man's first visit to Liszt, and was indeed most cordial.

On his way back Dvořák was warmly greeted by Leoš Janáček,
the young conductor of the Brno Choral Society, who was to become
the Mussorgsky of Czech music, and he found himself enthusiastically
welcomed in Moravia.

From now onwards Dvořák's life, with the exception of the English
and American journeys, is mainly a chronicle of composition. The
year 1879 brought a flood of orders of a kind for which he was unpre-
pared, for, with an eye on quick sales, Simrock, and other publishers,
begged for short and easy pieces. Dvořák, who was not interested,
drew attention to his early operas, symphonies and chamber music,
but of these larger works he only succeeded in unloading, on Simrock,
the A major Sextet, the overture to *The Peasant a Rogue* and the newly
composed E flat major Quartet, Op. 51, which was the answer to a
request from Jan Becker, first violin of the Florentine Quartet, for a
Slavonic work.

Conductors, choral societies and chamber-music organizations all
besieged Dvořák, and a very obvious danger confronted him—the
commercial exploitation of what was Slav in response to the demands
of publishers and these bodies. In later years he told Sibelius—who
might have said the same thing: 'I have composed too much.' Both
of them had to provide a lot of drawing-room music which does not
amount to much more than pleasant note-spinning. But in the
things that matter there is no betrayal of their national heritage.

Joachim again gave the first performance of the Quartet in E flat
major (including also the A major Sextet) in his own house, and
Becker made it well known on his concert tours. Besides these
works Dvořák composed a setting of the 149th Psalm for the famous
Prague Choral Society, Hlahol, which was given at its spring concert
in March 1879, and in the same month a *Mazurek* for violin and small

[1] Dvořák had just been awarded the Austrian State Prize for the fifth
time.

THE NATIONAL THEATRE, PRAGUE

orchestra, dedicated to Sarasate, was heard at the first performance of Smetana's *Scenes from my Life* Quartet (E minor).

It is pleasant to record that Dvořák got some of his own back in his relations with Simrock. Like Beethoven, though probably without intention to deceive, he had promised works to another publisher, though he had given Simrock an option on all his future compositions. Dvořák found an easy way out of this difficulty by giving a low opus number to the *Czech Suite* in D, Op. 39, which Schlesinger unsuspectingly published in 1881 as an early work. It is, at any rate, a most delightful one.

The publisher may have full marks for demanding piano scores of the various orchestral works, and it is to be wished that the habit of playing these and chamber music in fourhanded arrangements had not gone out of fashion. There are few more delightful and profitable exercises. Many of the piano scores were arranged by Dvořák's friend, Dr. Zubatý, orientalist and professor at Prague University, who wrote the first biographical sketch of the composer.[1]

After dealing with the orders for small things and giving himself some time off in May and June, Dvořák went into retreat in July at the house of his friend Göbl, on Prince Rohan's estate at Sychrov, in order to devote himself to the writing of the violin Concerto in A minor, Op. 53, for which Joachim had asked. He finished the score in September 1879, and sent it to Joachim, not, as Brahms sent his work in this same medium, for the counterpoint to be looked over, but for general criticism. Dvořák followed Joachim's suggestions as regards the solo part and the instrumentation, and the Concerto received its first performance in Prague in the autumn of 1883— when it was played by František Ondříček—and again in December the same year in Vienna with the Vienna Philharmonic Orchestra conducted by Richter.

It was Dvořák's sensible practice to turn to the composition of small things after writing a work of large dimensions, and he now wrote five collections of short piano pieces for his publishers. In order not to arouse the suspicions of Simrock, to whom he was, as has been said, under contract for all his future works, Dvořák gave the first

---

[1] This was published, in German, by Hug Brothers, of Leipzig, in 1887.

of these collections, *Silhouettes,* published by Hoffmeister, the early number of Op. 8. It must be confessed that it sounds like it! Simrock had to be content with eight *Waltzes* for piano published as Op. 54, but he received as well the violin Sonata in F major, Op. 57, and, best of all, the *Seven Gypsy Songs,* Op. 55. The fourth of these, *Songs my mother taught me,* was a little gold mine, and still disputes with the *Humoresque* in G flat the first place in the affections of the public.

After these labours Dvořák took two months' holiday, spending July and August on his brother-in-law's [1] estate at Vysoká (where he was eventually to find a home for himself), with Göbl at Sychrov, and with Ehlert at Wiesbaden.

Refreshed by his holiday and with commissioned work behind him, Dvořák's mind turned in its natural direction, towards the composition of large-scale music. It was five years since he had written a symphony (the F major, No. 5), and after conducting at a concert given at Zlonice in September to raise funds for a memorial to his old teacher Liehmann, Dvořák returned to Vysoká and began to compose his Symphony in D major, Op. 60, which became erroneously known as his first. It was dedicated to Hans Richter, the kind friend who from now onwards always tried to include one of Dvořák's works in his programmes, and published in 1881 by Simrock. The great conductor was delighted with the Symphony, as well he might be, and punctuated the composer's run through on the piano, when he took the score to Vienna in November, with effusive embraces. Dvořák's old student friend, Adolf Čech, conducted the first performance at Prague in March 1881 and Manns gave the first English performance at the Crystal Palace in March 1882, Richter following with another performance in London on 15th May. The Symphony proved an immediate success and at the Prague performance the scherzo was encored.

Dvořák's fame was spreading. The Society of the Friends of Music heard a performance of the Symphony in 1883, conducted by Gericke, and it reached New York in the same year, where it was conducted by Dvořák's constant admirer, Theodore Thomas.

[1] Count Kaunitz, who married Josefa, sister of Dvořák's wife.

D major Symphony—'Dimitri'

After completing the Symphony Dvořák found, as usual, relaxation in composing—but not to order—small things: ten *Legends*, Op. 59, for piano duet, which found almost as much favour with the public as the *Slavonic Dances*. The *Legends* were dedicated to Hanslick, and both he and Brahms were enthusiastic about them. The ever-vigilant Simrock wanted them orchestrated as soon as possible, and Dvořák completed the task at the end of the same year, as well as orchestrating, at his publisher's request, five of Brahms's *Hungarian Dances*.

During March to October of 1881 and February to September of the following year Dvořák was occupied with the composition of *Dimitri*—another opera—to a libretto by Marie Červinková-Riegrová. The story begins where Pushkin and Mussorgsky leave off, but unfortunately the good lady was no Pushkin and Dvořák was no Mussorgsky; and the opera is, in spite of many beauties, lacking in dramatic grip. Dvořák, sensitive as ever to criticism, submitted it to several revisions in the next few years, but without really improving it. The first performance was intended to have taken place in the Czech National Theatre (Národni-Divadlo), which had been opened on 11th June 1881, with the first performance of Smetana's *Libuša*, but the building was burnt down in August and *Dimitri*, when completed, had to be produced (on 8th October 1882) at the new Czech Theatre, the provisional home of the destroyed building. It had a success there, but for political as well as artistic reasons, did not succeed in crossing the frontiers. World-wide operatic success ever eluded Dvořák.

The other works of 1881 were a string Quartet in C major, Op. 61, and some incidental music to a drama by Šamberk, *Josef Kajetan Tyl*. (Tyl was the founder of the Czech Theatre.) There is a nice spark of humour in Dvořák's remark about the Quartet. In November he wrote to Göbl: 'I see in the papers that on 15th December Hellmesberger is to perform my new quartet which does not yet exist! There is nothing left for me to do but compose it.'

Dvořák found plenty of ideas always at call, and the Quartet, dedicated to Hellmesberger, and too consciously attuned to the environment in which it was to be played, was duly performed in Vienna on the advertised date.

The remaining works of 1882 were an *Impromptu* for piano not published until 1916, twelve years after his death, and five choruses for mixed voices, Op. 63, entitled *Amid Nature*.

Composers are usually held to be irritable beings, but they seem to be remarkably charitable to their librettists. Marie Červinková-Riegrová, though not a Helmina von Chézy, was far from being the ideal librettist, yet not long after the first performance of *Dimitri* Dvořák told her he would like to discuss a new subject, as two important impresarios, Schuch of Dresden and Janner of Vienna, had let it be known they wanted to produce an opera by him. They had, however, made one condition: the libretto was not to be on a Czech, nor even a Slav subject: it was, in fact, indicated quite clearly that Dvořák should set a German text.

The temptation to enter the international field of opera must have been great, though at this period of Czech history it would have looked like a betrayal of the national cause which he was implicitly vowed to serve. Dvořák's inward disturbance of soul over this problem was enhanced by the death of his mother on 14th December 1882, at Kladno. This unsought suffering, a condition of artistic growth, caused him to write his two most deeply felt works, the pianoforte Trio in F minor, Op. 65, composed in the early months of 1883, and, when the emotional storms had subsided, and after his very successful visit to England, the Symphony in D minor, Op. 70, which is undoubtedly his greatest work. It was composed (without dedication) between December 1884 and March 1885. Two other fine works, rarely heard now, belong to 1883, the *Scherzo capriccioso,* Op. 66, written in April and first performed under Adolf Čech at the New Czech Theatre, Prague, and the *Hussite Overture,* Op. 76, composed between August and September for the festivities in connection with the opening of the Czech National Theatre, and given there at the gala opening on 18th November.

In this overture Dvořák solves a problem which still eludes theologians by quoting both a Hussite and a Catholic tune, and pointing the moral by ending with the national anthem. In response to Simrock's unceasing and irritating demand for easy piano duets Dvořák produced the character-pieces, *From the Bohemian Forest,* which form a kind of musical travel diary. He had to call in the aid of Madame Červinková-Riegrová to find this quite obvious title, and she may have helped with the titles given to the various pieces, as Dvořák complained that Schumann had used up all the best ones.

In October Dvořák again visited Brahms and found him in excellent spirits. It has been suggested, and may well be the case, that Brahms's playing over of his new F major Symphony determined Dvořák to write another symphony himself. If so, the period of gestation was over a year. and in the meantime the composer was to experience perhaps the greatest public successs of his career. In England.

CHAPTER VII

THE BOHEMIAN IN ENGLAND

DVOŘÁK set out from Prague on 5th March 1884, accompanied by his friend, Heinrich von Kaan, a pianist, and travelled to London by way of Cologne and Brussels. He was met at the station by Oscar Beringer, with whom he was to stay, and by Alfred Littleton, head of the house of Novello, and an honorary secretary of the London Music Society, founded by Barnby in 1878 'for the practice and per-formance of the works of composers which are not generally known to the musical public.' It was this society which had already, in 1883, performed Dvořák's *Stabat Mater* under Barnby's direction. The Czech composer had in fact been well publicized before he set foot in the country. Attention had been drawn to his humble origin, his early struggles and his growing success, in such a way as to appeal to a well-nourished public always ready to shed a tear over poverty not too visible from its own doorsteps. England, further-more, always has a warm welcome for the foreign artist—in itself a pleasant trait—and the music that had already been heard whetted the appetite for more.

That excellent travel poster, the string Sextet in A (Op. 48), had been given twice at the Monday Popular Concerts in St. James's Hall in the spring of 1880, and from then onwards other chamber-music works were regularly produced, including the string Quartet in E flat major, as immediate a favourite as the *Slavonic Dances,* which came out at the Crystal Palace in 1880. This fresh and uninhibited music, spiced with national flavouring and not at all subversive, gave much direct and vicarious pleasure to a society whose manners were as tight-laced as its women.

Dvořák gave pain to some critics by such lapses as failing to bring back the second subject in the relative major; but the St. James's Hall audiences, in spite of the copious analyses to which they were accustomed, took no umbrage at such small violations of musical good behaviour. Instead they were quick to welcome a composer

46

who had got away from the conventional musical utterance of the time, while those of them who felt bound to wait until a sign had been given from on high received the *imprimatur* of Brahms with relief and joined in the universal approbation.

It is important to remember that the public for the 'Pops' was, as H. C. Colles pointed out, 'largely the preserve of cultivated Kensington,' the ground tilled by Mendelssohn. It must have been a really keen and discerning public for a typical programme consisting of Schubert's D minor (*Death and the Maiden*) Quartet, Beethoven's 'Archduke' Trio and Schumann's *Carnival* to be designated as popular and to cause a thousand persons to be turned away from the doors. But it was in no sense the general public.

Dvořák had been engaged by the Philharmonic Society for a concert in St. James's Hall, at which he was to perform the *Hussite Overture*, his Symphony in D major (No. 6), the second *Slavonic Rhapsody* and a group of the *Gypsy Songs* with the composer at the piano. Here again there was no question of an appeal to the general public. The Philharmonic Society gave only six concerts a year and 'was by its constitution an association of musicians professional and amateur, formed to provide music for its own associates and subscribing members, its programmes chosen by its elected directors. So to invite a composer to conduct his work at the Philharmonic was to secure for him the attention of the best informed and presumably the most critical of London audiences.' [1]

Dvořák passed this searching test with flying colours, and one should record that, apart from the fulsome praise of the daily press, one music critic at least, Joseph Bennett, in *The Musical Times*, 'showed that he really had got the measure of this new music.' He had written two articles on Dvořák in 1881. These are good, but his article written in the April number of 1884 is first-rate. It may attach undue importance to the national elements in the music, but it ably seizes upon and discusses the chief characteristics and qualities of the Czech composer's art.

The remaining two events for which Dvořák was engaged brought him to the generality of the music-loving public. These were an

[1] *Musical Times*, April 1940.

orchestral concert at the Crystal Palace, at which he conducted the
Scherzo capriccioso and the *Nocturne* for strings (Op. 40), and a performance of the *Stabat Mater,* given by the Albert Hall Choral Society
under his direction at the Albert Hall on 13th March.

Dr. Colles again reminds us that:

The regular hearing of orchestral music meant to the Londoner a Saturday
afternoon journey on the London, Chatham and Dover line to the Crystal
Palace in company with football crowds and other pleasure-seekers. The
lover of orchestral music of the finer type had to be an enthusiast. But the
habit of oratorio performance had long been indigenous, and though it
still rested on the reiteration of Handel, Mendelssohn and Spohr, its
audiences were ready to be awakened to new experiences.

The 'new experience' of the *Stabat Mater* was welcomed with terrific
enthusiasm, which one would like to think was partly a reaction
from the copious draughts of Gounod's Catholicism *sucré* then being
imbibed. But the facts do not justify such an assumption.

It is worth while giving Dvořák's account of his reception in his
own words:

As soon as I appeared, I received a tempestuous welcome from the audience
of 12,000. These ovations increasing, I had to bow my thanks again and
again, the orchestra and choir applauding with no less fervour. I am convinced that England offers me a new and certainly happier future, and one
which I hope may benefit our entire Czech art. The English are a fine
people, enthusiastic about music, and it is well known that they remain
loyal to those whose art they have enjoyed. God grant that it may be so
with me.

There were the usual banquets and receptions, and at the one given
by the Philharmonic Society Dvořák managed to get out his first
speech in English.[1]

He reached home on 29th March, a well-contented man. Nothing
succeeds like success. Novello had offered him £2,000 for a new

[1] Herman Klein gives a pleasant little sketch of Dvořák at one of these
affairs: 'simple as a child, his dark piercing eyes rarely lighting up with a
smile . . . bearded like the pard and with a crushing handshake.' Edward
Lloyd's singing of *Songs my mother taught me* caused him 'to wipe the furtive
tears off his cheek,' as the song describes.

oratorio, and Simrock had been generous over terms for the *Hussite Overture* and the piano duets *From the Bohemian Forest.*

Dvořák had given England not only some beautiful music, but a guilty conscience. Much stress had been laid on the national elements in his work. What had been done, conscience hinted, to encourage the growth of a truly national art in England? A rather dusty answer to that question was given by men contemporary with Dvořák like Mackenzie and Cowen, Parry and Stanford, whose influence was more widespread. The response of the public was tepid, and England was no doubt fortunate to find a voice in 'Gilbert and Sullivan' and Edward German which did, and still does, command the ear of at least a portion of the public.

Back in Bohemia Dvořák lost no time in realizing one of his dearest wishes, to have a cottage of his own in the country. He knew just what he wanted, a bit of land on his brother-in-law's estate at Vysoká. Here, on the foundations of a shepherd's hut, he had made a simple house and garden. Hills and forests were around him, and he found the village folk of Vysoká entirely congenial company. It was a great pleasure to him to sit amongst them of an evening in the village inn and occasionally join in the conversation, but he found even greater pleasure in the rearing of pigeons. This was a subject on which he was always willing to talk, and if a host unwittingly provided pigeon at a meal Dvořák, protesting, forthwith left the table. His little country house became very dear to him, and after mid-June Prague never saw him again till the beginning of winter.

It does not need a high degree of imaginative sympathy to realize how he felt, with the years of poverty now well behind him, at waking up in his own house and amidst such beautiful surroundings. Gissing, who underwent even more severe poverty, has given an unforgettable picture of such an experience in his *Private Papers of Henry Ryecroft.*

Besides rearing pigeons and getting his house in order Dvořák now had to do some juggling with Simrock. That gentleman had to be prevented from getting wind of the oratorio promised to Novello. The composer had made up his mind that it was to be a work of a national character, but, as he could find no suitable text, he turned to K. J. Erben (1811–70), a Czech poet, whom he much admired and who had compiled an extensive collection of Slavonic legends and Czech ballads, and set one of these ballads, *The Wedding Shift*. (As the mention of this garment offended the modesty of the ineffable Rev. Dr. Troutbeck, to whom we shall return, this choral ballad is known in English as *The Spectre's Bride*. This is, at any rate, a better selling title!) The score was finished by the end of November 1884 and published by Novello, and the work was first performed by the Pilsen Choral Society on 28th March 1885, with the composer conducting.

While still at work on this score Dvořák made his second journey to England. He had been engaged to conduct his *Stabat Mater* and the D major Symphony (No. 6) at the Worcester Cathedral Jubilee celebrations in September. He again had enormous success, and this was repeated in Berlin a month or so later, where he made his début as a conductor in Germany with the D major Symphony.

His mind was now set on two large projects: the oratorio for Novello and a symphony for the Philharmonic Society of London, who had elected him an honorary member on 13th June 1884 and, as a *quid pro quo*, begged for a new symphony. His creative mind had been busy over this idea ever since he had heard Brahms's third Symphony, in F major, and as a letter to his friend Antonín Rus shows, he set to work with high ambitions. He wrote: 'Everywhere I go, I think of nothing else than my work, which must be such as to shake the world, and with God's help it will be so.' The composition of the Symphony in D minor, Op. 70, occupied him from mid-December 1884 to mid-March 1885. It bore no dedication. The first performance took place at the Philharmonic Society concert at St. James's Hall on 22nd April 1885, under the composer's direction, and was a huge success.[1] The work, which pleased conservatives and progressives alike, was favourably compared with Schubert's C major Symphony, and declared to be more immediately appealing than the Brahms F major.

In this Symphony Dvořák set out deliberately to show that he was a good deal more than merely a national composer, and it is indeed

---

[1] At the two other London concerts on 6th and 13th May the piano Concerto was played by Franz Rummel and the *Hymnus* performed (it was published by Novello under the title of *The Heirs of the White Mountain*).

only in the last movement that any national flavouring is perceptible.
Though complaining that Dvořák's major works did not sell, Simrock was anxious to buy this one, but demanded also another set of
Slavonic Dances, as a sort of makeweight. He offered three thousand
marks, and received the following pertinent reply from a composer
who was now beginning to realize that he was a good commercial
proposition, and not so easily to be bought as all that:

(1) If I let you have the Symphony for 3,000 marks, I shall have lost
about 3,000 marks, because other firms offer me double that amount. I
should very much regret it if you were, so to speak, to force me into this
position.

(2) Although such big works do not at once achieve the material success
we could wish, nevertheless the time may come that will make up for it, and,

(3) Please remember that in my *Slavonic Dances* you have found a mine
not lightly to be underestimated.

(4) If we look at this from a commonsense point of view, reconsidering
all you have indicated in your last letter, it leads to the plain conclusion:
that I should write no symphonies, no big vocal works, and no instrumental
music; only now and then perhaps a couple of 'Lieder,' 'Piano Pieces' and
'Dances,' and I don't know what sort of 'publishable' things. Well, as
an artist who wants to amount to something, I simply cannot do it! Indeed,
my dear friend, this is how I see it from my standpoint as an artist. . . .
Please remember that I am a poor artist and father of a family. . . .[1]

Simrock increased his price to six thousand marks, and extorted a
qualified promise that the new set of *Slavonic Dances* should be sent to
him the following year. Relations were also a little strained over the
printing of the composer's name. Dvořák wished his Christian
name to be printed as Ant.—which would stand for Anton or
Antonín—and for the titles of his works to be given in Czech as well
as German. Explaining his reasons he wrote:

After all, what have we either of us to do with politics? Let's be happy
that we can consecrate our services to the fine arts alone! And let us hope
the nations that possess and represent the arts may never go under, no matter
how small they are. Forgive me for this digression: I was only trying to
explain that an artist also has a homeland in which he must have firm faith
and to which his heart must always warm.[2]

---

[1] *Simrock Year Book,* vol. ii, page 109.   [2] Ibid., page 111.

With Teutonic obstinacy and singular bad manners Simrock, as before, printed the title of the D minor Symphony and the composer's Christian name only in German.

On his return from London Dvořák turned to the composition of smaller things—a new Overture to the second act of *Dimitri*, a *Ballade* for violin and piano (Op. 15) and a chorale in praise of Czech peasant life.

A suitable text for the national oratorio had been provided by Vrchlický (1853–1912), poet, novelist, critic and translator, on the subject of St. Ludmilla, but before he could get to work on this Dvořák had to go to England once again, this time alone 'just to see how it goes.' It went well. In a letter to Antonín Rus Dvořák gives an interesting account of this visit:

I arrived safely on Monday, 17th August, at six o'clock in the morning. London was still asleep. Everywhere was quiet. There was no one in the streets. I was quite tired after the journey, and on the same afternoon I had to go to Birmingham, where in the evening there was a rehearsal of *The Spectre's Bride*. It went off excellently, completely according to my wishes. The choir consists of five hundred people, and they had rehearsed the work perfectly beforehand. Before and after the rehearsal I was received with cheers by the choir, as well as by the assembled public. On the next morning I went back to London, and to-day, as I am writing to you [19th August], I am again in another place—in the beautiful sea-coast town of Brighton, where the richest class of Londoners go in the summer. The beautiful view of the sea from my lodgings, the spectacle of the thousands of people swarming everywhere, the beautiful English women bathing here (and in public), the men and children, the vast quantity of great and small ships, then again the music playing Scottish national songs, and all kinds of other things: all this so enchanting and fascinating that whoever has seen it will never forget it. Novello also has his beautiful house here, where I am staying, and where, thank God, I am in good health.[1]

After taking rehearsals of *The Spectre's Bride* at Birmingham Dvořák went off to stay with Littleton at Brighton. Then he submitted himself, at the Birmingham Festival, to the ordeal of eight concerts,

---

[1] This letter is quoted on page 38 of 'The Life of Antonín Dvořák,' a chapter by Viktor Fischl in *Antonín Dvořák: his Achievement*.

each of them four or five hours long, in four days, a test of endurance which he found 'simply terrible.' Wagner had made a similar complaint some years before.

Back at Vysoká Dvořák got to work on *St. Ludmilla,* dedicating the score, which he finished on 30th May 1886, 'to the Zerotin Choral and Music Society at Olomouc.'

On 1st October of this year the composer journeyed to England for the fifth time in order to conduct the first performance of the work at Leeds. Excitement ran high, and the oratorio, sung by a choir of 350 voices, had an enormous success.

It is hard for us to realize, in these days, what competition there was to have the honour of a first performance. We hear without emotion that Manchester or Birmingham will have the first performance of a new work by a modern composer and, if we are Londoners, we await its arrival with perfect composure. Dvořák thought he had taken the measure of the English public in making this large and impressive work sufficiently Handelian to appeal to them while retaining its appeal on national grounds at least to his own countrymen. This falling between two stools produced the usual result, final neglect; and the dust has lain thick on *St. Ludmilla* for many years. The Leeds performance took place on 15th October. London heard the work on 29th October and 6th November. Writing home to Bohemia Dvořák said:

Well, to-day it went off gloriously! The performance lasted from 12.30 p.m. to 3 p.m. All the same, no sign of weariness, not the very least. The interest kept going to the last note! I am still in the greatest state of excitement, partly the result of the remarkable performance of the orchestra (120 players), chorus (350) and soloists of the first rank; and also on account of a magnificent ovation on the part of the public. The enthusiasm—this English enthusiasm—was such as I have not experienced for a long while! I confess that I have never before been so strongly moved, nor so sensible of the flutter of excitement around me at the conductor's desk as after the first and third sections. At the close of the performance I had to bow my thanks again and again in response to a tempest of applause and the calling of my name. Then I had to speak a few words of praise in English, heartily congratulating the orchestra and chorus. Again the audience broke into tempestuous applause, waved their handkerchiefs and shouted my name. I heard that at Ludmilla's aria, 'O grant me in the dust to fall,' which the famous Albani sang divinely, the public was moved to tears.

(The oratorio was done in costume at the Czech National Theatre in 1901.)

Relations with Simrock were again becoming strained. Dvořák, ignoring the terms of his contract, had promised *St. Ludmilla* to Novello, and for a better price than Simrock would have paid. But in spite of protests Simrock wanted neither oratorios, operas or symphonies. He wanted a new set of *Slavonic Dances* or, he graciously intimated, some songs. He got both. Eight *Slavonic Dances, Op. 72* (second series), for piano duet were ready by July 1886 and were published three months later. Then the exigent publisher demanded that they should be orchestrated. This seems to have bothered Dvořák, for the orchestration took him six months and, according to the composer, sounded like the devil. There was no question of merely repeating a success in these dances. They are Polish, Serbian and Czech dance poems and a considerable advance on the first series.

Simrock got as well, in September, some of Dvořák's best songs, the set of four called *Im Volkston,* Op. 73, which were also published this year.

The *Terzetto* for two violins and viola, Op. 74, and the *Four Romantic Pieces* for violin and piano, Op. 75, belong to January 1887 and were written about the time that the committee of the Birmingham Festival suggested Cardinal Newman's *Dream of Gerontius* as a text for an oratorio. It might have been imagined that this poem would have appealed strongly to Dvořák, and certainly it would have been most interesting to see what he would have made of it. But he refused the suggestion and promised another work. In the meantime he devoted himself instead to the revision of the Quartets in A major and A minor, the arrangement of some of the *Cypress Songs* for string quartet, the completion of the second version of the opera *King and Collier* and the composition of a Mass in D, commissioned by Josef Hlávka, 'a wealthy patron of the arts,' and first given at the consecration of his private chapel. The first public performance took place at Pilsen in 1888. A Mass, however successful, was not much in Simrock's line, and the work was published (as Op. 86 instead of Op. 76, which Simrock had used for the F major Symphony, formerly Op. 24) by Novello in 1892.

After casually informing Simrock, in August 1887, that he had nothing new in mind, Dvořák began one of his finest chamber-music works, the piano Quintet in A major, Op. 77, but published by Simrock as Op. 81. Dvořák seems to have been in love with the key of A at this time.

Composers have, on occasion, to be commercial travellers for their own goods. In the autumn Dvořák journeyed to Berlin where he sold Simrock the Symphony in F major, the *Symphonic Variations,* the string Quintet in G major, the 149th Psalm and the A major piano Quintet. Simrock paid six thousand marks for these works and had the decency, this time, to print the titles in German and Czech, as well as following the composer's wishes in regard to his Christian name. This appeared as Ant. and might therefore be read as Anton or Antonín. Nothing if not tactless, the publisher thoroughly muddled up the opus numbers, making early works appear as if just written.

Dvořák was ready again for a large work and he turned hopefully to opera, choosing a libretto, *Jakobín* (to be called *The Jacobin* hereafter), which had long been awaiting him. Marie Cervinková-Riegrová was again the authoress and once more provided a rambling and un-dramatic text. Dvořák, for sentimental reasons, turned a blind eye to its deficiencies. The 'spirit of the old Czech musicians breathes from end to end of the work. It is an apotheosis of the Czech cantors of the past, a graceful tribute by the great musician to the teachers of his youth.'[1] The character of Benda, the village schoolmaster, organist and composer—so strongly recalling Liehmann—and the chance of painting genre pictures of the life of his beloved countryside proved irresistible. The opera was completed by November 1888, and first produced in Prague on 12th February 1889 under Adolf Čech. It had the usual success, underwent revision, in the Dvořák manner, and has rarely been heard outside Czechoslovakia.

There is a touching story of Dvořák revisiting his birthplace

---

[1] *Antonín Dvořák,* by Hoffmeister, page 97.

Nelahozeves in April 1889 and improvising for a long time on themes from *The Jacobin* on the piano in a girls' high school now housed in the Lobkowitz castle. The outcome of this experience was the composition of the thirteen *Poetic Tone-Pictures* for piano, Op. 85, which the parsimonious Simrock grumbled would be expensive to produce. In the event he was well repaid, as the collection proved extremely popular. Dvořák's greater skill in handling the piano is shown in this work and much more in the fine piano Quartet in E flat major, Op. 87, which he composed in the summer of this year.

Simrock, who was pleased to get this work—which he published at the end of 1890—had not long before written to Brahms that Dvořák's head seemed always full of music. It remained so after the piano Quartet was completed, and the composer now began his G major Symphony. When it was completed[1] publisher and composer began once again to haggle. Simrock offered only a thousand marks for the Symphony, making the familiar complaint that Dvořák's large works did not sell, and having the effrontery to add that he made very little out of the smaller ones, more of which, however, he demanded. Dvořák replied tartly that he had a lot of ideas for big works in his head, and what was going to happen if he could get none for small ones? 'I shall simply do what God tells me to do,' he said. 'That will certainly be the best thing.'

This reply alarmed Simrock, who pointed out that the contract of 1879 was still valid. Dvořák ignored the letter and sold his Symphony to Novello, who published it as Op. 88 in 1892. The score bears the inscription: 'To the Bohemian Academy of Emperor Franz Joseph for the Encouragement of Art and Literature, in thanks for my election.'

At the end of this year honours began to be heaped on Dvořák. He went to Vienna with his wife to thank the emperor for the award of the Iron Crown of the third class; the Czech University of Prague made him an honorary Doctor of Philosophy, and Cambridge University a Mus.Doc.

He was, however, fuller of ideas than honours, and now began the work which he had promised the Birmingham Festival Committee

[1] It was first performed in Prague in February 1890, the composer conducting.

A LETTER IN ENGLISH WRITTEN BY DVOŘÁK

MS. OF PART OF THE CANTATA 'THE SPECTRE'S BRIDE'

when he rejected *The Dream of Gerontius*. This was a Requiem Mass for solo voices, chorus and orchestra, which occupied him, with the interruption of journeys to Russia and England, from February to October 1890. It was first performed at Birmingham on 9th October 1891, under the composer's direction and, though successful, was rated, by the critics, lower than *St. Ludmilla,* a judgment history has reversed.

Dvořák has left an amusing account of his investiture with the honorary degree of Doctor of Music which took place at Cambridge on 16th June 1891. He had conducted his 'exercise,' the G major Symphony, and *Stabat Mater,* to which the dean made a flattering reference in his Latin oration to the vice-chancellor. Dvořák 'on pins and needles' listened to this, arrayed in the doctor's robes presented to him by the university choir. It was all 'frightfully solemn,' he said,

nothing but ceremonies and deans, all solemn-faced and apparently incapable of speaking anything but Latin. When it dawned upon me that they were talking to me, I felt as if I were drowning in hot water, so ashamed was I that I could not understand them. However, when all is said and done, that *Stabat Mater* of mine is more than just Latin.

In 1889 Dvořák had been offered a professorship at the Prague Conservatoire by the Society for the Furtherance of Music in Bohemia. At the time he was too much occupied with composition and concert tours to accept, but at the end of 1890 he felt able to undertake the post and started his duties on 1st January 1891.

The Conservatoire and the Organ School were now amalgamated, owing to the efforts of Dr. Josef Tragy, and Dvořák's task was to bring his composition class, for which he was allowed to select the most talented students, up to the high level of the classes in instrumental music. His fifteen students included Suk, Nedbal and, later, Novák, all of whom were to play an important part in modern Czech music. His students seem to have understood him well. He kept to no settled time-table, staying long after the appointed hour if he was interested. He was often testy and could say very hurtful things, for which he at once atoned if he felt they had been unjust. He had no more settled plan of instruction than he had followed himself, and no doubt 'God, the flowers and the birds, myself,' figured largely in his teaching. Perhaps the most delightful thing was his comradeship with his pupils. Nedbal said: 'Sometimes he's a comrade; then, again, he's a god.' When he was in the mood to be a comrade he was ready to discuss his plans and not only to give but to receive advice.

On his return from America he intensified the democratic character of his class. Every one in it was to be equal. He insisted on hard work, 'many sketches and long developments, otherwise you're no composer.' Severe in his judgments, whenever he refused to teach untalented pupils he would say: 'It hurts you now, but later on it will save you much suffering.' Pellegrini has given an interesting account of his ideas which may here be summarized as it throws light on his own methods.

The art of composition is to make a great deal out of very little. As an artist must be capable of much, he must learn a great deal. Invention was no special credit to the student, it came from God, but the really important thing was what the student did with his ideas. To make the best of them he should soak himself in the classics and so learn to be logical and intelligible. But Dvořák was by no means sure (and became less so as he grew older) that the classic forms were the right mould for contemporary music. 'Modern' music by his students was received with abuse or jokes, but secretly preferred to the safe and conventional. He himself showed great interest in com-posers then thought revolutionary, such as Richard Strauss and Bruckner, and carefully studied their scores. He had a wide know-ledge of musical literature, and was an excellent sight-reader of orchestral as well as other scores.

Dvořák enjoyed teaching, and his fame and original methods naturally made him much sought after. In fact if not in name his was a 'master-class,' and soon became known as 'The Dvořák School.' The class gave its first concert on 13th May 1891, when a piano Quartet by the seventeen-year-old Suk was performed and favourably commented on.

After his return from America in 1895 Dvořák continued with his teaching till 1904. His professional duties caused no interruption in his creative work. The so-called *Dumky* pianoforte Trio, Op. 90, followed the Requiem Mass and was first performed on 11th April 1891, with Dvořák at the piano and one of his colleagues, Hanuš Wihan, playing the cello. It became one of his most popular works and was published by Simrock in 1894.

This sonnet-sequence, a novel departure in form, must have given his pupils food for thought. His feeling towards programme music, fed by the study of Liszt and Wagner, which dominated the last years of his life, now found expression in the three overtures, *In Nature's Realm*, Op. 91, *Carnival*, Op. 92, and *Othello*, Op. 93, which were originally given the generic title of *Nature, Life and Love*.

These three tone-poems share one motive in common and to make their full effect should be heard consecutively. This is never the case in the concert-hall, and indeed only *Carnival*, the least good of the three, is heard now with any regularity. Suk and Nedbal prepared the duet-scores of these works for publication. These two, who were pupils in Bennevic's violin class, joined Karel Hoffmann and Otto Berger in a Conservatoire string quartet organized by Wihan. (The quartet, which first appeared before the public on 22nd October 1892, later became famous as the Bohemian String Quartet,[1] and did much towards the popularizing of Dvořák's chamber music. In 1897 Wihan himself replaced Berger, who had died, and was himself replaced, in 1913, by Zelenka. When Nedbal left, in 1906, his place was taken by Herold.)

Dvořák's fiftieth birthday on 8th September 1891 was the occasion of many ceremonies, speech-making and newspaper articles. Dvořák took part in the gala performance of one of his operas by remaining with his family at Vysoká and having a walk through the woods, thinking over, no doubt, all that had happened to him in his fifty years of life.

[1] Name subsequently changed to Czech Quartet.

CHAPTER VIII

THE AMERICAN JOURNEY

PERHAPS Anthony Trollope did as much as any man to disabuse the public mind of the idea that a writer only employs his pen when in a *raptus*. His honest and forthright statement that he turned out daily and at a regular hour so many hundred words came as a shock to the generally received notion of a literary man.[1] Bach, had the public studied him as a man, did much the same thing, as indeed any creative artist must on whom continual demands are made, or for whom a ready market exists. Dvořák had, as he now well knew, a high market value, and he was perfectly ready to exploit it. When the American composer Dudley Buck, whom he had met in London, had tried to persuade him to go to America in 1884 he had already made a great success in England and was becoming a name in the world. Now he was famous. This time a definite invitation, not merely an idea, was forthcoming.

Mrs. Jeanette M. Thurber, the wife of a well-to-do wholesale grocer in New York, wanted a big name for her National Conservatory in New York, and was prepared to pay for it. She had consulted a Viennese friend, Adele Margulies, who taught the piano at the New York National Conservatory, and this lady, on the advice of her master in Vienna, Anton Door, had suggested Dvořák and Sibelius. Geographical considerations determined the final choice. Miss Margulies did not feel equal to the journey to Finland. Her family lived in Vienna, and it would be easy to see Dvořák there or in Prague.

The offer of the directorship of Mrs. Thurber's institution was cabled to Vysoká in the spring of 1891. Dvořák declined.

Now the philanthropic Mrs. Thurber had lost a lot of money over an attempt to run opera in English in competition with the Metro-

---

[1] Sir Alexander Mackenzie, in *A Musician's Narrative*, relates that Dvořák said it was his habit to write and score forty bars daily—'that makes about three hundred bars weekly.'

politan, an attempt which proved as fatal as that of her countryman, Oscar Hammerstein, to make a going concern of the London Opera House. Undaunted by a failure which cost her (or, more properly, her husband), in two years, $1,500,000, Mrs. Thurber founded, in 1885, the National Conservatory of Music. She had been a music teacher, and knew something of the difficulties students of music have to undergo. And so the Conservatory was to be a non-profit-making institution, exacting fees only from those who could afford them, but in other cases providing free tuition. Because of this Congress allowed its title. Perhaps the most remarkable thing about the school was that the coloured races were admitted. This liberal policy may be taken as an indication of what was in Mrs. Thurber's mind, the creation of a school of American composition. So far, as Dr. Colles remarked, the Conservatory 'had followed the model of the Paris Conservatoire, at any rate to the extent of finding much virtue in the vocal practice of solfeggi under the direction of Jacques Bouhy, a Belgian baritone who had studied at the Paris Conservatoire.'

Bouhy's return to Europe a few years later caused a break, and the invitation to Dvořák to succeed him suggests that the question of how to repair it was the subject of much anxious thought.

Mrs. Thurber was not the sort of woman to be put off by Dvořák's first refusal. She wired from Paris. The post of director was offered for two years, the official duties taking up eight months in each year, with four months' vacation. Dvořák would have to conduct ten concerts of his own works. The salary was $15,000 a year. Dvořák weighed this large amount against the 1,200 gulden the Prague Conservatoire was paying him. He hesitated. He consulted Göbl. He thought with distaste of the long sea journey, the longer absence from his country, and in particular from Vysoká. More telegrams from Mrs. Thurber. Would it not do if he undertook the ten concerts? The wires again buzzed with the energetic American lady's reply. It would not do. Then the bait was dangled right in front of him, the arrival of a contract simply requiring his signature. The 28th of September 1891 was still some way off, half his salary was to be paid in the spring of that year, the Prague authorities had given him leave. And so, finally, he accepted.

Early in 1892 Dvořák went on a concert tour through Bohemia

and Moravia with the violinist Lachner and the cellist Wihan, who seems to have inspired him much as the clarinettist Mühlfeld did Brahms. He wrote a Rondo for piano and cello, Op. 94, for him at the end of 1891, and dedicated to him the cello Concerto in B minor, Op. 104, which he started during his last year in America, 1894.

With the prospect of Dvořák's prolonged absence in America in mind Simrock again opened negotiations with the composer and declared himself willing to publish at once the *Dumky* Trio—which had been played throughout the Bohemian-Moravian tour—and the just completed three Overtures. Dvořák replied to the effect that the matter could stand over until next season. He was in no hurry.

His coming journey made Vysoká, no doubt, more than usually attractive to him. He did not, in June 1892, attend the Prague National Theatre's performance of *Dimitri*, which was given in Vienna during the International Music and Drama Exposition. The previous night had seen a brilliant performance of *The Bartered Bride*. Certain elements—Hanslick, it may be, among them—engineered this juxtaposition not so much as a compliment to Bohemia as to oppose Dvořák, the friend of Brahms, to Smetana the (so-called) disciple of Wagner.

Soon after this event Dvořák felt the first effect of his signed contract. Mrs. Thurber wished him to compose and bring with him a new work for performance on 12th October, the fourth centennial celebration of Columbus's discovery of America. As the promised poem did not arrive until a few weeks before he sailed, Dvořák wrote instead a *Te Deum* for soprano and bass solos, choir and orchestra, Op. 103, and this was given shortly after the Columbus celebrations. He made some sketches for the other work, *The American Flag*, but did not finish it until January 1893, and it was not performed until after Dvořák had left America. It is quite understandable that he, in fact, forgot all about it.

Obedient to Mrs. Thurber's instructions Dvořák left Prague on 15th September 1892 to travel, via Southampton, to Bremen, where he was to pick up his ship, the *Saale*. Besides his wife he took two of his numerous children, and a young man whom he had met in a

Prague music shop, Joseph Kovařík. This proved an important contact, as Kovařík's father had emigrated to the United States and become choirmaster of St. Wenceslas's Church at Spillville, a Czech settlement in Iowa, Mass., where Dvořák spent his happiest days in America.

On arrival at New York, on 27th September, the secretary of the Conservatory and a delegation of Czech-Americans welcomed the party, and four days later Mrs. Thurber introduced the new director to the teaching staff of her Conservatory at 128 East 17th Street. They were delighted, and possibly relieved, to be greeted in excellent English.

The American public had been made very much aware of the famous composer in their midst. Mrs. Thurber had seen to that. She had also announced a prize for the best opera by an American-born composer, the works submitted to be judged by Dvořák.

The press had most thoroughly interviewed him and revealed to the public every detail they could extract, observe or invent. It was conceded that he was not so much of a backwoodsman as they had expected, indeed his face and manners were described as agreeable. Naturally enough extravagant speculations were made about the rise of a new American music, to be either produced by the Czech composer himself or conjured by him out of his pupils.

Dvořák kept his head amidst all this pother. He liked the enthusiastic, warm-hearted people, their democratic ways appealed to him, and he felt at home in a city as yet untroubled by fast-moving traffic or skyscrapers. The musical situation he did not like so well. Indeed, it astonished him. There were excellent institutions like the Metropolitan Opera, founded in 1883, and the Philharmonic Society, founded in 1842 and now conducted by Anton Seidl, a friend of Wagner's. Walter Damrosch conducted the New York Symphony Society (later merged into the Philharmonic Society) and Nikisch the Boston Symphony Orchestra. There were choral societies, such as the New York Oratorio Society and chamber music societies such as the Kneisel Quartet. There were plenty of recitals at which artists such as Paderewski could be heard. Standards of performance were good, money was plentiful.

But when it came to the question of training the future generation there seemed to be a complete lack of organization. Students behaved much as they liked in the music schools, and not one of these places was a real artistic centre. Mrs. Thurber's National Conservatory of Art, therefore, had a clear field before it, and offered great opportunities to a director of genius. Dvořák had already warned Mrs. Thurber that he might not be that.

His colleagues included James T. Huneker, who has given us in *Mezzotints* an amusing account of his association with Dvořák, and Henry T. Finck, both of whom taught the history of music; and Adele Margulies, the piano teacher really responsible for his being there.

The Dvořáks were not the sort of people to care for hotel life—which anyway proved very expensive—so they moved into an apartment near to the Conservatory. It was not long before Dvořák discovered the railway stations, but he found it much more difficult to study engines there than at home. His ardour, however, remained unabated, and he would take an hour's drive to 155th Street just to see the Chicago expresses thunder by. His passion for engines being somewhat thwarted by unsympathetic station-masters, he found a new attraction in the harbour, where one could board any vessel on sailing days. The determined little man inspected every outward-bound liner with the thoroughness usually attributed to royalty, and even when he was supposed to be at the Conservatory he did his best to see every ship sail.

Twice a week he went down to the docks, twice a week he visited a railway station, and the other two days he went walking in Central Park. Evenings were spent in fascinating speculation as to where a certain ship would be about that time and how many knots she could make. He knew to the day and hour what ships were arriving and departing, and prided himself on being able to address his letters to Bohemia, stating exactly on which ship they would be carried.

For the rest, his love of nature had to be satisfied with Central Park. There were pigeons, too, in this extraordinary town, though you did not get to know them so well as in Vysoká. [1]

It is doubtful that Mrs. Thurber appreciated these hobbies as much

[1] *Anton Dvořák*, by Paul Stefan, page 197.

as her director did, nor could she approve his habit of avoiding all
social functions, including concerts or the opera, that interfered with
his regular hour of bedtime, whether or not his own works were to
be performed.

Dvořák was scarcely a man of routine in his teaching, however
much that was the case with his personal habits, but he did try to
introduce some discipline into the rather haphazard methods of Mrs.
Thurber's school. Three times a week he gave a two-hour lesson in
composition and twice a week he conducted the Conservatory
orchestra.

He had some good pupils, who included a sprinkling of negroes,
greeted by him with innate sympathy for the underdog. He was a
success as a conductor of his own music, and that music was everywhere warmly received.

But of course there were difficulties. The Wagnerians dubbed him
a reactionary, interested parties pointedly alluded to a lack of 'results.'
It was Mrs. Thurber's job to keep the pot boiling, and she countered
rumours—perhaps inspired—of dissatisfaction with a statement of all
Dvořák had accomplished and praise of his qualities as a director.

There were soon, however, to be results which would silence
Dvořák's enemies and justify Mrs. Thurber's most sanguine expectations. He had come across Longfellow's *Song of Hiawatha* in a
Czech translation, and was enchanted by it. Had there been a
possibility of giving it dramatic shape there is no doubt that he would
have made an opera out of the poem. It seems strange that he did
not anticipate Coleridge-Taylor and make a cantata of it, one which
no Troutbeck could spoil! As it was, his note-books, five of them
used by turns, which contain dated and undated ideas for later
works, give convincing evidence of his interest in *Hiawatha*. The first
entry, dated December 1892, has, under the heading 'Legend' the
middle-section tune from the slow movement of the 'New World'
Symphony.

Ideas for the first three movements of this Symphony were sketched
out in the last three weeks of January 1893, and the work was completed by 24th May. While working on it, in New York, Dvořák
made up his mind not to go back to Bohemia in the early summer, but
to pay a visit to Kovařík's home town of Spillville. He cabled for

his remaining four children, and on the last page of the score, after his usual 'Thank God,' Dvořák wrote: 'The children have arrived at Southampton. We received a cable at 1.33 this afternoon.' What he did not write, in the excitement of the moment, were the trombone parts for the closing bars of the Symphony. In June 1893 the Dvořák caravan, eleven in all, set out for Spillville.

CHAPTER IX

'NEW WORLD' SYMPHONY

An interesting account of Dvořák's visit to Spillville is given in Kinsella's *Music on the Air*.[1] The first part of it is taken from the Iowa State Records:

That winter [in New York] was very trying for Dvořák. He was by nature a country gentleman, used to the serenity of rural life, and accustomed to the solitary enjoyment of nature. In contrast to such an environment he was suddenly the centre of great attention in New York. His social engagements were scarcely less numerous than his musical appointments. After meeting these private demands in addition to his duties as director of the National Conservatory, he had little time left for composing. And when he did try to make a tune, it was invariably accompanied by the roar of elevated railway trains and the general clamour of traffic.

As spring approached Dvořák wanted more than ever to escape from the noisy city. He was anxious to work on some new music that he had in mind. One day Josef Kovařík (son of the Spillville schoolmaster, and assistant and secretary to Dvořák) suggested that Dvořák accompany him on a visit to Iowa. Apparently his master did not hear, for he paid no attention to the remark and made no comment. A few days later, however, he quite unexpectedly asked Kovařík about Spillville. Kovařík explained that Spillville was a little Bohemian settlement, where his native language was spoken on the street; that it was peaceful and quiet, as well as beautiful; and most important of all, there were no railroads in Spillville. Several days passed. Then Dvořák asked his assistant to draw a map of Spillville, indicating every house, every street, every person who lived in each house, and what they did. That was all; Dvořák made no comments. But when some friends of his from South Carolina tried to persuade him to go there for his rest he said: 'No, I am going to Spillville.' So it was that a lovely day in June saw Antonín Dvořák, his wife, their six children, a sister, a maid, and his assistant, alight from the train at the little station of Calmar, eleven miles from Spillville. Kovařík sent the family on to the village while he remained to look after the baggage. Upon

[1] Garden City Publishing Co.

his arrival, he found Dvořák strolling around, smoking his pipe, quite at home, and apparently very much pleased with his surroundings.

Kovařík continues the story of Dvořák's visit:

One bright day, 5th June 1893, found the Dvořák *ménage* in the little town. Not only did the natural scenic beauty of the place appeal to the great composer, but also the fact that he was among his own countrymen reminded him of his mother country and he felt he was at home. But he barely got settled when his creative genius was at work, and on 8th June, three days after his arrival, he was at work on the first movement of his new composition, the string Quartet in F. He completed this movement in the early hours of the next morning and at once started the second movement, and even started the third in the evening of the same day. The next day he did the fourth movement, so that by 10th June the entire quartet was completed. With a clear conscience and with much satisfaction he put a notation below the last line of the last movement: 'Thank God. I am satisfied. It went quickly.'

He then went to work on the score, which he finished in a short time, writing each movement in about three days, so that the entire score was finished by 23rd June. Dvořák was so pleased that his new work was accomplished in so short a time that he felt a desire to hear it played, and so he formed a quartet of himself and members of my family, he playing first violin; myself, second violin; my daughter Cecilia, viola; and my son Joseph, cello.

Dvořák was a very plain man, and a great lover of nature. During this visit at Spillville a morning walk through the groves and along the banks of the river was on his daily programme, and he particularly enjoyed the warbling of the birds, in fact he admitted that the first day he was out for a walk, an odd-looking bird, red plumaged, only the wings black, attracted his attention, and its warbling inspired the theme of the third movement of his string quartet.

Neither I nor my son were pupils of Dvořák. When my son was at the Conservatory of Prague in the violin department, Dvořák was an instructor of composition there, and, when my son was returning to America, Dvořák also came to America. You ask whether I ever heard Dvořák talk of the source of the material he used in his 'New World' Symphony. I must say that Dvořák was very reticent in regard to his compositions. He gave one the impression that he did not like to discuss them, and I never gathered enough courage to ask him directly about them and cannot therefore make any authentic statement. I can say, however, that Dvořák was greatly interested in the Indians, and one day while he was still at Spillville a band of Indians came to town selling medicinal herbs. We were told they were the 'Kickapoo,' and belonged to the Iroquois tribe.[1] Every evening they gave a little performance of their music and dancing and Dvořák was so interested that he made it a point always to be present.

The *Humoresque*, which has become so popular with the public at large, was composed on 16th August 1894, a year after Dvořák's visit to Spillville.

Dvořák took great interest in the church music at Spillville. In fact, the first day he came there he visited the church just at the time the people were gathered at the morning mass, and without hesitation he walked up the choir and commenced a prelude to the hymn, 'Bože Pred Tvou Veleb-ností' (O Lord before Thy Majesty), so well known to the Bohemian settlers, and it did not take long before the entire congregation joined in, and evidently Dvořák liked it because it reminded him of his congregational singing in his mother country. And after that, every morning found him at church playing for the service. His wife, Mrs. Anna Dvořák, had a fine contralto voice and she, too, contributed to the music at church on Sunday.

Perhaps the quiet and peace of Spillville led Dvořák to feel more kindly disposed towards Simrock. In June he had curtly replied to the publisher's anxious inquiries for new works—of which, he said, he heard only from Hanslick: 'From now on, thank God, I compose only for my own pleasure; I am practically independent. . . . I can therefore wait for publication'; but he offered Simrock the three Overtures, the 'New World' Symphony, the F. major Quartet, the E flat major Quintet and two lesser works, for 7,500 marks. Simrock, in his anxiety to publish these works quickly, asked Brahms to do the proof-reading. The great man's reply, in agreeing to undertake the task, deeply moved Dvořák. Brahms wrote to Simrock: 'Please tell Dvořák how much I rejoice to hear of his joy in composing,' and Dvořák in a letter to his publisher said: 'I can scarcely believe there is another composer in the world who would do as much.'

Dvořák had to make two expeditions from Spillville, one in August, to conduct some of his works on Czech Day at the Chicago World's Fair, and the second in September to Omaha to visit a wealthy compatriot, Mr. Rosewater, who owned a paper with the engaging name of the *Omaha Bee*. From there he went on to St. Paul to visit a Moravian priest, Father Rynda.

[1] They were, in fact, Algonquins.

On all these occasions the Czechs, of course, made a tremendous fuss of their great composer. He had to attend innumerable festivities, suffer ovations and submit to being serenaded, all of which he could hardly fail to enjoy. But the most important thing was his visit to the Minnehaha Falls. Their beauty so moved him that he wrote down on his starched cuff the tune he used in the slow movement of the Sonatina for violin and piano.

Dvořák was even more impressed by the Niagara Falls, which he visited on the way back to New York, and declared to Kovařík that he would make of them a symphony in B minor. Of the themes he noted down only one saw the light, the scherzo theme of the eighth of the *Humoresques* for piano.

Back in New York Dvořák had little time to miss peaceful Spillville. He was soon caught up again into a heavy round of work, and he wanted to give special thought to his hundredth composition. He hit upon the charming idea of giving two of his children, Ottilie and Antonín, a work simple enough for them to play, and this was the Sonatina with the Minnehaha Falls tune in it. The composer was certainly right in prophesying to Simrock that grown-ups would delight in playing the piece.

There were matters of greater moment to be attended to. Mrs. Thurber wanted to know if he proposed to renew his contract—which was due to expire in the summer of 1894. There was a great demand for the first performances of the new works, in particular the 'New World' Symphony.

The public had been well primed for this event. Already in May an article, over Dvořák's signature, in the *New York Herald*, had directed American composers' attention to the treasury of Negro music that lay at their door, unused. It did not seem to have occurred to the 'onlie begetter' of this article, Mrs. Thurber, or to Dvořák, that the songs of a race so despised and kept down were hardly a basis for a national art. The article certainly aroused the interest intended, and those who assembled for the general rehearsal in the Carnegie Hall on 1st December 1893 no doubt expected a symphony truly American in all its parts.

The *New York Herald*, in reporting the concert, pokes fun at Dvořák's study of Indian melodies, and at the awe-inspiring earnestness of the young women in the audience, but found the Symphony a distinctive American work of art in so far as it gave the Czech composer's impressions of the country. 'What the spirit of Indian music is I do not know,' says the paper's critic; 'if this movement (the *Largo*) breathes the genuine native atmosphere then certainly the future is in the hands of the Red Man.'

Of the event itself Dvořák sent a naïve account to Simrock:

The papers say that no composer ever celebrated such a triumph. Carnegie Hall was crowded with the best people of New York, and the audience applauded so that, like visiting royalty, I had to take my bows repeatedly from the box in which I sat. It made me think of Mascagni in Vienna.

The true value of the Symphony was at once seen by musicians, but they realized they had been listening to a Bohemian and not an American work of art. Dvořák made his point of view perfectly clear in 1900, before the first performance of the 'New World' Symphony in Berlin. Kretzschmar's analysis in his *Führer durch den Konzertsaal* had spoken of the composer using 'original American melodies,' and Seidl had called the Symphony—somewhat vaguely—'a lot of Indian music.'

Dvořák sent the conductor Oscar Nedbal—who had been one of his pupils—Kretzschmar's analysis with the refreshingly direct remark: 'but leave out that nonsense about my having made use of original American melodies. I have only composed in the spirit of such American national melodies.' In fact, as he himself said, whatever he wrote either in America, England or elsewhere was simply 'genuine Bohemian music.'

The next important work Dvořák wrote—for the Suite in A major, Op. 98, later orchestrated by the composer, is of small account—bears no trace of any foreign influence. Dvořák chose the words for his *Ten Biblical Songs,* Op. 99, from the Czech translation of the Bible made by some Bohemian friars in the sixteenth century. One has only to look at the uneasy fit of the English translation to realize why the composer insisted that Simrock should print the Czech text together with the German translation. These highly original works were his last contribution to solo song. Stefan thinks they may have been inspired by several motives, the deaths of Gounod and Tchaikovsky,

the ill-health of his father and the season of the year, Easter. However that may be they are moving religious documents. Dvořák
scored five of the songs for small orchestra (and conducted them in
Prague in 1896), and the remaining five were orchestrated by Dr.
Žemánek, sometime conductor of the Czech Philharmonic Orchestra.

Mrs. Thurber, intent on getting really American work out of her
director, tried hard to find someone to make a libretto for an opera
out of Longfellow's *Hiawatha*. Failing to discover any one in
America able or willing to do so, the determined lady applied to
Vienna. Nothing more, however, came of this plan.

Dvořák settled the question of the renewal of his contract by
promising to return in the autumn of this year, 1894, after five months'
leave in his own country. He set out for home on 19th May and
found a tremendous welcome prepared for him when he arrived on
30th May; but he was so impatient to see Vysoká again that he did
not wait for the gala performance of his opera *The Jacobin*. Possibly,
too, it would have meant his staying up too late.

The welcome Vysoká gave him—they carried him off to the inn
after a parade with lanterns and music—was more congenial to him
than the acclamations of Prague, and his delight at being amongst his
pigeons and in his garden again knew no bounds. He fell at once
into the old routine of early rising, a walk and attendance at six
o'clock mass—at which he played the organ—breakfast at seven and
then some hours of work alternating with quiet times in the woods
or the garden. His evenings were often spent at the inn 'playing
cards or telling the peasants and miners all about America.'

He seems to have been content to sit back and rest from creative
work on a big scale. In August he used up some of the material in
his American sketch-books in the shape of the eight pieces for piano
known as *Humoresques,* the seventh of which became known in its
original form, or in some arrangement or another, all over the world.

Dvořák screwed four thousand marks out of Simrock for the
pieces. They proved cheap at the price. There had been a time
when Dvořák could not afford a piano, but on his birthday, 8th
September, he was able to give the village church a new organ, on
which he duly played at the opening ceremonies. Three days before
he sailed again for America he conducted the first performance in

DVOŘÁK'S STUDY IN PRAGUE

Europe of the 'New World' Symphony. This was given at the National Theatre, Prague, in a programme consisting of his own works.

Dvořák's second visit to America proved, to him at any rate, an unhappy experience. He had tasted the joys of Vysoká again and felt desperately homesick. He had left all his children but one behind him this time and, perhaps, as a result of mental worries, he was not in his usual good health.

Mrs. Thurber expected, no doubt, a successor to the 'New World' Symphony, but no kind of American music emerged from the composer. He gave the world something much better and America the honour of its birthplace. This was the cello Concerto in B minor, Op. 104, which was written between November 1894 and February 1895. Either the hearing of a cello concerto by the solo cellist of the New York Philharmonic Orchestra, Victor Herbert, or a request from his friend, Hanuš Wihan,[1] provided the initial inspiration for one of Dvořák's best works. He was so sure of the solo writing that he refused to allow Wihan to make any but minor alterations in it, or even to use that gentleman's cadenzas. This sets up an excellent precedent for other composers to follow.

The only other music he wrote during this time in America was the opening of the string Quartet in A flat major, completed in December 1895. On 16th April of that year he left America for good. Artistically his second visit had been a success. The New York Philharmonic Society had made him an honorary member, much of his music was being played in the country and America would have been glad to keep him. He spoke vaguely to Mrs. Thurber of returning, and she made an attempt, through Miss Margulies, to induce him to do so; but he always had some objection ready. He was not without guile.

[1] In later years Dvořák said he only wrote the Concerto because Wihan had asked for it. So far as he was concerned he did not consider the cello a solo instrument.

CHAPTER X

CLOSING YEARS

THIS time Dvořák arrived without fuss or celebration, for he had only told his closest friends about his return. He was tired, and all he wanted to do was to rest at Vysoká. The unfinished Quartet remained on the shelf and he seemed to have lost all desire to compose. But in the autumn of this year, 1895, he took up his teaching work at Prague. He had always enjoyed this, and with it he resumed his old routine, the early morning walk in the Karlsplatz Park and the inspection of the railway engines. Then there was the meeting, several evenings a week, in a special room at Mahalik's restaurant in Myslik Street, nicknamed 'The Trunk,' where young musicians and theatrical folk gathered together. Dvořák was made chairman of this institution and always left punctually at nine however promis-ing the evening looked. He also enjoyed being at the more decorous musical evenings given by Professor Hlávka, president of the Academy, where notable people of all kinds were to be found listening to his music.

Soon the urge to compose visited him again, and he completed the string Quartet in A flat major, Op. 105, begun in America, and composed another, his last Quartet, Op. 106, in G major. The impatience of chamber-music societies all over the world to play these works—which many a composer to-day might well envy—caused Simrock to publish them in the summer of 1896.

Dvořák was now well on the way to becoming a 'grand old man.' Vienna received his 'New World' Symphony, conducted by Richter, on 16th February 1896, with extraordinary enthusiasm, which was acknowledged by the composer from the directors' box, where he sat with Brahms.

March found him on his ninth and last visit to England, where he conducted, at Queen's Hall on 19th March, his cello Concerto, Symphony in G major and the *Biblical Songs*. But just as in the case of his return visit to America, he felt out of tune with London. The food was nasty, the fog worse. Perhaps a disordered liver made him declare this time that 'the English do not love music, they respect it.' There is some truth in this remark; but Dvořák really could not complain of the reception—as enthusiastic as ever—given to his concert.

In Vienna, after the English visit, Brahms made a final effort to induce him to become a teacher of composition at the Vienna Conservatory. Dvořák again said he could not afford to live there, and Brahms again offered to put his entire fortune at his disposal. Whether or not Brahms and Hanslick really wanted to use Dvořák to put a spoke in Bruckner's wheel is not clear, but the quite unpolitical Czech was much moved by so generous an offer.

He had been distressed by Brahms's lack of faith—'such a great man! such a great soul! And he believes in nothing'—but now he was proposing to commit what Brahms was bound to regard—for in this matter he had abundant faith—as artistic heresy. Dvořák in his last nine years of creative life turned away from the classical highway, and went into the romantic bypaths (or rather, now, main roads) blazed by Liszt and Wagner. We shall have to consider this deviation later on and have here to note events rather than causes. On 6th January 1896 he began three of the five symphonic poems he was to write. These were *Vodník* (*Water-Goblin*), *Polednice* (*Noonday Witch*) and *Zlatý Kolovrat* (*Golden Spinning-Wheel*), all of them based, for programme, on folk-ballads in the collection *A Garland* by J. K. Erben. The fourth of these symphonic poems, *Holoubek* (*Wild Dove*), a subject very congenial to the composer, was composed towards the end of 1896 at Vysoká.

Brahms was perhaps too ill to take notice of Dvořák's change of direction, and Dvořák, for his part, seems to have avoided meeting him until a few days before his death on 6th April 1897. But the younger generation of Czech composers, now becoming quite an imposing array, men such as Fibich, Suk, Janáček, Foerster, Novák and Nedbal—some of them Dvořák's own pupils—would certainly have been sympathetic to the new venture. Brahms's death dried up in Dvořák, for the time being, the springs of creative activity, and it was not until October 1897, after orchestrating a revised version—with a completely new third act—of *The Jacobin*, that Dvořák began his last symphonic poem and an orchestral work *Píseň Bohatývská* (*Hero's Song*), which had its first performance on 4th December 1898 in Vienna, with Mahler conducting.

Needless to say comparisons were made with Strauss's *Heldenleben,* not altogether in Dvořák's favour; but, apart from the autobiographical nature of the two works, there is as little in common between the music of these two 'heroes' as between themselves. The final section, 'Triumph of the Idea,' was not, moreover, autobiographically correct. Dvořák had not yet triumphed in the way he most wanted to. He had not sent a successful opera out into the world.

He had plenty of recognition now. In February 1897 the Viennese Society of the Friends of Music had elected him an honorary member, together with Ambroise Thomas, Grieg, Gevaert and Reinecke, though this was hardly equivalent, as Stefan seems to think, to joining the ranks of the immortals. Some of these wreaths look a bit dusty today.

Then the Viennese Ministry of Education, in raising the grant to the Prague Conservatory, stipulated that Dvořák's pay should be steppedup to that of the highest paid professors. But what delighted him more than anything was being made a member of the Austrian State Commission which had helped him in his hour of need and brought him into touch with Brahms, whom he now succeeded. The other members were Ignaz Brüll and Eusebius Mandyczewski. It was now Dvořák's privilege and pleasure to aid poor and talented composers.

The picture of these last years, apart from teaching and composition, is little changed. His routine remained the same. His music was being heard everywhere, new works as well as old. One source of irritation remained, the itch to write an opera which would have a success comparable with that of the 'New World' Symphony. Possibly, Stefan thinks, the success of Humperdinck's *Hansel and Gretel* and similar fairytale operas directed his attention to Czech folktales of this kind. He found a good subject in *Čert a Káča* (*The Devil and Kate*), a libretto by a young Prague schoolmaster, Adolf Wenig.

The composition of the opera, interrupted by preparations for the wedding of his daughter Ottilie to his pupil Josef Suk, and the sub sequent festivities, was spread over a long period, May 1898 to February 1899. The first performance, on 23rd November of that year, at the Prague National Theatre, had more than the usual success and the opera, though certainly not his best, crossed the frontiers. It was heard at Oxford in 1932 with a refurbished plot. In this same month of November, on the occasion of Francis Joseph's jubilee, Dvořák was given the high and rare distinction of being awarded the Medal of Honour for the Arts and Sciences, which only one other musician, Brahms, had held before him. He called this imposing ornament his 'big golden platter.'

No sooner was *Kate* off the stocks than Dvořák was searching, as impatiently as Puccini used to do, for a new libretto. It was no use Simrock asking for chamber music or symphonies or even symphonic poems. It was opera or nothing. The stage and the singers waited patiently while the composer cast frantically round for a 'book.'

On 20th December 1899 Dvořák was in Budapest, and two interesting little incidents are reported of this visit. He heard the famous gipsy orchestras and said: 'It's extraordinary how much gipsy music is like modern counterpoint; every one plays what he likes, but it all comes out together and it sounds all right.' Then the papers described how, when he conducted, he seemed to get twenty years younger; and how beautiful the expression on his face became.

The tide of Czech music was now running strongly, and Dvořák had really no need to make a 'personal appearance' in order to recommend his wares to the public. His pupil Nedbal had set out upon a highly successful tour as a conductor and, with doubtful artistic judgment but sound common sense, always included the 'New World' Symphony in his programmes. It always captured the house. About this time a young Italian conductor, Arturo Toscanini, gave it with great success at La Scala, Milan.

Between *The Devil and Kate* and his next opera, *Rusalka*, Dvořák wrote only a commissioned piece, a *Festival Song* for the seventieth birthday of the Prague Conservatory's president, Dr. Josef Tragy. In this work, performed on 20th May 1900, he made his last appearance as a conductor.

Meanwhile a shy young poet, Jaroslav Kvapil, was hawking round a fairy-tale play, which was a variation of the Undine legend. It had been rejected by Nedbal, Foerster and Suk, and the author was too diffident to send it to Dvořák. He got to hear of it in April, however, took it with enthusiasm and finished the score by December. *Rusalka,* his Op. 114, deserves to be, as it is in Czechoslovakia, Dvořák's most successful opera. There is little reason why, if imaginatively done, it should not become as popular as *Hansel and Gretel.* But more of this later. In his own country it ranks second only in popular favour to Smetana's *Bartered Bride,* and it triumphed from the start.

The opera, owing to various mischances, was not heard in Vienna until 1924, when the beauty of the music was at once remarked. It was to have been done at Covent Garden in 1938 had the war not intervened.

Great as was the success of *Rusalka,* Dvořák was not satisfied, for it was still only a local and not a world-wide success. So he went off to Kvapil, now assistant stage director at the Czech National Theatre, and demanded another libretto from the poet. As he had nothing ready, the composer asked him to write one that would stimulate him to compose and contain a good part for Maturova, the Rusalka of the *première.* Kvapil, however, could not work the oracle, and Dvořák was left high and dry.

His sixtieth birthday was approaching and there was plenty in a worldly way to distract him. The Austrian Government, always generous to him, named him and Vrchlický life members of the Austrian House of Lords. He was the first musician ever to receive this honour, and he attended the House exactly once, on the occasion when he was sworn in. He hated debates and politics, but he was charmed with some sharpened pencils that he found on his desk and brought these home as souvenirs.

There is a delightful story of his journey with Vrchlický to Vienna on this occasion. The poet remarked on the clouds of midges overhanging the marshes at Wittingau. Dvořák, a man of few words at any time, made no reply; but hours later, when the two were walking along the Ringstrasse he suddenly said: 'That's probably because there's so much water!'

If Dvořák was an anomaly in the House of Lords, he was scarcely less so as director of the Prague Conservatory, which he became on 6th July 1901. But of course he was not required to take either honour seriously in a practical way. Bennevic, the former director, wished to retire, and it would not have been possible to pass over Dvořák, so the board made him a nominal director while entrusting all business affairs and organization to Professor Knittl. The in-quiring stranger would be told that the director was not there—'What would he be doing here?'—and, had he made the journey, would have found the composer leading his quiet and ordered life at Vysoká.

But not all the gardening and pigeon-breeding and gossip at the inn could still his ardent desire for a new libretto. The only music he could bring himself to write, failing this, was a setting of a poem by Svatopluk Čech, *The Smith of Lešetín,* which appealed by reason of its social implications.

On 20th August Dvořák's old friend and enemy, Simrock, died, the last of his line. The circle of those who had lived with him through the difficult days was narrowing, and soon his own time would come.

The fuss over his birthday disturbed him, though he could not fail to be affected by the scope and warmth of the celebrations. The Czech National Theatre put on the whole cycle of his operas from *The Pig-headed Peasants* to *Rusalka,* ending with a dramatic version of *Ludmilla,* a handsome tribute indeed.

Nelahozeves, of course, surpassed itself and we have been left a picture of the composer roaring, through his tears of emotion: 'Tell them to stop shouting,' as they cried 'Long live Dvořák!'

It should be recorded that at the one function at which he felt bound to appear, the banquet given by the Umělecká Beseda, Dvořák actually made a short speech in the following words: 'When I first heard about what you were planning to do, I was very much upset. But then I thought to myself that I would probably survive this, too.'

The opera question, when all the tumult and the shouting died down, remained to be solved. He considered a Cinderella libretto, rejected a sequel to *Ludmilla* on the subject of St. Adalbert, and an idea of oratorios on Nazareth and Golgotha.

Dvořák began to wish he had Wagner's talent as a versifier. In the end he accepted from Vrchlický—who had proposed the sequel to *Ludmilla*—a libretto on the subject of Armida; Lully, Handel,

Gluck and Rossini (amongst others!) notwithstanding. Besides the attraction of a story which opposed Christian Europe to the pagan orient and love to duty, Dvořák perhaps thought that an opera on a subject devoid of local colour would be more likely to succeed abroad. On 11th April 1902 he wrote at the end of the first act: 'Completed at Vysoká on 30th June, after the fair, in very hot weather.' The whole score was completed on 22nd August 1903, and the first performance took place in the Czech National Theatre on 25th March 1904. The work was ill-fated from the start of rehearsals. No one seemed enthusiastic, Dvořák's temper was uncertain, and, feeling unwell, he had to leave before the end of the *première*.

He had, in fact, an organic disease, uraemia and progressive arterio-sclerosis, though the nature of the disease was kept from him. He was not able to take part, much to his disappointment, in the first Czech Music Festival which began in Prague in April 1904, and opened with his *Ludmilla*; and to complicate matters he caught a chill standing about the railway station on his regular visit to the locomotives.

The doctors promised he would be well enough to conduct *The Spectre's Bride* at Kremsier in May, when his daughter Magda was to sing the soprano solo, and there was no reason to suppose he would not be able to go. But on 27th April he had a relapse. The engagement had to be cancelled, and it was doubtful if he would be well enough to be moved into the new and larger flat the family had persuaded him to take. For himself he much preferred the one he had been in so long: small as it was, no one near played the piano!

The first of May was a day of brilliant sunshine, everybody was in good spirits, and Dvořák was so much better that the doctor allowed him to have luncheon at the table with his family. He was feeling rather weak from lying still for so long, and in order to restore his sense of balance, made a tour of the dining-room. He sat at the head of the table and ate his soup with appetite. Suddenly turning pale, he muttered that he did not feel at all well, and was helped back to bed. Almost immediately he lost consciousness. Dr. Hnátek, who lived across the way, hurried over, but could only establish that the end had come swiftly with a brain-stroke. It was early afternoon.[1]

---

[1] *Anton Dvořák*, by Paul Stefan, page 302.

Death of Dvořák

This brilliantly fine May Day found half of Prague out in the country, and it was only in the evening that the news got round. The audience assembling at the Czech National Theatre for a performance of Smetana's *Brandenburgers in Bohemia* found the house draped in black, and soon all Prague knew that their great composer had died.

Expressions of sympathy came from all over the world, and on 5th May enormous crowds lined the route of the funeral procession. After the lying in state in the church of the Saviour, Dvořák's body was buried in Vyšehrad Cemetery, the funeral oration being delivered by Professor Knittl.

CHAPTER XI

DVOŘÁK AS MAN AND MUSICIAN

THE chapters of criticism following on this one must be considered mainly in the character of a *catalogue raisonné*, and the inquiring reader will find there something, if only a line, about practically all of Dvořák's works. The present chapter serves as a basis for the judg‑ ments that are passed and endeavours, also, to give a portrait of Dvořák as man and musician. In a brilliant chapter contributed to a recently published book[1] Gerald Abraham takes Dvořák into his laboratory, places him under the microscope and very throughly examines him. Those who know Dvořák well will find this chapter of absorbing interest and those who know him little will end up, if they provide themselves with a bundle of scores, by gaining a very clear insight into his musical personality. Now, apart from the fact that Mr. Abraham has said, better than I could, much of what I had intended to say, the present chapter has the modest purpose of treating Dvořák in a more general way and of indicating the reasons for the curious mixture of styles and changes of direction which his music shows from start to finish. This is of the greatest importance to our understanding of him, and so it may as well be the first point of discussion.

Dvořák was, and remained, a peasant; but is it true, as Daniel Gregory Mason remarks,[2] that he went forward in his steadfastness of aim, with a dumb persistence and an unthinking doggedness that didn't weigh motives or foresee obstacles? Is it true that he forged ahead hardly knowing where he was going or what he was doing, canalizing torrents of music? The evidence by no means shows this to have been the case. As we have seen, Dvořák knew very early on in his life that he wanted to be a musician and that he would have to fight for his goal. For ten years he submitted himself to intense

[1] *Antonín Dvořák : his Achievement.* Edited by Viktor Fischl (Lindsay Drummond).

[2] *From Grieg to Brahms*, by Daniel Gregory Mason (Macmillan), in which there is a chapter on Dvořák.

artistic discipline, during which time hardly any one knew what he was at. He learnt his trade by close study of great models—Beethoven, Schubert, Mendelssohn: doubtless several others, but above all the first two—and he was, at this time, intensely critical of his own efforts. He was not yet country-conscious, and it was certainly the influence of Smetana which made him so. *The Bartered Bride* had been produced in 1866 and *Dalibor* in 1868. Perhaps, he may have argued with himself, the obscure orchestral player could get a hearing on the operatic stage. He had grown to mistrust the chamber music he had written, and it might be that opera was his true medium of expression. What happened has already been told; and doubtless it would have happened even if Wagner had not obscured his vision. But the really important thing for us to note—and the point of this recapitulation—is that the failure of *Alfred* left Dvořák with a heightened sense of personal mistrust.

There is a revealing sentence in Hoffmeister's book [1] to which sufficient attention has not been given:

He [Dvořák] spoke of his genius as 'the gift of God' or 'God's voice.' I remember that after completing a great work he was always afraid lest that voice might not be heard again; lest the gift of God should fail him, the boon of his creative faculty should be withdrawn.

Such a statement from a composer who has been called 'the most inventive and spontaneously musical of all national composers' might merely be excessive modesty. But Dvořák, when he did speak, meant what he said. Nothing is more certain than that.

And so I part company with Daniel Gregory Mason. Dvořák knew where he wanted to go quite soon in his creative career, but he was not certain of the means of getting there. Smetana, on the other hand, was single-minded. He submitted himself, in the event, to a martyrdom to give his people, in the form that most appealed to them, the opera, music that would reflect their highest thoughts and aspirations, as well as their lighter moments and national customs. It would be impertinent and untrue to suggest that Dvořák loved his country less; but fair, I think, to say that the order of his artistic ambitions was different. He had not, therefore, Smetana's

[1] *Antonín Dvořák*, by Karel Hoffmeister (John Lane), page 104.

single-mindedness; he wanted to give the world music that would be recognized as cosmopolitan first and Czech second. Politics and propaganda of any sort were alien to him. How much personal ambition was included in his vision no one can say. The enormous success he had in England might have ruined a man of less integrity. And *St. Ludmilla* stands as a warning sign to a downward path. The huge success of the *Slavonic Dances* might, again, have tempted him to exploit the national vein, but this too he resisted and, instead, in his use of it he enriched all music. And it must not be forgotten that when Vienna offered him thirty pieces of silver for a German opera he did not hesitate to refuse. Nevertheless the ambition remained and was with him until the end of his life. One notes his frequent use of the term 'Slav.' He would not be hemmed in behind the frontiers. He was more race- than nation-conscious. Of the works of the greatest period of his creative career only one, the *Hussite Overture,* is distinctly national: the others are personal documents.

The problem that faced Dvořák, therefore, was that of finding a style through which he could fulfil his ambition of conquering the frontiers and showing the world that a Brahms could be found in Bohemia. If the *Slavonic Dances* can be taken as the types of his national style there is the fact, which has defeated so many composers, that the folk-tune is not susceptible to development, being self-contained, lacking generative power, and therefore unsuitable for large-scale works. But the music he had grown up with 'moved in his veins like blood,' it was his own dialect, his natural method of speech. He did not imitate folk-tunes as, for example, Rimsky-Korsakov confessedly did, he created in the spirit of them. He thus showed that he understood the difference between nationalism and the national spirit. We see him, then, as a sort of Eliza Doolittle, rich and racy as his own self—and an infinitely poetical Eliza too—learning painfully how to speak with the voice of the musical *haut monde* and apt, sometimes almost as disconcertingly as Eliza, to relapse at any moment into his native speech.

I do not, therefore, recognize different periods in Dvořák's development so much as these restless changes of direction, aimed at solving an acute problem. We cannot know just how far he was actually conscious of all this; but I do suggest that the impurity of style which is bound to strike unfavourably any one who looks over the whole corpus of Dvořák's work arises from the fact that he never wholly succeeded, in his larger works, in forging a style which completely satisfied him.

The casual listener, to whom Dvořák means the 'New World' Symphony, one of his most 'impure' works, will find all this an un-necessary pother and, doubtless, will be merely irritated by the evidence—which it would be tedious to repeat here—adduced in the following pages. But, others may reflect, which of the early national-ist composers, Chopin, Borodin and Smetana apart, ever succeeded in the larger instrumental forms without writing highly repetitive works, such as *Scheherazade*, or compromising as Dvořák does? He was not, as was Rimsky-Korsakov, essentially a writer for the stage: he was a composer of absolute music, and yet he was too much of a Czech and too different a man to adopt, and continue in, the cos-mopolitan but yet very personal style that we find in Tchaikovsky. He was, in my opinion, always seeking and often coming very near to finding a wholly integrated style, a harmonious marriage of two opposed worlds. If great success had not robbed him of the severe critical faculty of his youth he might have found and kept it.

Did, then, any nationalist composer of Dvořák's time, with the exception of Borodin named above, ever use classical symphonic form without relying over-much on the facile charms of orchestral colour, and on the stock devices of sequence and repetition as op-posed to real organic development? Tchaikovsky's 'Little Russian' Symphony (No. 2, in C minor) was indeed a work of distinctly national character, but it resembles those brightly coloured Russian boxes each of which conceals another. You never find what you are looking for, the Russian soul, only another charming box. But in Borodin's symphonies we are given not only the outward and audible sound, but the inward and spiritual meaning. Than the B minor Symphony, as Gerald Abraham remarks, 'no more thoroughly Russian music has ever been written.' Borodin is the only true symphonist of the 'Five,' and he alone of all the national composers, the chemist-musician, discovered the secret of saturating every bar of his Symphony with the Russian spirit without going over the frontiers.

The remarkable figure of Leoš Janáček emerged in the next generation of Czech composers. Within his chosen field he solved the problems that troubled Dvořák and carried Smetana's realism many stages further. But the causes of Dvořák's honourable failure must now be examined.

Dvořák imitated folk material as little as did Borodin, but the Russian material was more primitive, more suggestive, richer than the Czech—which shows only too many signs of the foreign domination, and not only cultural penetration of the country. That had never been suffered by Russia. But the chief reason lies in the fact of Borodin's advantages of education and his superior mental apparatus; and also in the fact that music was not his profession. The mental factor tells in the sheer intellectual effort of symphonic creation, the economic in the time that may be given to it. Dvořák had the building power, but had he put down his fiddle more often and thought harder and more fastidiously, it is possible that he might have become as skilful an alchemist as Borodin. It is possible. Borodin's profoundly original mind is felt at work in nearly all his small output —not only in the symphonies, but in *Prince Igor,* the chamber music, the songs and even in the small piano piece *Au Couvent.* Dvořák lacked that originality, among his many and great gifts, and in face of his greater problem, it is perhaps to be marvelled at that he should have achieved so large a measure of success.

In many of his smaller works, and in movements and moments of his larger ones, one can hear a very individual voice. Then it fails; and one becomes conscious of an exquisitely musical and most skilled craftsman, well read in the classics and familiar with modern literature. There is ample proof of this thesis in the fine works of the years 1883–5. If the most perfect, in the sense of the most individual of them, is the greatest, then the palm must be awarded to the *Scherzo capriccioso* for orchestra, written the same year as the Pianoforte Trio in F minor, in which Brahms exercises undue influence, and the *Hussite Overture* (both 1883), which is one of Dvořák's rare political documents and not a wholly satisfactory one. Two years later came his Symphony in D minor, a work which he declared 'must be such as to shake the world' and be inspired by 'God, love and motherland.'

The tremendous effort, on a cold analysis, muddies the stream sufficiently to put this splendid work on a lower plane of achievement, as a perfect whole, than the *Scherzo capriccioso*. Going backwards and forwards in either direction we find a Beethovenian Quartet (the C major, 1881) and a 'grand' opera, *Dimitri* (1881–2), with very mixed elements, the Handelian *St. Ludmilla* (1885–6), an unhappy compromise, and the second set of *Slavonic Dances* (1886), in which again he is completely himself.

In the old days of the music-hall a familiar turn was the quick-change artist. He was now Napoleon, now Gladstone, but always unmistakably himself behind the disguises. Dvořák is never convincingly disguised, and one is therefore bothered by the assumed personalities. This process continues up to the end of his life; and it does not seem to me possible that it can be written down by the serious student of Dvořák's music, however great his sympathy with its causes, as other than a severe limitation.

I do not feel able to discuss how much, precisely, Dvořák's music owes to Czechoslovakian folksong. Any one who cares to turn up the appropriate section in the *Botsford Collection of Folk-Songs* (Schirmer) or, when it is again available, to examine the tenth volume of Dr. Heinrich Möller's impressive collection, *Das Lied der Völker* (Schott), will find all the evidence he wishes for the identification of certain tricks of style that are met with over and over again in Dvořák. Thus *The Little Dove* provides the source for Dvořák's (and Smetana's and Janáček's) habit—which can be charming or merely irritating—of phrase repetition:

Out a-mong the cliffs a lit-tle dove did fly, dove did fly

And the 'Three Blind Mice' phrase which, as Mr. Julius Harrison says,[1] turns up so frequently in the fourth and fifth Symphonies, is present in *Weeding Flax-fields Blue*:

Weed-ing flax-es blue   Lit-tle then I knew

[1] *Antonín Dvořák: his Achievement*, edited by Viktor Fischl, pages 264–5.

Here, too, is the type of the displaced accents of the *furiant* (*The Farmer*):

Mr. Frank Howes, in the best chapter on the subject which has so far appeared,[1] shows that the Slovakian tunes are, on the whole, fuller of 'rhythmic excitements' than the Czech ones; but I think he would find Dvořák's music (particularly in the operas) as full as these tunes are of one-, two- and four-bar phrases. His rhythms are, in fact, often surprisingly square.

It is natural enough that all these folksong idioms should fertilize Dvořák's melodic speech and—as folksongs are all, basically, very much alike—that he should have been able to mix all types of Slav folksong into his music with far greater success than he mixed Czech and German speech. It is not for a foreigner to judge how much or how little he is truly Czech, but if Dr. Bartoš brings him to trial as being 'a musical exotic,' I suggest that both Fibich and Suk must also stand in the dock with him. Smetana's greater purity of style and nobility of purpose, Janáček's realism, represent, no doubt, higher national ideals. But may it not be allowed that Dvořák expressed the homelier aspects of the Czech genius?

If English nationalist composers have never really caught the public ear, it may well be because there is nothing now in our national life that corresponds to the conditions in which our folksongs took shape. With us, indeed, folksongs are an exotic. In the case of Czechoslovakia, I am told, this is not so. It must therefore be the marriage of the Czech and the Teutonic, the fatal admixture of styles, which caused Dr. Bartoš to say: 'Our national style is something far deeper than his sonorous exoticism; therefore for the sake of truth we must be prepared to renounce before future generations even so distinguished a musical personality as was Antonín Dvořák.'

We can now pass on to the natural talents and acquired skill which Dvořák brought to the practice of his art. They are of a high order.

[1] Op. cit., page 241.

We should do him a grave injustice in supposing that there is no growth in the music that poured so unendingly from him. We think of him, and rightly, as we think of Schubert, as above all a sweet singer, and of sweetness of sound as his chief concern. But in many of the early works, the F minor Quartet, the early D minor Symphony, there is nothing very striking about the melodic vein; and even as late as 1876, when Dvořák was thirty-five, it can be as flat and undistinguished as we see it in the Trio in G minor, Op. 26. Yet oil has been struck; and once the machinery for refining it gets into thorough working order, how rich a stream pours out! The most constant quality of this lyric melody is joyousness: it is full of a sensuous happiness which goes beyond mere freshness and gaiety and is without parallel in music. Perhaps this, coupled with his strong rhythmic sense, is what writers mean by calling Dvořák elemental. His sadness is not the childlike pathos of Schubert or the world sorrow of Beethoven: it is the sadness of the exile, of an acute nostalgia. Humour he has but rarely—and it is a characteristic quality of Czech folk-music—and there is little passion but much tenderness in his tunes. One other quality his melody possesses which is harder to define, but which must be described as intoxicating. It is to be found in the soaring phrase of the *Dumka* in the F major Quartet, or in Rusalka's second aria in the opera of that name, and it is intoxicating from excess of sweetness. It may be this quality, present in smaller or larger quantities, that makes some people hostile to Dvořák's music. But they cannot deny him, when he is out in the open air, a unique gift of enchantment, of communicating his joy in 'the birds, the trees and the flowers' to which he owed so much.

The luscious quality of his harmony is, naturally, a result of his preoccupation with sweetness of sound. Sometimes it stiffens into a cliché of this too familiar kind, the result of a habit of taking the easy course:

But generally one feels its fundamental rightness. Dvořák, however, is by no means always sweet. He is often decidedly adventurous, as in this cadence from the twelfth *Slavonic Dance*:

And in the last music he wrote there are some harmonic clashes that must have seemed very daring at the time:

So non-schematic a composer as Dvořák is inevitably full of inequalities. One so often reflects, in one and the same movement, or even phrase: if only he had thought twice, if only he hadn't done that! The severe critical faculty of the earlier years would never have passed intact things like the slow movement of the E flat pianoforte Quartet or the last movement of the 'New World' Symphony. And Dvořák's modulations, like his harmony, suffer from taking an easy or a quite unplanned course. Sometimes, as in the first movement of the B flat piano Trio, his indecision sounds almost comic; but when he takes trouble and thinks ahead how lovely the results are! The classic example is the exquisite modulation from the *Scherzo capriccioso* quoted on page 151. The same criticism applies to a method of development which is peculiar to him, the seizing on a suggestive passage of notes in a main tune and developing that to the exclusion, entirely or for the moment, of all else. Compare the opening move-ment of the G minor Trio with the similar movement of the string Quartet in E flat major. In the Trio the semiquaver figure which

first appears on the piano breaks out like a rash over the whole movement. But in the Quartet the little suggestion thrown out by the
two semiquavers in the opening theme is adopted with great subtlety.
One could continue the inquisition in every part of Dvořák's technical equipment. The practice, for example, of quoting themes
previously used in other movements, which he perhaps learnt from
Liszt, can be as meaningful as he makes it in the early E major
string Quartet or in the last string Quartet, in G major, or as mechanical as its employment in the 'New World' Symphony or the
American Suite for piano.

But let us look at one of the greatest gifts bestowed on Dvořák, one
that has the power to float his music even when it is dead weight: the
gift of movement. His music never sags as sometimes does the music
of a composer in whom so many of his faults of style and construction
are found in an unpleasantly over-ripe form—I mean Mahler—for
whatever is moving, whether it be a finely shaped tune, a soggy stream
of sixths and triplets, a formula of dotted quavers, continues to
move. With this gift, as has been well said, he vitalizes the entire
mass of his tone and gives rhythmic individualization to under parts.
His never-failing store of counter-melodies are no better, and no worse,
as counterpoint, than Wagner's in, say, the *Mastersingers* Overture
or the Dance of the Apprentices, but they both fulfil their purpose
effectively and give plenty of jam to those who have to play them. He
has, indeed, an endearing habit of distributing good things to all and
sundry. A second oboe or a second violin is made to feel that he
is of importance in the scheme of things. The sum of this rhythmic
genius, plus a wide and often sharply contrasted range of dynamics,
gives Dvořák's music the vitality that is one of its most delightful
qualities.

Some mention is made of his orchestration in the chapters that
follow. How much he learned from Liszt and Verdi I should not
care to say, but how much he remembered of the village fairs and
dances is plainly told us as late as the slow movement of the G major
Symphony or in the less admirable score of the *Carnival* Overture,
in which, as Julius Harrison says in his most interesting chapter on
Dvořák's orchestra,[1] 'woodwind, brass and percussion seem intent

[1] Op. cit.

on slaying each other, so desperate is their fight for survival, so heartless their conduct towards the strings.'

He learnt his orchestration, as Elgar did, in the most practical of schools, by playing in an orchestra, and, I think, he really did learn his lovely use of the woodwind from his love of birds. I can imagine that it was one of his beloved pigeons that he thought of when writing for the flutes. We have the evidence of the conductor quoted above that his string passages, though often difficult to perform, nearly always fall gratefully under the fingers of the player. He carried, Mr. Harrison says, the principles of string-quartet writing into the richer fields of the full orchestra and was able to impart to each instrument a life of its own.

It was sound instinct that led Dvořák to the composition of chamber music at the outset of his career. His improvisatory genius needed the discipline of classical form, and his attempts, made at all periods throughout his life, to modify it are of great interest. One of these, the habit of theme quotation, we have already glanced at. Another is the short-circuiting of which the recapitulations in the first movements of the D minor Symphony, the E flat pianoforte Quartet and the cello Concerto all afford excellent examples. If he is diffuse —which is undeniable—he is never disorderly. Little is thrown away, everything, if not developed, is given a logical twist; and it is another of the paradoxes that we meet with in Dvořák that his skill in the art of diminution makes him, from one angle, a most economical composer.

This sketch portrait would not be complete without some reference to a term which is as personal to him as the use of *nobilmente* is to Elgar. *Grandioso,* in Dvořák's scores, can cover anything from the literally grandiose measures of the first *Slavonic Rhapsody* to the triumphant outburst, truly grand, in the slow movement of the last string Quartet. (It is curious that Dvořák nowhere uses the direction in the big D minor Symphony.)

Dvořák the man has been the subject of the previous chapters. If he vacillated and changed direction in his music he did not do so in his private life. He was consistent in his habits, strong in his attach-ment to his family and home. In his *Variations on a Theme* James Huneker gives an entertaining and, one suspects, rather a highly

coloured account of 'old Borax' (as he and Horatio Parker affectionately called him) in New York: 'He scared me with his fierce
Slavonic eyes and yet he was as mild-mannered a musical pirate as
ever scuttled a pupil's counterpoint.'

In his communications with the world, as in his own home, he
wanted simply to be and to be accepted as himself.

And that is what he strove to be in his music. I have endeavoured
to indicate why he never succeeded to his satisfaction and why he
sometimes fails to our dismay—particularly if we have inconvenient
memories. But now that the writing of this book is done,[1] and, with
it, the long period of examination of his whole output, I rise from it
with the feeling that I have been in the company of a good, sane and
healthy man whom one has grown to love for his faults as well as his
virtues: for indeed, his weaknesses are a condition of his strength.

[1] The above chapter was the last to be written.

CHAPTER XII

SONGS

DVOŘÁK's solo songs, fifty or so in number, show that not by melody alone can a composer enter into this kingdom. There is, indeed, much more than melody in the best of his songs, but not enough to put him in the category of great song-writers.

In earlier days such a man as he would surely have given spontaneous utterance to many a folksong and, as always in his music, it remains true that the closer he is to that spirit, and the farther he is away from his German or Austrian models, the more successful he is. He has the born song-writer's feeling for the vocal phrase, but only rarely the born lieder-writer's feeling for a song as a work of art; that is, something perfect as a whole and in all its parts.

The earlier songs, when he found words intractable and could only, and often clumsily, deal out conventional formulas to serve as piano accompaniments, contain little over which we need go into detail.

Dvořák had a great and natural affection for his first essay in this field, the song-cycle—about eighteen numbers in all—to words by G. Pfleger-Moravsky, *The Cypresses*. He composed this work in 1865, the year in which he met and fell in love with Anna Čermáková. Four of these songs were revised and published in 1882 as Op. 2. Eight more of them, also revised, came out as *Love Songs*, Op. 83, in 1888. The tenth was used as an aria in the opera *King and Collier*; one found its way into the *Silhouettes* for piano, and twelve were rearranged for string quartet in 1887, under the title *Evening Songs*.

By 1880 Dvořák had written one of his finest sets of songs, the *Seven Gypsy Songs*, Op. 55 (to say nothing of big works such as the sixth Symphony and the violin Concerto), and had obviously passed his apprenticeship in song-writing. Either sentimental reasons or an insufficient degree of self-criticism must have caused him not to revise more drastically than he has done.

The first song of Op. 2, *Go forth my song, delay not*, opens with a phrase to delight every singer and hearer and then goes to pieces over too literal tonal representation of words—in this case 'speed' and 'haste'—which are each provided with what seems to the composer an appropriate form of accompaniment. The shape of the song is spoilt. Both the next two songs have rather clotted accompaniments but, as nearly always, Dvořák seizes and holds the general mood of the song, and conveys expressions of grief in major keys convincingly. The third song, *Nought to my heart can bring relief*, has a dimly national character and contains a really bold stroke which foreshadows the great soaring phrases in later songs:

Here sleeps a brok - en heart

The last song is a charming exercise in the light Schubertian manner.

The revisions which resulted in the *Love Songs* of Op. 83 were evidently more thorough, and by this time Dvořák was able to insist on the printing of the Czech text along with the English and German translations. The first song of this set, *Never will love lead us*, is superb. It has a fine soaring tune which begins:

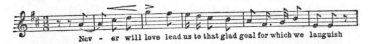

Nev - er will love lead us to that glad goal for which we languish

and rises to a thrilling climax. The composer does not here move rigidly in the bonds of the words: he uses phrases of five and six bar lengths with great freedom, and there is no easy acceptance of harmonic clichés, as in the earlier set. The promise of this song is not fulfilled elsewhere, except possibly in the fifth and the eighth songs, *Nature lies peaceful* and *Thou only dear one*, both of which deserve honourable mention. The other five, in spite of some good points, are disfigured by impurities of style, irritating (and time saving) *tremolandi*, dominant seventh fixation, and so on. But it is interesting to note a foreshadowing of the *dumka* in No. 7.

The next songs Dvořák composed were an answer to an appeal for national music, made in 1871, by Dr. Ludovic Procházka. He chose words by Eliska Krašnohorská and Karel Jaromír Erben, but he did not, or was perhaps not yet able to, rise to the occasion; if we may judge by two of the songs that were published nine years later by Schlesinger, with two numbers from a set of twelve *Evening Songs* to words by Vítěslav Hálek. Of these Hoffmeister published four in 1881 as Op. 3, and five more were published by Urbánek in 1883, as Op. 31. These *Evening Songs* all date from 1876.

None of these songs can be said to advance the national cause, but they do show the composer in an experimental frame of mind. The first Krašnohorská song, *Darum* (they have only German words), deliberately varies its phrase lengths, and the second song, *Die Erwägung,* does so less obviously, more happily, and receives a much more independent accompaniment. The process is carried farther in the first of the *Evening Songs—Es schweigt der Blätter Abendlied—*which has the look of one of Wolf's Italian songs. The second of these, *Der Frühling flog aus Weitem her,* merely looks like what it is, bad Schumann. The five songs of Op. 31 show a steady growth in actual song-writing, even though the models are, with one exception, not out of sight and the national note is absent. The third of these songs, *Like to a linden tree* has great charm and a well-contrived climax, but the fourth, *All ye that labour come to Me*, is the most original Dvořák had yet written. It has real and unsuspected power and can stand easily with the best of the *Biblical Songs*.

The J. K. Erben song, *The Orphan,* Op. 5, shows only that Dvořák could not deal with the ballad form without becoming dull. The song is unwieldy and fails to gain sympathy for the child's woes.

The four Serbian folk poems which Simrock published as Op. 6 were composed in 1872, that is, four years before the *Evening Songs.* It may be true that Dvořák ceased here to copy foreign models and that he felt much more at ease with this peasant poetry, but the songs are almost the worst he wrote. The accompaniments are very lumpish and the composer is even deserted by his usual copious out-pouring of melody. Interest lies only in the curious tonality of the opening phrase of the first song and in the unconscious humour of the English translations, which quite unseat the Rev. Dr. Troutbeck. Here is a sample from the first song, *The Maiden and the Grass:*

> Wrangling full long and sore thus each did each implead;
> Until the Judge deemed parting their only remede.

Poems from the famous Königinhof manuscripts 'discovered' by Václav Hanka in 1817 and denounced as forgeries by Masaryk in 1886, provided Dvořák with the material for his next songs. He worried as little about the authenticity of the text as any Scottish nationalist, not a literary man, might be expected to worry about Macpherson's Ossian. He set six of the poems, of which Starý published the whole set as Op. 17, and Simrock four as Op. 7, omitting, in his usual impolite manner, the Czech texts. There is little to choose between the English versions by Mrs. Natalia Macfarren (Simrock) and Dr. Troutbeck (Novello). Troutbeck rhymes; Macfarren doesn't. The first song, *The Nosegay,* is dull, and both the German and English texts leave one in doubt as to what is supposed to be happening. *The Rose* starts with a charming idea but lapses into the commonplace, and the cry of the cuckoo, in the song of that name, is followed by a heavy bass chord as comic in its way as the volley on the drums each fourth bar of the *allegro* of Wagner's Overture in B flat major. *The Lark,* actually Dvořák's first published work, since it appeared in 1873 as a supplement to the musical periodical *Dalibor,* has a pronounced flavour of folksong and a charm which lifts it above the rest of this set.

The history of the once famous *Moravian Duets,* composed for the most part in 1876, has already been related. In the thirteen duets of Op. 32, for soprano and contralto, which contain the pick of the bunch, Dvořák at once finds his form. He is far from the crude experimentation of the *Serbian Songs,* and his melodic inspiration flows freely and freshly throughout. He even manages to invent quite satisfactory piano accompaniments, though there is rather too much doubling of the voice parts. Stefan says that the melodies, though Dvořák's own, 'betray the peculiarities typical of Moravian folk-poetry and song; wide leaps in the melody, gliding of a motive in the interval of the major second, modulation in the minor second.' I do not pretend to understand this statement, particularly the latter half of it. There are a few quite ordinary leaps of an octave or a seventh in some of the duets, but nothing that seems in the least bit characteristic of Moravian folksong. No doubt Czech singers would present the duets most acceptably, but it would hardly be possible to listen to them unmoved, sung in English on the concert platform, the contralto addressing the soprano thus:

> Rosemarine or lily, fairy queen is Nelly,

and the soprano replying:

> I'm no rosemarine love, I'm no fairy queen love.

With all due respect to I. Bernhof (sex unknown), such a translation could only be gravity-removing. Even, however, with a serviceable translation this particular kind of domestic music has become un-fashionable and cannot be satisfactorily transplanted into the concert hall. One may notice, in passing, an early example of one of Dvořák's odd harmonic clashes in the dance-like section of the sixth duet, *Holub na Javoře* (*The Forsaken Lassie*).

Dvořák's next essay in song-writing were the *Tři novrecke básne* (*Three Modern Greek Songs*), Op. 50, for baritone, composed for a concert of his works in the winter of 1878, at which he made his first appearance as a conductor. The poems, by Václav Nebeský, were in Czech on Greek themes. By this year Dvořák had sounded the national note loud and clear in the *Three Slavonic Rhapsodies*, Op. 45, the first set of *Slavonic Dances*, Op. 46, and the two dance movements, *Dumka* and *Furiant*, of the A major Sextet, Op. 48; so perhaps he was glad to try his hand at something different. In these three songs, *Koljas, Naiads* and *Lament for a City*, Dvořák returns to the ballad form he used for *The Orphan* and was to use once again towards the end of his life. The first song is a dramatic affair about the rebel Koljas, the second relates the efforts of some water-maidens to charm a shepherd, who is duly warned by his mother to resist, and the third is a lament for the city of Parga, betrayed by fifth-columnists to the Turks. The last song is the best and should prove moving in the hands of a good singer. The other two are restless and episodic, the accompaniments again too anxious to be illustrative.[1]

With the *Cigánske Písne* (*Gypsy Songs*), Op. 55, composed in January 1880, Dvořák reached his highest pinnacle as a song-writer.

---

[1] These songs are published in English in the Hinrichsen edition as well as in German by Hainauer. The English translations by E. G. Porter are singable and the best that Dvořák's songs have so far received.

Gypsy Songs

The words, by Heyduk, are based on folk sources and the open-air, freedom-loving spirit which fills them obviously made a deep appeal to the composer. Everything is in place here. In the first song, *I chant my lay,* Dvořák is not led astray by such words as 'My courser skims' (I quote the poor translation), but keeps a steady keel in the chosen figure of accompaniment. He uses his dance-like opening measure to bind the verses together and maintains a perfect balance between voice and accompaniment. The workmanship is unusually careful. In *Hark how my triangle* the two verses are not only connected by a dance-measure, but that is also taken over by the voice in a charming little coda.

The third song, *Silent Woods,* is the only one to owe a debt—to Brahms—but it is so very beautiful that one feels grateful to its foster-parent. Dvořák is so sensitive, in this song, to the changing mood of the words that though he keeps his accompaniment the same in the second verse, he takes care to give expression to the heightened emotion of the words by varying the voice part. There is a cadence at the end of each verse, a rising ninth, of remarkable beauty.

The next song and, of course, the best-known of any that he wrote, *Songs my mother taught me,* is uniquely his own. It is truly inspired writing, a perfect little work of art and a most moving one. The marriage between voice and piano is of the happiest kind, and the accompaniment itself clashing delicately against the voice part (6-8 against 2-4) is beautifully devised. The song reaches its climax in the second verse, with a phrase of unforgettable beauty.

Of the remaining three songs, *Tune thy strings, O gypsy, Freer is the gypsy* and *The cloudy heights of Tatra,* the last deserves special mention as a bold and well-planned song. The accompaniment variation is dramatically right and the extended phrase in the voice part of the last verse not only makes a fine climax to the cycle but lies most gratefully for the voice.

During one of his London visits, in 1885, Dvořák wrote two songs, *A Lullaby* and *Disturbed Devotion,* which were published posthumously in 1921 by Hudební Matice. Dr. Stefan says they are delightful songs. Dvořák alludes to the *Lullaby* in the last act of his opera, *The Jacobin.* It was six years before he wrote a set of songs as considerable as the *Gypsy Songs,* and then only in response to a request from Simrock. *V národním tónu* (*In Folksong Style*), Op. 73, are settings of one Czech and three Slovak dance rhythms and imitate, in the second song, folk melody with great success. *Dobrou Noc* (*Good night*) can at once take its place in the best serenades of the great lieder writers. It is tenderly passionate and eminently singable. *Žalo Dievča* (*The Mower*) is a charming idealization of folk melody, and then comes the gem of this collection, *Ach neni tu* (*The Maiden's Lament*), which is one of the best songs Dvořák ever wrote. The two-part counterpoint for voice and treble piano part is beautifully contrived. As the girl laments her love the accompaniment carries the inner intensity of her emotion. In the second verse the accompaniment—and not as in *Silent Woods* the voice part—is subtly varied, and in the exquisite final verse Dvořák uses the thematic material of the opening bars of the song, kept over until then. The whole song is most moving, and it is extraordinary that it is not better known. The last song, *Ej, mám já koňa faku* (*Loved and Lost*), makes use of a vigorous dance rhythm and is in no way remarkable.

The German poetess Ottilie Malybrok-Stieler, who provided the translations of Dvořák's Op. 73 under the title of *Im Volkston,* gave him the material for his next set of *Four Songs*, Op. 82. It comes from her book, *Lyric Poems and Translations based on Bohemian Literature and Folk-Poetry,* and, owing to one of his periodic complications with his publisher, which it is of no interest to relate, Dvořák set the songs in German for Simrock without bothering to have translations made into Czech. These were added later. The songs are disappointing. The first, *Kéžduch můj sám* (*Leave me alone*) drags its way through two long verses with the piano accompaniment, liberally sprinkled with thirds and sixths, chained remorselessly to the voice part. The next song, *Prí vyšíváni* (*Over her Embroidery*), opens enchantingly in E flat major, is conventional in its middle section, returns, in D major, to its opening strain and ends, surprisingly, in that key. *Jaro* (*Springtide*), is a great improvement on the *Spring Song* of Op. 31: it is more than that, a really lovely song with a lift of the melody in its second phrase which is ravishing. The last song, *Ul poloka* (*At the Brook*), might well be called, from the style of its accompaniment, *Margaret at the Brook,* an attractive echo, a sad one too, of a great song.

The *Biblicke Písne* (*Biblical Songs*), Op. 99, are usually spoken of

as Dvořák's best songs, a claim which must be seriously examined.
As a nation we are—or were—predisposed towards settings of words
generally so well known and loved as these. Dvořák used, oddly
enough for a Catholic, the traditional Czech Protestant Bible of
Kralice, published in 1613, as the source of his texts.[1] The songs,
issued in German, French and English translations, have become
known and loved in their English dress, as is natural enough, but it
is easy to see from the one volume—why only one the publishers alone
can say—of the English edition which has the Czech vocal line
printed below the English one, what harm has been done to the
vocal line. (In the second volume of this unintelligent edition the
German text is wedded to the English!) Note-values and phrasing
suffer; but these blemishes apart, there are good reasons for not agreeing with the generally accepted verdict concerning the songs. In
style they are—though this is speculation—influenced by the simplicity
and inner urge of the Negro spiritual. In some cases, as we shall see,
the melodic simplicity is marked. If these songs are to be compared
with the finest things in this field of song-writing one has to come to
the conclusion that the workmanship is often hasty and careless.
Religious songs, of all types, should not take the easy way out of the
dominant seventh or thirteenth or, in illustrating perturbation of the
soul, of the diminished seventh unless these chords are felt to be
absolutely in place. His attitude towards tonal illustration again
leads Dvořák astray. The lightnings are childishly pictured in the
first song, *Clouds and darkness are round about Him,* and no great phrase
(and harmony) supports the greatness of God declared in the last line
of the psalm.

The cadences of this first psalm are really obtrusively conventional and the treatment of the words is over-literal. And if this
verdict of conventionality be thought harsh observe the start of the
next psalm, *Lord, Thou art my refuge. Hear my prayer* offers no reason

[1] First: Psalm xcvii. 2–6. Second: Psalm cxix. 114, 115, 117, 120.
Third: Psalm lv. 1, 2, 4–8. Fourth: Psalm xxiii. 1–4. Fifth: Psalm
cxliv. 9; Psalm cxlv. 2, 3, 5 and 6. Sixth: Psalm lxi. 1, 3, 4; Psalm lxiii.
1, 4; Psalm lxiii. 5, 6. Seventh: Psalm cxxxvii. 1–5. Eighth: Psalm
xxv. 16–18 and 20. Ninth: Psalm cxxi. 1–4. Tenth: Psalm xcviii.
1, 4, 7, 8; Psalm xcvi. 12.

for revision of this verdict, but rather for a grateful remembrance of Mendelssohn; but No. 4, *The Lord is my Shepherd*, is a really charming piece of baroque decoration of the simpler kind—a little too sweet but most appealing.

No. 5, *I will sing new songs of gladness*, with its characteristic repetitions, offers a fine bit of tune, differently harmonized on each of its four appearances and furnished with a good climax. No. 6, *Hear my prayer, O Lord*, is little better than a commercial ballad with its *arpeggio* concluding chords and poverty of invention, but the Negro-spiritual-like *By the waters of Babylon* is on a far higher level, though the composer forgets Jerusalem—and his right hand its cunning—and puts a stale chord of the thirteenth at the point of cadence.

Turn Thee to me, No. 8, is not the work of a man who has felt real spiritual desolation and remorse—as, for example, Wolf felt it—but it is a moving song with beautiful and well-contrived modulations and a really lovely use of an upward major third after leaving the minor key ('for my hope is in Thee'). In No. 9, *I will lift mine eyes*, Dvořák, as in the third of the *Four Songs*, Op. 52, begins in one key and ends in another, quite evidently of set purpose and not merely because the music takes him there.

Negro-spiritual influence is again very strong in the tenth and last song, *Sing ye a joyful song*, which illustrates the emotion of the words adequately. If the Negro spirituals were indeed Dvořák's models, it can only be said that he comes nowhere near the profound feeling of things like *Steal away* or, supremely, *Were you there?* Great religious songs these *Biblical Songs* are not—most of them are not even very good Dvořák.

His last song, written in 1901 but not published until after his death, was *Lešetinský Kovar* (*The Smith of Lešetin*), the poem by Svatopluk Čech, for tenor and piano. It is of no great consequence, another essay in ballad form with a couple of tunes, one fast and vigorous, one lyrical, that would have served well for another Slavonic Dance.

The best of Dvořák's songs would make but a small volume—'few, but roses.' Grieg—the composer who is the obvious choice for comparison—wrote more than double the quantity and nearly always surpassed the quality of the Dvořák songs. He was a pianist, and his accompaniments are invariably effective. He was perhaps a more fervent nationalist than Dvořák, and one gains a more vivid picture of Norway, physically and spiritually, from his songs than of Czechoslovakia from Dvořák's (but it is only fair to remember that Norway has a seaboard and the fiords).

One can say that a few of Grieg's songs equal the best of Schubert and that about half of the rest come not far after him. That is too large a claim for Dvořák, but music would certainly be poorer without his best songs. These few have a lyric beauty which Grieg would have been the first to acknowledge as being of very high quality.

CHAPTER XIII

PIANO MUSIC

OSCAR WILDE speaks, somewhere, of Dvořák's piano pieces as 'curiously coloured scarlet music,' a statement which reads oddly to-day. Some of these pieces may well have seemed 'curiously coloured' to Wilde's generation, and no doubt Dorian Gray might have been inspired to scarlet sins by Dvořák's innocuous *Witches' Sabbath* in *From the Bohemian Forest*. Looked at from another angle than that of the *Yellow Book*, Dvořák's piano music is curiously unequal. He had no degree of antipathy for the piano such as Elgar had, and his thoughts are piano thoughts, but he rarely knew how to set them down in the most effective way. He reminds us that no great music for the piano has been composed by only moderate pianists. Dvořák knows his Mrs. Beeton, he weighs out his ingredients more or less correctly, but he has not the skilful hand of the born cook, and his fare is sometimes very indigestible. A look at the printed page is enough.

Much of this piano music was, of course, written to satisfy a publisher constantly eager for small and quick-selling pieces, and some of it, no doubt, to help balance the budget of a growing family; but as late as 1894, when he was a famous composer, Dvořák could allow the commonplace and lazily written *American Suite* for piano, Op. 98, to be published and even, a year later, to be orchestrated.

As always the composer is most successful when he is most simple, and there is a small number of really charming little pieces buried away in his many occasional piano works, which deserve to be resurrected for domestic use.

The *Furiant*, Op. 12, No. 2, is an example of how thoroughly bad Dvořák's writing for the piano could be. As a realistic picture of an indifferent village band, thumping bass and squeaking treble, it is a success: from any other point of view it is a failure. (We may note here, in passing, Dvořák's almost pathological attraction to the upper register of the keyboard.)

This *Furiant* was composed in 1884, by which time Dvořák had written a good deal for the piano, including his largest work, the *Theme and Variations.* The earliest opus number, 8, was a pious fraud on Simrock,[1] for *Silhouettes,* twelve piano pieces, were written in 1879 and not seven years before. The tunes of the pieces are, however, genuine antiques, for they are taken from the youthful symphonies in C minor and B flat major and from the *Cypresses* songs. It is not to be wondered at that the results are patchy. No. 2, without the silly and disfiguring little cadenza, is a really charming page with a faintly Lisztian perfume. No. 3 has an attractive tune and rhythm, and could be made to sound effective. No. 6 is a lapse into sloppy sentimentality and feeble writing, though not so feeble as the octaves in similar motion which take up a whole page of No. 7. No. 10 is unashamedly Schumannesque, and so is No. 11, but so delightfully that it is worth while forgetting *Papillons* when playing it. The final number, *Allegro feroce,* is funny without being vulgar. Dvořák wasn't much good at being ferocious.

The *Two Minuets* of Op. 28 have much of the appeal of Schubert's *Valses*—they are waltzes really. No. 1, which someone appears to have scored for the orchestra, consists of five short sections, with a coda. The first section has a haunting little tune, which Dvořák had used before in *King and Collier*:

The *Dumka,* Op. 35, is a sad example of trying to give full value

[1] See pages 41–2.

for money. Had it been half the length one would have welcomed it as a pleasant little sketch for the larger pictures Dvořák painted later on. As it stands it is diffuse and overwritten.

We now reach Dvořák's most considerable work for the piano, the *Theme and Variations* in A flat major, Op. 36. The theme, marked *tempo di minuetto,* is obviously derived from the theme of Beethoven's first (variation) movement in the piano Sonata, Op. 26. It is in the same key and time, with the same kind of repetitiveness and with its chromatic opening suggested by the bass phrase of Beethoven's fifth and sixth bars. Dvořák cannot weld the two contrasted sections of his theme together with the same art; indeed the feeling is rather that of a simple *Musikant* replying to a complicated *Kapellmeister.*

The first two variations are of little account, and each modulates three times to E major, which is twice too much. There is, however, a genuine feeling of growth in the third variation in the minor key, and the two sections of the theme are now in a closer relationship. Dvořák's atonality, perfectly unconscious, was alluded to by Hadow years ago and still is by other writers. This variation provides an excellent example of the whole-tone 'scale' and no doubt would have seemed scarlet to Wilde. Variation 4 is a Moravian scherzo, and Beethoven's octaves are copied in Variation 5. The tranquil sixth variation is as beautiful as the seventh is fussy and fabricated. Dvořák has provided rather too impressive a finale, though quite an effective one. The work then is unequal, but certainly deserves more performance than it gets. I have not been able to see the *Scottish Dances* or the *Two Furiants* which make up Opp. 41 and 42, and the *Slavonic Dances* are best considered in the form we most usually hear them, though it must be said, in passing, that Dvořák obviously feels much happier in writing for four hands than for two.

The enormous success of these dances brought a flood of orders, especially for small pieces, and it is not surprising to come across hack-work such as the *Four Eclogues,* only published posthumously by Hudební Matice, in 1921. It would have been better to leave these chips from the workshop in manuscript. On the other hand the first of the *Two Impromptus,* without opus numbers, would have been a loss had it not seen the light. Griegian it may be, but it has a wistful questioning quality all its own and is effectively written for the instrument. It is certainly one of the pieces against which we must put a star. The second is attractive but not outstanding.

Sketches for a new series of *Scottish Dances* survive only in *Three Album Leaves* published by the same organization in 1921. The middle one of these, in F sharp minor, is a little gem, simple strains of a tune repeated to changing harmonies in the style of the episodes in Chopin's mazurkas. Pianists must not neglect this exquisite little piece, which seems to prove the point that the simpler Dvořák is the more successful. The third number is an endeavour to be humorous.

All these essays led to Dvořák's almost hitting the bull's-eye with his Op. 52, *Impromptu, Intermezzo, Gigue and Eclogue.* The *Gigue* alone is off the target—right off. The influence of Schumann is easily to be discerned in the vigorous and rhythmically alive *Impromptu,* good piano writing except for one weak passage of sixths in the opening section. The *Intermezzo* is original, not Schumann-esque at all, but real Slav music, and lovely from every point of view. Two stars for this. The final number, the *Eclogue,* uses the opening tune of the third of the *Four Eclogues* for its thematic material; giving it out first of all in G minor and then, rhythmically altered, in G major for an expressive section of contrast.

Six Mazurkas, Op. 56, and the *Eight Piano Waltzes,* Op. 54, are delightful to play and full of melody. Nos. 1 and 4 of Op. 54 have also been scored for string quartet. This is excellent *salon* music. And so we come to the *Ten Legends* for four hands, Op. 59.

Dvořák undertook this work after completing the D major Symphony with, we are told, 'special affection.' The duets are carefully written, with enough contrapuntal interest to keep the bass player on the look-out and enough harmonic interest during the process of modulation to keep both players alert. The form is the usual three-fold one Dvořák uses in his piano music, with a good deal of time variation. No. 3 might easily take a place as one of the quick *Slavonic Dances,* with a tranquil wood-wind middle section. It is in the manner of a scherzo. The one following, No. 4, has long been popular as an organ solo, but its heroic pomp has worn thin to-day. Grieg did this sort of thing better and at shorter length in his *Lyric Pieces.* Nos. 3 and 4 are frequently heard in their orchestral form, but when duet playing becomes fashionable again (if ever) players will turn to No. 3, at least, with pleasure. Of the rest, every one will stop in No. 6 and wonder if the slashing seconds are what Dvořák has really written. They are. They will play the Chopinesque No. 8 in F major—recalling the *Ballade* in that key—with pleasure and interest: it has a dramatic episode with some typical modulations back to the first section, and dull pages before will be forgotten with the really charming final number.

The next piano work was again a series of pieces for four hands called *From the Bohemian Forest,* Op. 68, but only one of these 'wood-land pieces' was orchestrated (cello solo and orchestra). Dvořák fixed titles to the pieces after they were written—he was now thinking towards his last works, the five orchestral tone-poems—and they have no particular relevance. (He grumbled that Schumann had used the best ones.)

These pieces are thoroughly romantic, so much so that they hit one well below the belt. One surrenders to the luscious middle section of *On the Dark Lake* (homage to Chopin) and to the languorous tune of *Silent Woods* (homage to Liszt), which comes out beautifully as a cello solo. The horrors of the *Witches' Sabbath* are limited to a few shudders on Dvořák's faithful friend, the diminished seventh, and there is a luscious tune which appears in a more attractive form in the slow movement of the A major Quintet, Op. 81. In the last piece, a stirring march, the composer quotes from the scherzo of his early D minor Symphony.

Unfortunately Dvořák did not maintain his form in the three books of *Poetic Tone-Pictures,* Op. 85. He wrote for two hands only, and that meant preoccupation with the left-hand part whenever he de-parted from simplicity (he is happiest in dance forms when the left hand can take care of itself), and he was becoming title-conscious. He called these pieces 'a sort of programme music.' Resemblance-hunting is as poor a game as reminiscence-hunting, but it is im-possible not to ejaculate 'Brahms' as one begins the first piece, *Twilight Way.* The piece is far too long and its contrasting sections have no particular relevance. The overwriting to be noticed here disfigures nearly all these pieces. *Spring Song,* the last in the first book, is a near miss: its figuration grows monstrous, but the initial idea and the harmonic clashes are delightful. After an inflated *Peasants' Ballad* (Book 2) comes a wistful piece, *Sorrowful Reverie*, which makes its due effect because it is kept simple. The *Furiant* which follows sounds brilliant and has one of its composer's unfailingly tuneful trios. Naïvety is carried to extreme lengths in the *Serenade* with which the book ends. Dvořák must have been listening to *Santa Lucia*. In the last book the pleasant tune of *Tittle-tattle* is quite humorously treated, and there is a massive dignity in the opening of the funeral piece, *At the Hero's Grave*, which is entirely absent in the Lisztian decorations with which Dvořák covers up the emptiness of his middle section. In spite of its too patent debt to Chopin there is a real appeal about the five-four measures of *The Holy Mount*.

If in these pieces Dvořák is too obviously trying to write effectively for the piano, he certainly did not bother to do so in the *American Suite*, Op. 98, a very curious production. In 1893 he had declared that thenceforth he would compose only for his pleasure, so that he had no special reason for writing this suite unless he wanted to console Mrs. Thurber for his not composing an opera on the subject of Hiawatha, for which no libretto was forthcoming. The opening phrase is well plugged—it also closes the Suite—and it is unfortunate that it so resembles 'Vissi d' arte,' though perhaps that is its chief recommendation. Dvořák is being consciously American, and this lends distinct interest to the Suite. He evidently thinks the Americans a very sentimental race. But the G.O.M. disarms criticism again with his third number, a sort of 3–4 cake-walk which is enchantingly vulgar. A pleasant 'Indian' *Lullaby* follows, and the final number, a badly written *Gavotte*, ends with an absurdly pompous flourish. Was Dvořák pulling the American leg?

Fortunately this poor work is not his last word in piano music. With the *Humoresques* he returned to simplicity in most of the pieces, and to the true springs of his melody, and gave the world in the famous seventh number, in G flat major, a really moving and beautiful piece. It is the most original thing Dvořák wrote for the piano: absolutely and unmistakably his own.[1] And this is something which

[1] I entirely dissent from the view that this piece is more effective as a violin solo.

can be said of very little of his piano music.   In this field not only Smetana far surpassed him—why do we so rarely hear his brilliant polkas and lovely Czech dances?—but also Fibich, whose hundreds of minatures for the piano have been lost sight of in the enormous popularity of one of them.

CHAPTER XIV

CONCERTOS

I HAVE been unable to see the score of Dvořák's early cello Concerto
in A major (June 1865), which only came to light in 1929, when it
was edited and published by Günther Raphael and, according to
Stefan, 'suffered some drastic changes and elisions.' If we accept the
story that Wihan asked Dvořák for a cello concerto—the later work
in B minor, Op. 104—it can be said that all his works in this form
were the result of requests. Joachim asked for the violin Concerto
in A minor (1880), and the piano Concerto in G minor, Op. 33,
was written for the pianist Slavkovský in 1876. The first of these
works is said to be 'typically romantic, neo-Wagnerian, yet' (why
yet?) 'beautifully warm-hearted.' [1]

The piano Concerto has not so much a warm heart as cold feet
and, in spite of its national flavour, most pronounced in the last
movement, it seems unwilling to let go the hand of Beethoven. The
cold feet arise from Dvořák's fear that the piano writing may not be
effective. Over this score might well be written 'a warning to young
composers. The piano passage-work sounds as if Dvořák had
again got down a musical Mrs. Beeton and weighed out his ingredients fairly accurately, but mixed them with the heavy hand of
the inexpert cook.

After a short exposition, with no hint of a second group of themes,
the soloist enters, and the pages begin to grow black with notes. In
the slow movement asphyxia almost sets in. It is all but impossible
for Dvořák, even in his poorest works, to write for long without somehow disarming us with a charming phrase, but such phrases as make
an appearance in this Concerto are immediately smothered in notes
by the piano. The B major episode in the final movement, very
Slav in harmony, comes nearest to escaping the process. The
pathetic thing is that all this elaboration is lamentably ineffective and
unpianistic. In recent years a new version has been made by some

[1] *Anton Dvořák,* by Paul Stefan, pages 36–7.

person unstated for Rudolf Firkušný, who has played it with success. But the work will never take a place in the repertory or in the Dvořák canon.

The composer had not to agonize over the violin Concerto in this way. Here was an instrument he understood, and if he had any doubts about the writing for the solo part Joachim was at hand to solve them. This, in fact, he did, and he also suggested several changes in the orchestration. Dvořák, moreover, had been rapidly advancing in his art. There is little real development of material in the piano Concerto, and a great deal of thematic repetition. Much technical advance is shown in the violin Concerto, though it is only in the magnificent B minor cello Concerto that Dvořák solves all his problems. The first movement of the violin Concerto falls between two stools. Too long for an introduction to the extensive slow movement, it is too short for what is called first-movement form. No doubt Dvořák, in the modern way of the time, wanted to avoid a long exposition of the Beethovenian type, but he does not yet know how to do the short-circuiting so brilliantly carried out in the cello Concerto.

Then the style is mixed. The main theme is of Czech cast, but Beethoven and a typical eighteenth-century formula are called on to get it moving. With the entry of the solo violin Dvořák proceeds under his own steam and throws off some lovely phrases. Whenever he uses the flute we can be almost sure of enchantment—and so it is here.

One does not have to be a detective to hear Brahms take hold of the second subject:

but he is allowed only this one appearance. The passage-work is rather what is expected than what is inevitable, but the brief cadenza, ending on a pause, brings at the first hearing the totally unexpected little episode with which Dvořák decides to forget the first movement. It is a beautiful moment, the solo violin low down in its compass, with high writing for the woodwind; flute and oboe leading into the slow movement. This movement opens with a lovely tune which has, for its second limb, one of Dvořák's most endearing fingerprints, derived from Czech folk music, the repeated refrain:

The orchestral tutti at the end of this section offers the conductor one of the problems of balance not infrequent in Dvořák's orchestral writing. He gives the tune to flute and oboe with amply filled-in string parts below. These, if not carefully handled, are apt to blur the outline.

This long rhapsodic movement contains a wealth of ideas, put down just as they occur to the composer; one of them, as actors say, is just thrown away. Brahms rightly said Dvořák's leavings would keep other composers going for years. The quick minor section is conventionally introduced, but there is real art in the unexpected burgeoning of the refrain, quoted above, in the middle of the third section of the movement. Perhaps the effect of the whole movement is rather too improvisatory but it is very enjoyable.

The presentation of the high-spirited finale—a *furiant*—is original and effective, and it is graced with one of Dvořák's enchantingly gay tunes:

The revels are interrupted by a *dumka* somewhat artificially worked up to the point of recapitulation. This last movement might be regarded as another, extended, Slavonic Dance, rather than the final movement of a concerto with an organic life of its own.

No such criticism can be made of the similar movement of the cello Concerto in B minor, Op. 104, composed fifteen years later, which shows that Dvořák had got concerto form just where he wanted it. The finest tribute to its worth came from Brahms, who said on a first reading of the score: 'Why on earth didn't I know that one could write a violoncello concerto like this? If I had only known, I would have written one long ago!'

A first theme presented by soloist and orchestra in thirds indicates congenital weakness and, as we saw, the opening movement of the violin Concerto expired prematurely. But there is no such weakness in the strongly drawn melodic line of the first theme of this Concerto. Perhaps absolute purity of style is not to be found here, or no more than in any other of Dvořák's large-scale works. Wotan has his say and Weber inspires the brilliant tutti after the horn solo has sung the second subject, that exquisite tune which has become a *locus classicus* of horn writing.

The entry of the solo instrument, preceded by a careful hush and a sufficiently arresting modulation from D major to B minor, is splendidly dramatic. This section is marked *quasi improvisando* and does not belie this description. The series of short phrases is like a chain of thoughts and afterthoughts suggested by a fertile mind. There is much endearing detail in the rich orchestral writing; for example, the little fountain of notes thrown up by flute and clarinets, as if out of sheer happiness, when the soloist is playing the second subject.

Profiting perhaps by Liszt's device of theme transformation in his A major piano Concerto, or, for that matter, Schumann's work in A minor, Dvořák, for his development section, modulates to the distant key of A flat minor, and gives us another viewpoint of his first subject:

This episodic development presented a problem which the composer most ingeniously solves. To have worked to the usual recapitulation would have been a dangerous possibility; to present us, after a brief cadenza, with the second subject in the tonic major, 'triumphant in the full orchestra,' is a brilliant actuality. The first subject, in this tail-first process, carries its *grandioso* marking without any of the vulgar strutting which disfigures a similar movement in the Liszt Concerto, and we can fully share the composer's apparent pleasure, expressed in the last four bars, at having cleared all the obstacles so successfully.

The poetic slow movement is so rich in material that only a wealth of quotation would make writing about it of any value. This time the contrasted central episode is not just pushed at us, though it arrives quite suddenly. The point is that it is felt to be inevitable and to have grown out of what has gone before.[1] This is partly achieved by shaping the cadence in the same way as the cello or the flute—most beautifully—have done.

Two lovely details must be mentioned, the duet for oboe and solo cello, which comes after the appearance of the central episode in G minor, and the flute solo which leads to the tranquil version of that same central episode with which the movement concludes.

The gradually organized last movement is full of good things, from the lively march the horns give out at the start to the 'glorious series of epilogues' with which Dvořák reluctantly, it seems, concludes the work.

[1] This episode is founded on the first phrase of the song, *Kéžduch můj sám* (*Leave me alone*), the first number of Dvořák's Op. 82.

Dvořák

It is surprising that we hear this masterly and beautiful work so seldom. Perhaps our soloists fear to challenge the superb performance of Casals, which is happily perpetuated in the recording made by him.

CHAPTER XV

CHORAL WORKS

THE vocal scores on the dust-laden shelves of second-hand music shops bear silent witness to changes of fashion. Here, now unperformed, lie works which once stirred thousands, works into which much fine music has been poured. But the mould has been modified very considerably. The qualification is important. *Messiah,* the *St. Matthew Passion, The Dream of Gerontius, Hiawatha,* show no disposition to be remaindered. They represent different musical levels, but the lesser works keep their place with the great not only by reason of an inherent vitality, but because words and music are so perfectly mated.

Now words were always a hindrance rather than a help to Dvořák. Even if this were not so the English translations by the Rev. Dr. Troutbeck would be a hindrance to us. It is doubtful whether either *The Spectre's Bride* or *St. Ludmilla* would bear revival, in spite of much fine stuff in them; but now that the anti-Roman translations of the worthy doctor can be ignored, it is extraordinary that performances of Dvořák's Latin works are so rarely given. The Requiem is, in my opinion, a masterpiece, and if *Stabat Mater* is unequal, it is none the less full of lovely music and a remarkable first essay for its composer to have written.

Domestic loss was added to religious feeling when the work was in process of composition (1876), but in any case all Dvořák's religious music is purely subjective. He knew Palestrina, but his approach had to be different from the selfless one of that great master. The *Motu proprio* had been promulgated, but the rulings embodied in it held little interest for Dvořák. His forms are unliturgical—there were also material and practical reasons for that—and his manner is baroque.

He had to fill a large canvas, to space out the words into movements which would give his soloists more or less equal opportunity. Handel's heritage lay heavy on all composers who took the English market into their calculations, but in facing his task Dvořák shows considerable imagination and avoids some of the conventions very successfully.

'The first Czech oratorio' opens with a poetical prelude, pictorial in its widely spaced unisons in the first bars, which suggest the Mother gazing up at the Cross, emotional in its chromatic theme and rising tide of feeling. The melodic appeal is perfectly frank and sincere and fresh:

Occasionally one is pulled up by Dvořák's use of commonplace harmony, facile sequences and casual treatment of words.

The opening chorus, twenty-five slowly moving pages of vocal score, exhausts patience with its overworked chromatic theme and its verbal repetitions—this is too ample an expression of grief. Composers rarely remember the emotional economy of the New Testament. In the succeeding chain of solos, concerted pieces and choruses one is alternately enchanted by the sheer melodic beauty of the music and by Dvořák's feeling for the voice, for which he always writes beautifully and effectively, and disturbed by his insensitivity to words.

It is not carrying naïvety too far to set the words ('In amando Christum Deum') 'ut sibi complaceam' to a slow Slavonic dance—there are plenty of parallels in baroque art for that kind of thing; but to write this kind of tune, with the words only too obvious a peg, is being naïve in quite the wrong way:

The final movement, 'Quando corpus morietur,' is closely related thematically to the opening chorus. At the words 'Paradisi gloria'

the mystical exaltation of Palestrina gives place to a burst of sensuous splendour. The candles are blazing on the altar at Benediction, the incense rises, the bishop is in full pontificals. A concession to Handelian tradition is made in the setting of the potent word 'Amen,' but Dvořák is so patently enjoying himself that it would be churlish to interrupt him. He remembers in time to end quietly and beautifully.

Fourteen years more of creative life gave Dvořák all else that he needed, and the Requiem, which he composed in 1890, is a most moving and lovely work.

The 'leading motive,' given out at the very start, by the cellos, which runs through the whole work, might well have been suggested by the first notes of the plain-chant setting of the Introit in the Mass for the Dead:

One quotation must suffice to show the resource with which it is used throughout:

Dvořák's manipulation of the text is, as usual, quite unliturgical, but extremely original and effective. Thus he links the 'Kyrie Eleison,' set to his leading motive, on to the Introit, making no break, and telescoping it amongst the voices. It matters not to him that he ends with the middle petition.[1]

The Gradual, 'Requiem aeternam,' is also set to the leading motive, in augmentation, the unaccompanied solo soprano moving upwards a semitone at the repetition of the words. The men's voices are reserved for the unaccompanied close in four-part harmony, the orchestra then taking the prayer upwards in a series of quiet chords, a most poetical conclusion.

[1] Verdi did the same thing in his Requiem Mass.

Dvořák rejects the overworked plain-chant theme of the 'Dies irae' in favour of an original tune in the style of a march. This section of the Mass is the weakest, for the composer is not good at suggesting supernatural terror and is apt to lapse into melodrama; but the prelude to the 'Tuba mirum,' in which the leading motive is taken gradually up three semitones,[1] is finely imaginative, and so is the modal setting of 'Liber scriptus proferetur,' with its unexpected pendant phrase:

For sheer sweetness and eloquence the quartet 'Recordare Jesu pie' stands out, and the too literal illustration of 'Confutatis maledictis'[2] is forgotten in the beauty of its ending and the moving pathos of the final number in this part.

With the Offertory Dvořák leaves the horrors of hell behind him, and one seems to sense his relief in the phrase, worthy of plain-chant, which the bass sings to the words 'Domine Jesu Christe, rex gloriae.' This serves as a lesser leading motive, for it is used also in the next number, 'Hostias.' At the end of the Offertory, to the tune of a traditional Slav hymn, comes a rather manufactured fugue ('Quam olim Abrahae'), the least inspired portion of the work. Its repetition is required at the end of 'Hostias,' but a conductor should take it upon himself to circumvent this at all costs!

The 'Sanctus' is originally treated. The solo bass begins and is followed by a small chorus of altos, the full chorus entering only after the solo tenor and soprano. The same idea is carried on in the

[1] Composers familiar with the liturgy of Holy Week have probably copied this device, unconsciously or otherwise, from the threefold singing, at a higher pitch each time, of *Ecce lignum Crucis*, on Good Friday. Verdi's priests in *Aida* use it also.

[2] Dvořák here imitates the opening of Verdi's 'Dies irae.'

MS. OF PAGE 19 OF THE 'HYMNUS'

'Benedictus,' which ends in a blaze of sound. Then comes an exquisite quartet, 'Pie Jesu,' for divided men's chorus, solo soprano, alto and tenor, in which the unaccompanied voices are answered antiphonally by an orchestral version of the leading motive.

Dvořák only sets the last petition of the 'Agnus Dei,' as if to assure himself that the dead will be granted eternal rest, and just as he linked the 'Kyrie' to the Introit, here he links the Communion to the 'Agnus.'

The music reaches a splendid climax, a blaze of light, and then dims to the quiet singing by the solo soprano of the motive which has proved such a fine unifying influence and been productive of such great spiritual beauty. With this motive the grand work very softly ends.

The Mass in D major, Op. 86, was commissioned in 1886, by Josef Hlávka, a president of the Czech Academy of Emperor Francis Joseph, for the consecration of a chapel on his estate, and is dedicated to him.

It is not an important work and has less melodic appeal than is usual with Dvořák, but he shows his accustomed originality in handling the problems of setting the Mass. Thus four contralto voices sing the clauses of the 'Credo' ahead of the remainder of the choir. This is effective, although it involves some foreshortening. For example the choir sing 'Credo in unum Dominum Filium Dei unigenitum.' The four hammer-strokes of the 'Crucifixus' are dramatic, and there is some beautiful harmony at 'passus et sepultus est.' Who but Dvořák would have set the 'Credo' to a soft phrase of this character?

This movement and the Handelian splendour of the 'Gloria,' a veritable flourish of trumpets, are the best things in the work.

Dvořák is still defiantly unliturgical, the priest's intonations are given to the choir, and the second petition of the 'Kyrie' contains a repeated 'Christe' to fit the musical phrase. This is not, however, a happy departure from tradition.

His last piece of church music, the *Te Deum,* Op. 103 (1892), for soprano and bass solos, choir and orchestra, was written for performance in America, and is perhaps the most original contribution to sacred music he made. It is spaced out like a symphony and contains a slow movement and a scherzo as well as the two outer movements. It is joyful open-air music, Franciscan in its exquisite wood-wind details, which suggest that the birds are there to praise God with men. It is indeed Dvořák's truest confession of faith, and the splendid opening theme, used also in the last movement, has a Bach-like strength and rhythm:

The motive which runs through the Sonatina for violin and piano, Op. 100, written a year later, appears in embryo here:

If the opening suggests Bach, the flute and English horn in the 'Sanctus' suggest Blake's happy piper, playing a variant of the main theme while the birds and beasts gather round to hear:

There is some remarkable 'whole-tone' harmony in the unique Scherzo, and in the lovely soprano solo in the final movement (which ends with an 'Alleluia!') Dvořák's oboe and flute foreshadow the diminution of the main theme in the slow movement of the 'New World' Symphony. From all points of view this *Te Deum* is a little masterpiece.

The first of Dvořák's non-Latin works of importance is the *Hymnus* for choir and orchestra, Op. 30, composed in 1872 and revised in 1880. This was published by Novello in 1885, with the title *Patriotic Hymn*, in a translation made by the ubiquitous Dr. Troutbeck. The simple heart-felt music movingly expresses the unconquerable soul of the Czech people and their aspirations to freedom. There is no jingoism in the hymn. To hear it sung by a Czech choir must be a thrilling experience.

The Spectre's Bride (1884), the good doctor's bowdlerization of the original title, *Svatební Košile,* aroused extraordinary enthusiasm when it first came out, and Dr. Victor Hely-Hutchinson assures us that 'in performance its dramatic illogicality does not matter. Dvořák holds his audience in a musical enchantment as secure in its way as Mozart's in *The Magic Flute*.'[1] This is a large claim, and it would be interesting to have it substantiated. Before that can happen someone must do for the libretto what Professor Dent has done for Mozart's opera. But in this case much of the music would have to be re-written also, if the Gilbert and Sullivan echoes are to be expunged. One could do better for the heroine than pseudo-Wordsworthian lines of this sort:

> Not one year old my sister died.
> War took my brother from my side,

but no amount of verbal felicity could overcome the fatal suggestions of the Savoy operas:

> *Bass:* And she behind, she might not wait.
> *Chorus:* And she behind, she might not wait.

There are thirteen pages like that, announcing the general feeling that there is a ghost around.

Not only Dr. Troutbeck is to be blamed for the lack of enthusiasm one feels for this work. Dvořák's arrangement of four soprano and

[1] 'Dvořák the Craftsman,' *Music & Letters,* vol. xxiii, No. 4, October 1941.

tenor duets interspersed with baritone solos with chorus must surely prove wearisome in performance. One cannot forget that Schubert's supernatural drama on this kind of theme occupies but four pages of music for voice and piano and contains more terror than Dvořák can conjure up in all his hundred and ninety-three pages.

There are, of course, charming lyrical moments, such as the soprano solo, 'Mine did I once a lover call,' and the prayer, also for soprano, 'O Virgin Mother'; but Dvořák was to surpass these numbers in later years. On the whole, and in spite of some fine pages, there seems to be no reason to disturb the dust that gathers on the shelves where this work reposes.

In the oratorio *St. Ludmilla* (1885-6) Dvořák found a really poetic text. He wanted to give England a new choral work and at the same time his own people a national one. The work had a terrific success with the public in the north of England (though not with all the critics) as well as in Czechoslovakia, where it has also been produced on the stage.

Looking over the first part of the work one is amazed that it should have been neglected for so long. Handel is obviously Dvořák's master here, and he is an apt pupil. The fresh beauty of the choruses in *L'Allegro* and *Acis and Galatea* lives again, with Dvořák's unmistakable touch on it, in such numbers as 'Blossoms, born of teeming springtime' (the reverend doctor's translation, of course), and the more massive choruses have all Handel's strength and simplicity.

Ludmilla's air, 'I long with childlike longing,' and the peasant's song, 'Come, let us garlands bring,' are exquisitely lovely. None of the solos or choruses in this first part is overlong or overburdened with verbal repetition, and they are exceptionally well varied. Why then is the work neglected? The answer comes with the arrival of the missionary priest Ivan. He might have inspired Swinburne's words:

Thou hast conquered, O pale Galilean; the world has grown grey from Thy breath.

With his entrance the happy pagan joy of the music vanishes. He is not only depressing: he is a bore, and the second part of the oratorio shows that he might well have given points to Gurnemanz. Lud-

milla retains her sweetness of disposition in spite of Ivan's gloomy
reminders of the 'hard and thorny way' she has to travel and the load
of sin she carries. Matters brighten up a bit with the arrival of Prince
Bořivoj, who is out hunting. He immediately falls in love with her.
The old pest Ivan allows this only on condition that he too becomes a
Christian. The music, even, imitates the banality of the translator,
and we are back at the Savoy opera:

> Convinced we are, deny who can,
> It is the wondrous holy man.

It is indeed! A pasteboard angels' chorus concludes this section of
the work. The last part is concerned with the baptism of Ludmilla
and Bořivoj in the cathedral of Velehrad. The choruses of this
part, in Handel's full-bottomed-wig manner, are magnificent, and
the English choirs, for whom they were intended, must have revelled
in them.

Dvořák founds a processional march, with chorus, on the ancient
Slav chorale, 'Hospodine pomiluj ny.' Too much elaboration of
detail makes the baptismal duet, 'The hour I long for,' sound fussy,
but apart from that there is a perceptible drop in melodic freshness
and charm. The chorus at the end of the work cannot fail to make
a terrific effect, sung by a large body of voices, but all the time one
thinks regretfully of the springtime paganism of the first part, now
overlaid with convention.

Dvořák's remaining choral works include a setting of the 149th
Psalm, Op. 79 (1887), a cantata written for America, *The American
Flag*, Op. 102 (1893), and various partsongs. The second of these
works is a joyful affair in the Handelian tradition with, Stefan
tells us, reminiscences of Gluck's Overture to *Iphigenia in Aulis* and
Wagner's *Mastersingers*—an odd combination. Of *The American
Flag*, a *pièce d'occasion* 'recalling in patriotic terms' the war of 1812
and the ultimate triumph and freedom of the United States, Stefan
writes:

Its form is similar to the *Te Deum* with the conclusion the same as the
beginning . . . there is a Hymn to the Eagle and a Hymn to the Flag,
sung by the brave fighters—infantry, cavalry and marines—who gather
round it. This is followed by a poetic apotheosis of the Flag that shall

become a Symbol of Freedom to the World. The March introducing the Soldiers' oath of allegiance to the Flag is remarkable for its Czechish [*sic*] colouring: it sounds almost like a polka, a message of greeting from Bohemia to the New World.

Dvořák's lack of regard for this work is probably the best critical verdict on it.

Only one group of Dvořák's several sets of partsongs has, so far as I know, been issued with an English translation. This is the setting of five Lithuanian folk poems, Op. 27, which he wrote in 1878 on the way from Prague to Vienna to see Brahms.

These English versions—the translations by Rosa Newmarch— are issued by Messrs. J. & W. Chester. One of the little songs, *The Sparrows' Party*, is delightfully humorous. A cock-sparrow, throwing a party, gets drunk on cider and, in a polka, treads heavily on Miss Owlet's big toe. She sues for damages, but he flies off. Another of the group, *The Lost Lamb*, stands out for its pathos.

I have not been able to see the other sets of partsongs. *Amid Nature*, Op. 63, five choruses for mixed voices to words by Hálek (1882), are said to be impressionistic, especially the second number, *Evening bells in the grove*, and one would be glad to hear the hymn in praise of Czech peasant life, Op. 28 (1885), words by Dr. Karel Pippich, set for mixed choir and orchestra or piano duet accompaniment. It is a very popular repertory piece in Czechoslovakia. Three Slovak Folksongs for Male Choir (1877) are also provided with piano duet accompaniment.

CHAPTER XVI

OPERAS

IT has been said that the history of Czech opera is the history of Czech music; in which case most of us know very little, at first hand, about it. We know, indeed, that Smetana wrote the first effective pages of that history; that, as the late Dr. H. C. Colles truly said:[1]

> [He] alone among the musicians of Europe perceived the possibilities of using national opera as a means of training his people, binding them together through their love of their traditional music, dance, and language —(the *Ton, Tanz und Ticht* of Wagner's aphorism) enabling them to recover their lost national consciousness through the presentation of their own life on a stage which should hold a mirror up to their own nature.

Smetana was single-minded in his great and arduous task, and only once, in *The Two Widows,* swerved aside from it. Dvořák, in his operatic strivings, was actuated by mixed motives. His great, perhaps his greatest, ambition was to write an opera that would cross the frontiers as surely as did his orchestral and chamber music works. And his last opera, of the ten he wrote, shows him still intent on this task.

It is often assumed by writers on opera that librettos based on national customs and sentiments will fail to secure a visa; but the world-wide success of two such thoroughly national, if different, operas as *The Bartered Bride* and *Boris Godunov* would seem to prove the reverse. One village is, after all, much the same as another, and tyrants all have a family resemblance. Provided a composer can give his music that quality of universality which every one recognizes and no one can define, there need be no barriers to the most national-istic of work.

In a country where opera is regarded as not a luxury but a necessity Smetana's lovely light opera, *The Kiss*—which is in every way superior to *The Bartered Bride*—should not fail to succeed, and one would think that a great epic work like *Libuša* ought to make its way. Similarly

[1] *Antonín Dvořák*, edited by Viktor Fischl, page 137.

Dvořák's *The Devil and Kate* and *Rusalka*—at least—seem to be labelled for export, and it is to be hoped that they will one day enter the current repertory.

For obvious reasons this chapter has to rely for the most part on the opinions of others, and more particularly on those of Dr. Colles, who was lucky enough to witness the commemorative series of Dvořák's operas given at the National Theatre in 1929. To this synthesis of opinions I can only add a close study of the vocal scores of all the published operas, joined to a lifelong interest in opera itself. In the following account of Dvořák's ten operas I intend to give only—in most cases—a very brief summary of the plots, for what is so dull as the retelling of such things? One wonders, in reading them, how any composer could have contemplated setting such rubbish; or how these stories, so barren of incident, could have been padded out to fit the three or four hours' traffic of the stage.

Dvořák was attracted to his first libretto, *Alfred the Great* (by Theodor Körner), because it exalted the idea of freedom—albeit British freedom in a German text. And when that idea was uppermost the music, it is said, took fire. Nothing was heard of this essay except the overture, published posthumously in 1912, by Simrock, under the title of *Dramatic Overture* but styled 'Tragic' by Dvořák. It was performed by Nedbal in 1903 and contains the four main themes of the opera, presented in the Wagnerian manner.

The history of Dvořák's next effort, *King and Collier,* has been related earlier in this book. The sub-title, 'Make yourself at home with Mr. Matej,' is a clue to the nature of the 'book'—in Czech this time—by Bernhard Guldener. The plot concerns the hospitality of a charcoal-burner to a stranger who turns out to be a king. This beneficent monarch disposes of the jealousy he unwittingly causes to the sweetheart of the charcoal-burner's daughter by inviting them all to visit him. This means that their fortunes are made. In its final form it seems that Dvořák exchanged Wagner for Smetana as model, with admixtures of Weber and Lortzing. There is a cheerful but leisurely overture, a ballad for the king which exhibits one of the composer's most characteristic finger-prints,[1] a bagpiper who intro-

---

[1] See page 158.

duces 'a fragment of genuine Czech folk-music' and a further song for the king, in Lortzing's strophic manner, besides an enchanting waltz (quoted below) and a quite ordinary polka in the ballet music:

Stefan speaks justly of 'youthful vigour and intoxicating melody.' Nevertheless 'unnecessary and lifeless persons whose appearance interfered with the continuity of the third act' have imperilled the opera's chances of life. Someone should start a society for the exhumation of departed operas, so that their best numbers, at least, would be certain of occasional performance.

These two abortive essays caused Dvořák to pursue his apprentice-ship more modestly, and he followed his second version of *King and*

Collier—which, after all, was a move in the right direction—with a little one-act opera, *The Pig-headed Peasants,* for which Dr. Josef Štolba provided the libretto. With this opera may be linked—but not for performance, since the operas are too much alike to go into one bill—*The Peasant a Rogue,* for which a more gifted author, but a poor dramatist, Josef Otakar Veselý, provided the libretto. It must be remembered that the first version of *The Bartered Bride*—in two, instead of the later three acts—was a *Singspiel,* recitatives being added in the revised version. Dvořák set his libretti to continuous music, and though his series of operas shows continuous improvement, he really handles this matter with ease only in *The Devil and Kate,* the last but two of his operas. For the rest these two rustic comedies are full of charming music. Indeed, Dr. Colles thinks that one or the other, in an English translation, would prove the best possible introduction to Dvořák's operas. Perhaps they will one day appear as co-respondents in the 'Cav.' and 'Pag.' divorce case!

The choice might not be easy, for *The Peasant a Rogue* is saddled with a very mixed kind of libretto, 'sometimes excellent, and then again rough and faulty'; though its plot offers more variety in social grades and so in the music allotted to the different characters. The aristocracy, domestic servants, and peasants all appear, music of a Czech type being given to these last, while the rest express themselves in cosmopolitan terms. Between these two small works Dvořák tried his hand at a tragic opera, *Wanda,* for which Zákrejs and Beneš-Šumavský provided a fearsome five-act libretto. Smetana had turned—though as yet with small success—from *The Bartered Bride* to *Dalibor* and *Libuša,* works on an epic scale, so Dvořák would not be less bold. But this Polish opera was to go the way of *Alfred the Great.* A real tragedy, the death of his daughter, cast a shadow over the writing of the second act, but the opera was ill fated from the start. It was performed in 1876, but soon disappeared from the repertory. If the overture, the only part of the music published by Cranz, to whom Dvořák sold the score, is any criterion, *Wanda* deserved its fate.[1] Dvořák never wrote anything else so utterly uninspired and conventional.

[1] It was revived for the commemoration of the twenty-fifth anniversary of the composer's death (1929).

Four years after the composition of *The Peasant a Rogue* Dvořák again challenged the operatic stage with a work on an epic scale. It was also a challenge to himself, for the epic was never in his line, nor had he learnt the secret of true dramatic concentration. Being per- haps unwilling to enter Smetana's now clearly chosen field, Dvořák selected a libretto, by Marie Červinková-Riegrová, on the subject of the false Dimitri, claimant to the throne of Russia. The story, which owes something to a Czech drama and to a fragment by Schiller, begins where Mussorgsky's opera ends. Dimitri, at the head of his Polish forces, is at the gates of Moscow as the opera starts. He is married to the Polish Princess Marina, and by the end of Act I is acclaimed as tsar. In rescuing Xenia, the only surviving child of Boris, from his soldiers, he falls in love with her, and thus the usual triangular situation is created. Marina and Xenia become rivals, but Xenia does not realize that her saviour was her father's worst enemy. Not unnaturally, when she does discover this, she refuses to marry the tsar and enters a convent. Her humility has won over the jealous princess, but Marina is determined to revenge herself on Dimitri, and denounces him as an impostor to the assembled people. Dimitri has a chance of being saved by Marfa, widow of Ivan the Terrible, but refuses to take it and is shot by Shuisky, Boris's chief minister. Such is the bare outline of a plot rich in incident and moving much more coherently than Mussorgsky's opera.

It concerns not only a clash of individuals, but also one of faiths; but Dvořák is far happier in the great crowd scenes of the contesting parties than in the characterization of his principal characters. His intention to present Marina as an imperious and headstrong woman is plain, but this cannot be done merely by the use of mazurka-like rhythms. The weakest scene in Mussorgsky's opera is the Polish one, and for much the same reasons. Xenia is more faithfully delineated; but even so much of her music, and that of Dimitri, runs on conventional lines. At its best it is exquisitely tuneful, at its worst absolutely uncharacteristic and manufactured. The duet for Dimitri and Xenia in Act IV contains a pale shadow of the *Tristan* love duet (page 274), and later comes a quintet in the vein of *The Mastersingers* (page 308):

But the real Dvořák shines out in simpler moments, such as Xenia's little air in the vault of the tsars—broken into by the drunken Polish soldiers (p. 138). The honours go to the magnificent choral writing in the first and third acts, great set pieces which should prove most effective in the theatre, and to the glowing colours of the orchestral score.

It is not difficult to see why the opera failed to realize Dvořák's hopes for it. Wagner was all the fashion, and this work was felt to be built on the old-fashioned lines of Meyerbeer. That verdict we can reject. The fault lies in the very nature of Dvořák's art. Sensuous beauty is out of keeping with epic themes. Mussorgsky's opera holds the stage by virtue not of its beauty, but of its vitality and truth to life. In later years Janáček was to give the Czechs unmistakable evidence of the same thing in a series of magnificent operas, at present quite unknown here.

The great attempt made, Dvořák, though tempted by an offer from the manager of the Vienna opera to set a German text, left opera alone until 1887, when he was a world-famous composer. But he revised *Dimitri,* both in 1883, when he added the brilliant dance music that opens the second act, and in 1894, when in America; and he went carefully over the entire work under the influence of the Wagner addict Seidl, 'eliminating all repetitions and pointing up whole scenes into lengthy recitative.' His opera had now become a music-drama. But as soon as he heard this latest version he sorely missed the beauties of the earlier *Dimitri.* It looks as if a de-Rimskying will have to be undertaken! *Dimitri* had, obviously enough, not conquered the world, and for his next effort Dvořák was content to write for home consumption and his own enjoyment. Paradoxically enough the result, *The Jacobin,* is an opera which might well bear transplantation: for 'Dvořák was at ease only with what he knew, his own people as he had grown up with them at Nelahozeves and

Zlonice, the little people who took life as they found it, made merry with song and dance, recounted their tales of devils and pixies and water-sprites, bargained with their neighbours in the market-place and exercised their cunning in defeating the petty tyranny of their overlords.'[1] Dvořák turned to a libretto which the authoress of *Dimitri* had suggested to him six years before when he was looking beyond the confines of Bohemia.

The central figure of *The Jacobin* (called Benda, Bohemian for Bach) is a typical Bohemian *Musikant,* who lives only for his daughter and his art. Add to this fact the stage directions for the first act, and it will be clear enough why the drama so appealed to Dvořák:

On the right a church with large steps.
On the left an inn. In the background the view of a castle.
When the curtain rises the stage is empty. From inside the church comes singing.

It might almost have come from a guide to Nelahozeves.

The Jacobin—the action takes place during the French Revolution —is the son of the local bigwig, in disgrace for his political views. Turned out of home he has sought his fortune and married abroad. When he returns home he finds a cousin seeking to supplant him in the count's affections. So he enlists Benda's help and eventually succeeds in regaining his rightful place. There are various other stock characters to provide a sub-plot, and the whole thing would wear a conventional air were it not for Dvořák's mellow and beautiful score.

The introduction—*allegro, tempo di valse*—to Act I literally waltzes us into church, and there they are singing a mixture of one of Dvořák's own gypsy songs and a carol. There is a tender beauty in the dialogue between Bohus—the Jacobin—and Julie, his wife, which was far to seek in *Dimitri*; and here the chief motive is introduced (page 9), one which Dvořák handles with much skill:

---

[1] *Antonín Dvořák: his Achievement,* edited by Viktor Fischl, page 141.

This becomes, for example, in the finale of the second act (page 258):

Lovely things, gay, humorous and tender, are scattered up and down this enchanting score. It is all most characteristic Dvořák, even when he shows us he has heard *Carmen* in the march-finale of Act I (page 126):

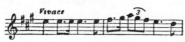

Here too, in a love song, is a faint foreshadowing of the famous tune in the slow movement of the 'New World' Symphony (page 170):[1]

How fresh this music is can best be shown by a quotation from one of the most delightful scenes in the opera, the rehearsal, in the school house, of a serenade by Benda. His preoccupation with his music, the love-making that takes place under cover of it, all this rings absolutely true (page 148). There was no question as to the success of this opera—albeit a purely local success—but Dvořák revised it after his return from America, working particularly at the third act. If he added the ballet music at that time he made the one mistake in the score, for it is an unwanted and unnecessary concession to convention.

[1] See also the duet on page 204.

'The Devil and Kate'

Eleven years passed before Dvořák again turned to opera, and his views on many matters had undergone a profound change. At the time of composing the 'New World' Symphony his faith in the form was shaken. The future, he thought, lay with the symphonic poem, and he wrote five to prove it. But one thing remained unchanged —his desire, as he himself expressed it, 'to compose an opera which, like some of Verdi's works, should live in the people'—and I think he meant the people everywhere and not only in his own country. This desire found fulfilment, potentially at least, in the two operas, *The Devil and Kate* (1898) and *Rusalka* (1900).

The libretto for *The Devil and Kate*, which was provided by a young Prague schoolmaster and writer, Adolf Wenig, is refreshingly out of the ordinary. There is no love interest. The heroine is 'a stoutish and elderly maid, well known for her extraordinary gift of the gab' —a description which every prima donna would recognize as blas-phemous—and the devil of the title, Marbuel, is a timid creature and no kind of Mephistopheles. The story, put into the setting of a country fair, turns on Kate's failure to secure a dancing-partner. She says she'd dance with the devil himself if he turned up; and so Marbuel appears and asks Kate for a dance, which begins as a polka and ends up as a galop. Kate thinks this is grand; and when the devil describes the fun they have in his abode she declares she'd like to pay him a visit there. To the horror of all they vanish down a hole.

The sub-plot too is excellent. The lady of the manor is an oppressive employer and this — another original touch — upsets Lucifer, the ruler of hell. Marbuel has really come to find out the truth of the matter and to deal appropriately with it. One of her employees, a shepherd called George, has been made to work overtime and cannot join in the dance. Goaded by the steward, George answers back and gets the sack. Hearing of Kate's disappearance, he offers to bring her back, and jumps into the hole through which she vanished.

The next scene is in hell—apparently a very jolly place. But Marbuel, saddled with the garrulous Kate, is far from happy: in fact, the general opinion in hell is in favour of getting rid of her. So George is given a great welcome. But Kate has spotted some gold and will not leave. However, Lucifer, on hearing about the tyranny of the lady of the manor, decides that she must be banished to the less pleasant parts of hell and the steward be given a chance to reform, but first of all Marbuel must take Kate back. Sooner than do this the poor devil offers George a rich reward—which the steward will have to give him. But he must not do any rescue work with the lady. He agrees. There is a dance and George manages to waltz Kate out of hell before she realizes what is happening. So ends the second act.

The third act discloses her ladyship quaking with fear—she knows what is coming to her. She repents, and begs George to save her. He requires her to have a proclamation read abolishing serfdom—then, and only then, will he rescue her from her fate. George tells Kate that Marbuel is on the way, and she makes up her mind to be revenged on him. Such is the situation when Marbuel makes a dramatic entrance, in scarlet splendour, through the open window of the castle hall. Out he quickly goes, however, when he hears Kate is after him. And so the lady is saved and makes George her first minister while Kate gets a big house which—it is assured—will attract to her plenty of dance-partners and one for life.

This delightful story made a new call on Dvořák. The purely lyrical numbers are few—a song for George in Act I and one for the lady in the last act; the dances, choruses and ensembles, of which there is a good supply he could do standing on his head; but could he manage the humour and could he set the libretto to continuous music, symphonic in texture, not the old divisions of arias and concerted numbers with rather manufactured pages of recitative-arioso in between, which do not always conceal the joins?

The Jacobin showed improvement in this matter, but *The Devil and Kate* is a great step forward. 'What distinguishes this opera from *King and Collier*,' Dr. Colles said, 'is the suppleness with which each act flows. There is no halting or bungling in getting the story told in the music.' So perhaps those five symphonic poems, which are always considered failures, served their purpose as sketches for Dvořák's last operas. There is another interesting point of con-struction: instead of the rather obvious use of leading motives in *Dimitri* and *The Jacobin*, those employed in *The Devil and Kate* are

MS. OF FRONTISPIECE AND FIRST PAGE OF SLAVONIC DANCES

collective. There is one motive for the people with variants for Kate and the Shepherd (*a*):

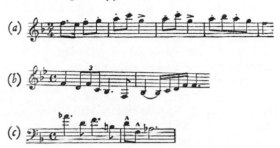

another motive for the castle group (*b*) and another for the devils (*c*). This idea works out extraordinarily well. Dvořák's new and frank return to his old love, Wagner, brings a great harmonic richness to the score, especially in the hell scene. (In the prelude to that act he writes a bit of whole-tone scale—as before in the *Te Deum*—but not for the benefit of theorists!)

The music of the opera is fresh and gay and, I imagine, sufficiently humorous although not witty. It was produced, in modern dress, by the Oxford University Opera Club in 1932, and proved a success. But it is an opera which needs professional resources to bring out all its qualities. So performed it would make Weinberger's *Švanda the Bagpiper* look the cheap and shoddy thing it is.

There is one thing about *Kate* which must have appealed to Dvořák. She represents the unconquerable optimism of her race. And to hell with hell, she got what she wanted!

From this rollicking opera Dvořák turned to a story of a very different kind, and gave his people the best-loved of his stage works. This was *Rusalka*, which he began two years later. The libretto was the work of a young poet and dramatist, Josef Kvapil, and the plot was, of course, one by no means new to opera. Dargomizhsky and Puccini, to mention only two composers, had both used it, but Kvapil gave the story of the water-sprite who fell in love with a man an original twist. The Vodník (water-goblin) is a sort of benevolent Alberich who typifies nature, a figure who must have immediately appealed to the nature-loving soul of Dvořák. And in the second act the introduction of a gamekeeper and a cook, a sort of Greek chorus representing the people, is as happy an invention, in its different way, as the trio of mandarins in Puccini's *Turandot*. It relieves, in the same way, a tragic atmosphere. The only weak part of the opera is the second act, in which Russalka's princely lover deserts her for one of the wedding guests, a duchess. Both the prince and the duchess remain lay-figures, and their love-duet is a singularly frigid and dull affair.

The supernatural beings, Russalka, the witch who transforms her into a woman, and above all the water-goblin, all come completely alive. We are not, therefore, greatly grieved when in the last act the prince, now repentant, comes to seek his bride and loses his life as the condition of Russalka's returning to her true nature. It does not really matter, any more than the doom that comes upon the gods and humans in the *Ring* mattered to the Rhine-maidens.

In this opera Dvořák mingles old and new styles. There are arias obviously detachable from their context, as for example Russalka's two exquisite numbers in the first act, of which the second, an invocation to the moon, is especially beautiful. There is an old-fashioned ballet in the second act. But the motives characterizing the different personages are used singly and in combination with considerable skill, and the texture of the music is even more defiantly Wagnerian than in *The Devil and Kate*. It is obvious enough that Dvořák had studied *Tristan* and the *Ring*. The glory of the opera is the imaginative orchestral writing devoted to the natural world which Dvořák has painted with the most loving care and attention to detail. All that Vysoká, his walks in the parks and the country, had meant to him, seems to be expressed here, and finds notable utterance in the lovely Russalka motive:

and he was particularly successful in the theme he found for the fantastic figure of the water-goblin:

The following quotation will show how effectively he combines these two motives:

Rusalka was an immediate success, and has remained a prime favourite. There is no reason why—with some judicious cuts in the second act—it should not repeat that success over here. There is just one thing that might make it seem overlong, and that is the squareness of the rhythms. The vocal parts are almost invariably in two- and four-bar phrases.

Dvořák was so stimulated by the reception given to this opera that he demanded another libretto forthwith, but as good librettos do not grow on every tree, it was two years before he found what he wanted. His last two operas had been works for the 'people.' Now he wanted to challenge the world at large, and so he chose the well-worn subject of *Armida,* of which the finest setting—and the only one still to be heard—was by his countryman Gluck, who had composed it when he was the same age as Dvořák. Although his librettist, the poet Vrchlický, had translated into Czech the whole of Tasso's *Gerusalemme liberata,* he provided Dvořák with a new poem, apparently a not very happy admixture of 'fable, fairy-tale and myth.'

In this, his last opera and last composition—if one may judge from the eight scenes which alone of the score are published—Dvořák took his most disastrous wrong turning. The subject, in any case, lay outside his range, but in his determination to grapple with it and produce an 'effective' score he changes direction with bewildering rapidity, being consistent only in the defiantly Wagnerian manner of the whole. Two of his main themes derive respectively from *Parsifal* and *Tannhäuser,* and we are given liberal doses of the latter:

The love duet at the end of the first act of Verdi's *Othello* is unashamedly quoted in one of Rinaldo's arias (Act IV, scene i):

It is only fair to say that Dvořák quotes himself as well. There is a lovely reminiscence of his 'American' period in the Rinaldo-Armida duet from the seventh scene of Act II:

and he draws on *Rusalka* for Armida's solo in the third scene of Act I as well as in the Siren's air and chorus of nymphs in Act III, scene i. This scene shows how uncertain his touch had become. The *Rusalka*-like music leads to a chorus which might have come from any one of his peasant operas and then, in a love duet, he gives us a great soaring phrase of Italian cast which it must be thrilling to sing:

This is followed by a waltz which Kate and the devil might have enjoyed, but which sounds incongruous in this classical story; and all these abrupt transitions take place in twenty-eight pages of vocal score.

The last thing in the opera—which ends with Armida's baptism and death—is a Meyerbeerian love duet; and it looks as if the curtain is going to fall both on Dvořák's opera and the close of his creative life, with him still in disguise, when suddenly in the last few bars he gets back to the enchanted garden, not of Armida, but of Vysoká:

And that is the end.

Dvořák had failed in his chief and most torturing ambition. He had, in his eager quest, gone after strange gods, and the public, with a sure instinct, rejected his offering. These eight scenes are, indeed, a most pathetic and fascinating document. His inspiration, as he always feared might happen, had deserted him. You have to stop your ears to the Circe-like beauty of this lyricism and coldly analyse page by page to discover how poverty-stricken the composer really has become. Brilliant orchestration failed to save the symphonic poems, enchanting if second-hand lyricism cannot save this opera.

But if Dvořák never developed a really individual operatic style, there is enough delightful and characteristic music in *King and Collier, The Peasant a Rogue, The Jacobin, The Devil and Kate* and *Rusalka* to make it very much worth while for some skilled Czech musician and literary man to edit and let the world hear these operas. It is little short of absurd that not even an aria has found its way into the current operatic repertory of singers and only the overtures to *The Peasant a Rogue* and *Wanda* into the orchestral one.

CHAPTER XVII

MISCELLANEOUS ORCHESTRAL WORKS

DVOŘÁK's smaller orchestral works cover all the usual forms. There are suites, serenades, variations, overtures, dances and symphonic poems. Not much of this music goes deep, but a surprising quantity of it is fresh and charming, and very little of it dull. For sheer charm the Serenades in E major for strings, Op. 22, and D minor, Op. 44, and the *Czech Suite* in D major, Op. 39, take a high place. They fulfil their tasks simply, unpretentiously and delightfully.

The string Serenade dates from May 1875. It is in five movements, of which the fourth is a beautiful little *Larghetto*. The string writing is admirable—as one would expect from the composer of the Noc⁄turne, composed five years before. The vein of melody is not yet very individual, but both the Waltz (No. 2) and the Scherzo follow⁄ing it have lovely trios.

The D minor Serenade (1878) is laid out for two oboes, two clarinets, two bassoons, one double bassoon, three horns, cello and double bass. This good⁄humoured work opens with a spirited march—repeated in the finale—and continues with a minuet in the form of a *Sousedská*. Then comes the most considerable number, a long and romantic slow movement preceding a gay finale. One of Dvořák's periodical jugglings with opus numbers accounts for the low figure given to the orchestral Suite in D major, known as the *Czech Suite*. Actually it is the latest of these three works and was composed in April 1879. Dvořák had found himself in the first set of *Slavonic Dances*, and his melodies, in this Suite, have an individuality that was lacking before. Three of the movements are dances: a *Polka* (No. 2), a *Sousedská* (No. 3) and a *Furiant* (No. 5).

In the middle section of the *Sousedská* 'clarinets and bassoons make their entrance just as they do in Bohemia.' The first movement of the Suite, sub⁄titled *Pastorale,* has a truly pastoral tune on a drone⁄like bass, and the *Romance* (No. 4), a song divided between flute and English horn, has all its composer's strong melodic appeal.

Dvořák's first set of *Slavonic Dances*, written in August 1878, was like an injection of monkey-gland into the concert-halls and drawing-rooms of Europe. The composer scored the music at the same time as he wrote it for piano duet, and though the dances need the colours of the orchestra, they are not only delightful to play as duets, but have the merit of giving an easy but sufficiently interesting part to the player of the bass. Louis Ehlert found the right phrase for the dances in describing their 'heavenly naturalness.'

It seems absurd to listen to such open-air music in the stuffy solemnity of the concert-hall. It provides the right background for good wine and food, and intermittent conversation, in the rural surroundings of Dvořák's native heath. The second set of *Slavonic Dances* followed in July 1886, but this time it took Dvořák six months to do the orchestration. It sounded, said the composer, 'like the devil.' A cryptic remark!

Stefan catalogues the various dances as follows:

1.	C major	*Furiant*
2.	E minor	*Serbian*
3.	D major	*Sousedská* (in orchestral version No. 6 is placed here)
4.	F major	*Sousedská*
5.	A major	*Skočná*
6.	A flat major	*Polka* (No. 3 in orchestral version)
7.	C minor	*Skočná*
8.	G minor	*Furiant*
9.	B major	*Slovakian Odzmek*
10.	E minor	*Mazurka*
11.	F major	*Skočná*
12.	D flat major	*Ukrainian* (begins in E flat major)
13.	B flat minor	*Špasírka*
14.	B flat major	*Polonaise*
15.	C major	*Serbian Kolo*
16.	A flat major	*Sousedská*

Brahms had been accused of 'stealing melodies' for his *Hungarian Dances*, though he gave these dances no opus number to show they were arrangements (actually two or three are original); but Dvořák could not be charged with theft, for all his tunes are original and his orchestration is so individual that even his scoring of five of Brahms's Dances (Nos. 17–21) makes them sound like more *Slavonic Dances*.

As Dvořák got engrossed in his task the dances become subtler and more idealized. But the elemental quality remains. Quite a large variety of mood is covered, from the terrific vitality of the *Furiants* (Nos. 1 and 8) to the charm of the *Sousedská* (No. 3), one of the most delightful of all the dances, or the wistful gypsy music of No. 10. The second set of Dances, as the list above shows, lives up to the general title more fully than the first set. No. 12 has a remarkable cadence,[1] and No. 16, *lento grazioso, quasi tempo di valse,* makes a lovely and regretful coda to the whole work.

There is plenty of evidence of loving care in the working out of the Dances. Dvořák is rarely content with straightforward recapitulation, but adds new detail and colouring, and nothing is more charming than his consideration for the secondary players—in No. 10, for example, the second violins are allowed their part in the tune and the second oboe is singled out at the recapitulation. His ample provision of counter-melodies never seems to fail, and from first to last the music is alive in every part and fascinating in melody and harmony. The composer's treatment of the main theme in No. 7 will show better than anything the variety and resource of his treatment:

After this free canonic opening for oboe and bassoon solos the seven repetitions are all orchestrated differently, three times canonic imitation is abandoned in favour of new counter-melodies, and the accompaniments are also delightfully varied.

Compared with the heavenly naturalness of the *Slavonic Dances* there seems something rather artificial and smelling of the concert-hall about the *Three Slavonic Rhapsodies* in D major, G minor and A flat major, Op. 45, composed in the same year. The best is No. 3, and

[1] See page 90.

unlike the case of the three overtures, it is the most often heard. It is a pre-Raphaelite hunting scene, beautifully coloured but rather too long and repetitive and inclined to be rhythmically monotonous. No. 1 sounds just like a selection from an opera. After a determined plugging of the theme Dvořák can think of nothing better to do than give a trite cadenza to the harp which runs the music, chromatically, into a commonplace march in B flat major. The rest is mere repetition, however concealed by diminution, *grandioso* blasts of sound and theatrical *stringendi*. There is more punch in the G minor, but here again Dvořák takes the easy way out of any real development by introducing an amiable waltz tune. The *presto* diminution, near the end, of a phrase in the opening section is embarrassingly naïve. Dvořák the academic *Kapellmeister* shows up badly in contrast with Dvořák the inspired *Musikant,* and these Rhapsodies, with the possible exception of an occasional performance of No. 3, can well be laid to rest.

The overture, *My Home,* published by Simrock in 1882 under a German title, *Mein Heim,* was composed in 1881 as part of the incidental music to a drama by Šamberk, *Josef Kajetan Tyl.* It is one of nine pieces, the rest consisting of two intermezzos and other music for each act. It is a pleasing but rhythmically a rather monotonous work, remarkable for the quotation of the song by Škroup (the words by Tyl) 'Kde domov muj?' ('Where is my native land?') which became the Czech national anthem. Much more important are the three overtures which Dvořák originally meant to call *Nature, Life, and Love,* but eventually labelled *In Nature's Realm,* Op. 91 (a title similar to that used for some partsongs, Op. 63, in 1882), *Carnival,* Op. 92, and *Othello,* Op. 93. The three overtures occupied Dvořák from the spring of 1891 to the beginning of 1892. The first of them is dedicated to Cambridge University, *Carnival* to the Czech University in Prague.

These works look towards the five symphonic poems which were Dvořák's last contribution to symphonic literature. They are variations on one pastoral theme. That the composer had, it is said, some difficulty in finding his chosen titles rather detracts from *Othello.* Otherwise we should have been happily busy in spotting jealousy and Desdemona motives—as it is we do so rather doubtfully.

All but the middle part of *Carnival* is noisy, obvious music, which any competent composer might as well have written, and Svendsen did. But after an unblushing visit to the Venusberg—one of the sights at the fair—we emerge into the cool clean atmosphere of Dvořák's central theme. A stab on the strings fades into a soft held horn-note and the woodland voices begin, English horn, clarinet (the theme), solo violin, mysterious rumblings in the undergrowth by the cellos and double basses, and then the dream ends and we are back in the pasteboard Venusberg and the bustle of the fair. This overture is the weakest of the three, but that sudden transition, though done better by Dvořák elsewhere, makes it worth while.

In Nature's Realm is a much more characteristic production. The common theme here, as in *Othello,* holds chief place and is not, as in *Carnival,* just an episode. But we get rather too much of it, and in the end the country walk has been little more than a pacing up and down the garden. The prospect is pleasing, but the view is restricted. It must, however, be admitted that the birds sing enchantingly.

Othello is a very carefully worked-out and dramatically effective treatment of the main theme. It is hinted at in hymn-like fashion by the muted strings and immediately challenged by a bold phrase for first violins, answered by violas and cellos, these phrases being marked *forte* but with mutes still on. Then the theme appears clearly on flute and two clarinets while the atmosphere grows more ominous, and so at length the *allegro con brio* breaks out. It proves to be based on the immediate opposition of the two themes of the introduction, relieved by some beautiful love music as a central episode. Dvořák strays down no by-paths, his concentration never flags, and this work takes a high place among his miscellaneous orchestral works. It is high time it displaced *Carnival.*

Dvořák's two most important miscellaneous orchestral works are the *Symphonic Variations* for large orchestra, Op. 78, and the *Scherzo capriccioso* (for a still larger orchestra), Op. 66. The opus numbers are misleading in the familiar manner. The Variations were composed in September 1877, and published, probably after revision, in 1887, but the Scherzo was composed in 1883 and published the year after.

The theme for the *Symphonic Variations* comes from a partsong for male voices, one of several without opus numbers, called *Guslar*. Dvořák is said to have been challenged to write variations on what a friend thought an intractable theme. To us, after the event and in the light of later variation-writing the tune, with its varied figuration, well-marked opening phrase and irregular periods (7 : 6 : 7) seems an excellent and fruitful choice:

Never before or after was Dvořák so happily inspired in his variation writing. These twenty-seven examples make the *Theme and Variations* for piano (1876) look like apprentice work, and subsequent examples, such as those in the A major Sextet (1878) or the G major Symphony (1889), seem unimportant if not dull. There is another most welcome quality about many of them which rarely invades Dvořák's music, and that is wit. The range of expression found here is indeed notable. The theme is presented in the barest outline for the first eleven bars, and with a sudden *crescendo* from double *piano* to double *forte* which dies away almost at once to a mere whisper.

After this rather ominous start the first variation strikes delightfully on the ear. Piccolo, flutes and oboe make witty comments on the theme, which is given to clarinet, bassoon, violas and cellos *pizzicato*. Dvořák had already learnt to write the effective counter-melodies that we find in so many of the *Slavonic Dances* a year later, and in movements such as the scherzo of the big D minor Symphony, and throughout the variations he shows himself a master of orchestral colour. His invention never flags, or hardly ever, for two variations —sounding as one (Nos. 25 and 26)—sound dull in relation to all that has gone before. Anyhow they are well placed, for they come just before the brilliant finale.

Dvořák alternates in style between Nelahazoves, Vienna and a purely individual utterance. Thus variations 9, 10, 13, 18, 21 are founded on native dance-rhythms while variations 3, 4, 5, 19 (the one in the form of a waltz), 23, 24 and the dull pair are cosmopolitan. There are obvious echoes of Brahms, for example the figuration for the strings in variation 6 which is that of the Brahms-Schumann Variations; and the lovely variation for solo violin, No. 12, might have come from a lost Mendelssohn concerto.

In variations such as 14, 15 and 18 the utterance is completely individual. Variation 14 is a little masterpiece of suggestion with original colouring which calls for quotation:

Variation 15 is the wittiest of the lot. A pompous outburst on the full orchestra, with the brass prominent, is answered by rude echoes from oboe, flute and clarinet. Most lovely is the music and colouring of variation 18 which, again, must be quoted:

The finale, led into by a whisper of a variation, begins with a most

effective fugue, with very nicely placed sequences, a bit conventional
in its working-out, but copied from the best models! But Dvořák
is not done yet. As in the cello Concerto, a series of epilogues
follow, a polka on the woodwind, the theme on the strings (violins
on their G strings), the scheme recalling the first variation. Then a
scurry of violins up to an *allegro con brio* and finally *più animato,* a
jubilant suggestion of bells pealing out all over the orchestra.

Fine as the work is, it is surpassed by the *Scherzo capriccioso,* which
can take its place amongst the greatest short orchestral works by any
composer. Had Dvořák ever written a symphony with three other
movements of equal quality one could say that he had reached the
snows. The work belongs to the period of the piano Trio in F
minor and the D minor Symphony, a period of 'doubt, defiance,
silent grief and resignation' which called forth his best music. Nowhere else is Dvořák so absolutely and defiantly himself as in this
magnificent work. The instrumentation is magical, from the opening
call on the horns to the enchanted coda.

Magical too is the modulation to the main waltz-theme. The
harmonies melt and dissolve into G major:

It is a mystery why some choreographer has not long ago used this idealized dance for a ballet. It is highly evocative music, flaming with energy and strong dynamic contrasts and picturesque detail, the child of Weber's *Invitation to the Dance*, but greater than its father.

To this period belongs also the *Husitská* Overture, Op. 67, which was 'intended as a prelude to a Hussite dramatic trilogy that never got farther than the first act.' It has the grand gesture and defiant energy of this great creative flowering in Dvořák's life, but the balance of the overture is rather disturbed by the composer's determination to hold the scales evenly between his two denominational tunes. They are both heard in the introduction, the Protestant Hussite chorale and some phrases from the ancient Czech Catholic *Song of St. Wenceslas*. These are combined with other themes and reach their apotheosis in the concluding section of the work which falls into four divisions: (1) The Hussite chorale—*grandioso*. (2) St. Wenceslas—*più animato* and marked *espressivo*. (3) A *presto* work-up to (4), *lento maestoso*, in which the Hussite chorale receives the full weight of the brass, drums beat urgently, and there are exciting string rushes upwards. The result is a slight feeling of anticlimax and a conviction of the triumph of Huss—which, of course, Dvořák means to be interpreted as the victory of freedom.

The remaining works include, beside the five symphonic poems which were Dvořák's last contribution to purely orchestral music, a delightful and gay *Mazurek* for violin and small orchestra, Op. 49 (1879), dedicated to Sarasate, and a *Romance*, Op. 11 (1873), for the same combination which takes as its first tune the second subject of the slow movement of the F minor Quartet of the same year, and then develops on its own. The chief melody is a Mendelssohnian 'Song without Words' of some charm, with which is contrasted a reminiscence of the second subject in the second movement of Schubert's B minor Symphony. They mix nicely, but the piece is overlong and betrays, in the decorative passages, too obvious a desire to make the violin part effective. The Rhapsody in A minor for large orchestra (1874), originally Op. 15, but published posthumously without opus number, is said 'to tend towards the type of symphonic poem created by Liszt and to be modelled on Smetana's *Vyšehrad*.'

Then there is a *Festival March*, Op. 54, composed in 1879 for the silver wedding of the Emperor and Empress of Austria, and a *Polonaise* in E flat major written in the same year for a ball.

More interesting than any of these pieces is the *Nocturne* in B major for strings, Op. 40, composed in 1870. The first half of this work is taken from the slow section of the unpublished single-movement Quartet in E minor, with a double-bass part added. After the clear, almost Palestrinian, part-writing of the opening bars comes melody and harmony of so Wagnerian a quality that we can surmise how Dvořák would have developed had he stuck to this style. Apart from its historical interest this is a lovely, quiet piece, which has recently again come into favour.

Dvořák's last will and testament, in the purely orchestral field, took the form of five symphonic poems, or, as he called them, 'orchestral ballads.' Begun on 6th January 1896, three of them were finished not many weeks later. These were *The Water-Goblin, Noonday Witch* and *The Golden Spinning-Wheel. The Wild Dove* and *Hero's Song* followed towards the close of the year.

All but the last of these symphonic poems take as their programme poems by K. J. Erben, who had provided the text for *The Spectre's Bride* and several of Dvořák's songs.

Unfortunately Dvořák had not the psychological insight of Richard Strauss, nor his power of characterization, nor even the tidy and picturesque approach of Saint-Saëns.

Nevertheless it is only in *The Golden Spinning-Wheel* that the course of the music is really difficult to follow, provided that one seizes on the general outlines of the stories and, as Dvořák himself does, ignores much of the detail. *The Water-Goblin* is, unlike his predecessor in *Rusalka,* a malicious creature to whom a village girl is irresistibly attracted, in spite of her mother's warnings. Once his wife, she becomes sick with longing for home and at last is allowed to visit her mother. The goblin keeps their child as a pledge of her return. As twilight falls he knocks furiously on the door. The mother refuses to let her go and immediately a terrible storm rises over the lake. Something is dashed against the cottage door. It is the headless body of the child.

The music takes rondo form and the details that are illustrated come out quite convincingly. The approach of twilight, for instance, is eerily suggested by the use of low chords for trombones and tubas with the girl's theme on the cellos. This section ends with the notes of a gong over low string basses *tremolandi*. The goblin's tune on the oboe, after this, has a very sinister sound, like the tapping of old Pew's stick in *Treasure Island*.

Some of the motives—such, perhaps, as the girl's lullaby sung to the child—are said to imitate exactly the metres of Erben's verses. This is also the case in *The Noonday Witch,* where the witch's demand for the child is set to a phrase that follows the scansion of the words. This is more important as indicating the spirit in which Dvořák set about his task than in its musical results.

The Noonday Witch is the simplest story among the five works, and relates how a mother threatens a fractious child with the Noonday Witch (this species of individual operates from eleven until twelve). The witch, 'a little shrivelled spectral woman leaning on a crooked stick,' materializes and demands the child. When the father returns home for his midday meal he finds the mother fainting on the floor and the child dead.

This piece is the most successful—perhaps because the simplest— of the symphonic poems, and well deserves a place in the repertory. There is delightful humour and truth in the musical picture of the mother at work and the child growing restless until at last it cries. The extract below will show how the impatient mother replies:

Dvořák is no less successful in creating the right atmosphere for the unexpected apparition of the witch and her gradual, sinister approach. This is done by the use of muted violins and violas (these last high in their register) with a sustained low note on a solo bass clarinet. The witch's demand is spoken through the bass clarinet and bassoon:

The use of that phrase in augmentation, with some alteration and given out double *forte*, then double *piano*, at the climax, cleverly suggests how large and menacing the witch has become.

The Golden Spinning-Wheel has the longest story and one which, on the face of it, is quite unsuited to musical representation. The heroine has her hands and feet cut off and her eyes put out, and to illustrate that would tax even Strauss's powers.

Suk made a shorter version of the piece, but nothing can overcome its too literal translation of a rather silly story. It is the only one, by the way, of the symphonic poems with a programme that ends happily—for the young woman recovers the mutilated portions of her anatomy by magic!

It is clear from a letter to Richter that Dvořák was anxious that the audience should be in possession of a prose synopsis of the various programmes, but *The Wood Dove* is the only one in which, on the first page of the score, the story is related to each section of the work. This process certainly makes for clarity and is worth showing here:

1. *Andante. Marcia funebre* An attractive widow follows her husband's body to the grave. (She is *The Beloved as Poison-mixer*—a title of one of Dvořák's partsongs.)

2. *Allegro—Andante.* She is easily consoled by a jolly peasant and becomes his wife.

3. *Molto vivace—Allegretto grazioso.* Wedding festivities.

4. *Andante.* The wood dove coos mournfully (and with malice aforethought) from an oak-tree overhanging the first husband's grave.

5. *Andante—Tempo I—Più lento.* Remorse of the guilty widow who, nearly driven mad by the dove, attempts to drown herself. The music, but not the original tale, provides a happy ending.

The widow is characterized in the theme of the first funeral march, and the different variants of her theme form the chief musical interest of the piece, besides unifying it satisfactorily. The result is sometimes distinctly amusing. Thus when the new love appears the widow, after a slight hesitation, changes direction:

The wedding music provides some more variants of the same theme, and the maddening cooings of the self-righteous dove are orchestrated in the following curious way: two flutes, oboe, cymbals struck with a drum-stick, and very high reiterated notes for harp.

Justice satisfied, the dove settles down into the major key at the end.

As we have seen before, the heroic lay out of Dvořák's range, and his *Hero's Song,* whether autobiographical or not, fails to gain one's sympathy. It opens with an admirably terse idea:

which, in the manner of most of these symphonic poems, undergoes various transformations such as this one:

The close, melodramatically heralded, is disappointingly commonplace. It reminds one of Elgar's most bombastic manner:

After this comes a Brock's display of chromatics.

There is something rather pathetic in Dvořák's effort to overcome, in these symphonic poems, the difficulties of what he thought was the new musical form. If he only partially succeeded, he has bequeathed a fine series of pamphlets on orchestration to the inquiring student.

CHAPTER XVIII

SYMPHONIES

Dvořák composed his first symphony in 1865—unless earlier works were destroyed in the holocaust which swallowed up nearly all the music written from 1863 up to this year. He was only twenty-four when he embarked on the task from which Brahms had abstained until he was in his forty-fourth year, and then, perhaps, he did so only because the Czechs needed not only national opera, given to them by Smetana, but chamber and symphonic music as well. I can only speak—in company with most English writers—of the first three Symphonies at second hand. No. 1, in C minor (February–March 1865), seems to have escaped destruction by accident. It was found only in 1923, first performed a few years ago, and has now been published. The work has a title, *The Bells of Zlonice*, and of it Stefan writes: 'The best movement of the Symphony is the scherzo, and the whole work speaks clearly of the hardships of youth, the undaunted will to live and the playful spirit of an original inventor.' The next Symphony, in B flat major, dates from the same year (August–October 1865) and was composed after the (early) A major cello Concerto (June 1865). This work is said to have been on the condemned list, but does not seem to have deserved the Gilbertian tag. Dvořák revised the orchestration and named the work Op. 4 in 1888. This Symphony has also been published, and has been performed. The Stefan-Šourek account speaks of it as having an almost cosmic joyousness, from which one concludes that it is a light-hearted affair. It pays tribute to Wagner in its orchestration and in its diffuseness. Perhaps its chief interest for us lies in the following:

This little phrase, reminiscent of the folksong-like lullaby in Smetana's opera *The Kiss*, appears, as a fingerprint, in Dvořák's opera *King and Collier*:

in the first *Slavonic Rhapsody*:

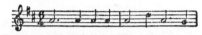

and, where it takes an important place, in the opera, *The Jacobin*:

The third Symphony, in E flat major, was not composed until eight years later, in 1873. As we have seen, it was given a performance by Smetana at a Prague Philharmonic concert in 1874, but Simrock published it only in 1912. It seems to have been a Wagnerian love-child, and, as such, was much loved by its begetter. The Wagnerian attraction which is so strongly evident in the *Andante religioso* [1] of the third string Quartet, in E minor, written in 1870, is apparently undisguised. The orchestration is said to be magnificent, the invention superabundant. It would be interesting to hear the Symphony performed. [2]

By 1874 the Wagnerian fever had died down and the composer arrayed himself (not without some backward glances) in the penitential garments of Beethoven and Schubert when he composed the early D minor Symphony (then called Op. 13). The whole work was not heard until 1892, under the composer's baton, Smetana giving only the scherzo (the least good movement) in 1874. The Symphony was published in 1912.

A glance at the score makes it obvious enough that, even at this early stage, Dvořák is a born symphonic writer. He has good ideas: strongly rhythmic, attractively melodic; he has plenty of them, and can marshal them. He keeps the music moving. He understands

[1] Arranged, by the composer, for string orchestra under the title of *Nocturne*, Op. 40.

[2] Since writing the above I have seen a score of this three-movement Symphony. Both themes and orchestration—which is thick—seem very uncharacteristic of Dvořák.

the art of deep breathing: his music does not pant. If, in this early and youthful work, he is eagerly diffuse, maturity, no doubt, will alter that. The orchestral instruments are his friends, and he knows how to make them talk, even if the talk is at present not on a high level. The Symphony has an impressive beginning:

In scaling the difficult symphonic cliff face Dvořák often leaps on to the safe ledges of thirds and sixths and diminished sevenths. As these hurry by there is time to discern the countenance of Beethoven, as displayed in the slow movement of his D major piano Sonata, Op. 10, No. 3, and here recalled by his disciple:

Any one who loves lyricism—that is to say, any one with a heart—will always be filled with expectancy about the second subject, or subject-group, of a first movement. With Dvořák you are rarely

disappointed, and so it is here. The development section of the
movement is based on the simple opposition of two rhythms:

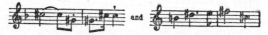

But development is really a misnomer. As Tovey says, Dvořák
never learnt the difference between development and exposition, and
so in his developments the cliffs of Dover (so to speak) are always
in sight.

Both rhythms—and particularly the first—outstay their welcome,
but we take leave of them with the affectionately indulgent smile
accorded to a young man who talks attractively, naïvely, and too
much. The slow movement is an early exercise in a form which
Dvořák rarely handled with complete success—variation form. The
theme [1] is one of great beauty and might well be labelled *nobilmente*,
not only for its general feeling, but in respect of the melodic line in
bars two to three:

Only a good craftsman would have delayed his cadence as Dvořák
does at the close of his theme:

Four variations and a lengthy coda follow. While the tune pursues
what in the end begins to look like a well-worn track, we are given

---

[1] Dvořák's admiration for *Tannhäuser* is made clear here.

a lot of manufactured and rather fussy detail. Dvořák is a long way yet from the glorious slow movement of his later Symphony in D minor (Op. 70), but in this movement, as in all the others of the work, coming events often cast their shadows before.

The scherzo proves that the young composer knows how to organize his stuff effectively. The three emphatic chords in the opening bars are skilfully used as binding material and rhythmic monotony is avoided except for an arpeggio accompaniment of the big guitar kind, of which there is far too much. The trio reminds Stefan of the entrance of the tailors in *The Mastersingers*. It reminds me, I must confess, of a Liszt Hungarian Rhapsody. (We meet again with the main theme of the scherzo in the piece called *In Troublous Times* from the *Bohemian Forest* set for piano duet.)

The last movement bids fair at its start to be terse and epigrammatic, but that was not Dvorak's way. He hammers his theme home relentlessly in bar after bar until he decides we are due for a spell in the woods. This we receive through a charmingly devised tune with, unfortunately, a triplet accompaniment clinging to it like a limpet. The work-up is conventional and somewhat Wagnerian, and the movement becomes unbearably repetitive and diffuse.

Probably Dvořák would not have consented to the printing of this Symphony had he lived to give an opinion, but although music would have lost little, since its best ideas are used elsewhere, the work is a useful yardstick to measure what came after.

It may be convenient here, before going on to the 'big five,' to put down the correct order of the Dvořák Symphonies:

No. 1. C minor, ('The Bells of Zlonice'). 1865.

No. 2. B flat major of about the same date.

No. 3. E flat major. 1873.

No. 4. D minor. 1874.

No. 5. F major (called No. 3). 1875.

No. 6. D major (called No. 1). 1880.

No. 7. D minor (called No. 2). 1884–5.

No. 8. G major (called No. 4). 1889.

No. 9. E minor ('From the New World') (called No. 5). 1893.

From this table it will be seen that the so-called third Symphony is, in reality, the first of the received group of five and the fifth in order of composition. Dvořák had just begun to dawn on Brahms and Vienna; and Hans von Bülow, handsomely acknowledging the dedication of the Symphony, had spoken of its composer as 'next to Brahms the most God-gifted composer of the present day.' This composer, then, abjuring the rather melodramatic gestures with which his previous Symphony had begun, puts down a quiet chord of F major and maintains it through eight bars, then turns a lovely, perfectly simple cadence. Nothing could be more ordinary in appearance, but few symphonies open so poetically; and if the proceeding is naïve—Dvořák's inescapable label—it is still quite unconsciously so.

Dvořák comes slowly, as is his way, up to his second subject, scattering rhythmic hints by the way; and it is typical of him to use the grandiose phrase of his exposition (the first subject group) not long before its recapitulation. The arbitrary divisions meant nothing to him. His highly inventive flow of music poured out, and if such a phrase was reborn out of due time, then down it went!

The slow movement, in the pastoral vein of the previous movement, is plaintively charming and notable as an example of the composer's habit of getting his tunes to throw out new shoots, clearly derived from the parent stem, and using these as binding material:

The scherzo goes ahead in the highest spirits, and is less beefy and sprawling than the corresponding number in the previous Symphony. The trio is conspicuously short.

Dvořák seems to have felt a need to give the Symphony a weighty finale, with the result that the movement seems at first a little out of character with the rest of the work, but he has a surprise up his sleeve. The essence of the movement is a struggle for mastery between A minor (the key of the opening) and F major, fought out over this theme:

The movement is sweetened with a most tuneful second subject, and a very keen listener would prick up his ears the first time this 'celestial' phrase is heard:

Eight bars of a tonic chord might carry the suspicious mind back to the opening of the Symphony, where the same phenomenon occurs; and sure enough it is this 'celestial' music which ushers in the initial theme of the first movement: a beautifully managed transition. After this surprise Dvořák rushes the music to an exciting conclusion, in which the two themes are merged and seem part of one comprehensive idea.

Five symphonies and five more years of creative work lay behind Dvořák when he wrote his sixth Symphony, in D major, Op. 60. Every bar of this work shows him at the height of his maturity. The village boy can move amongst the great of the symphonic world with ease and assurance. He speaks their tongue, albeit with his own accent; even when he pays obvious homage to Brahms's Symphony in the same key:

The romantic modulation into E minor (*a*) is a wholly personal touch, and another characteristic passage is the pendant phrase to the second subject—a double one—sung by the oboe. The effect is as lovely as the opening of a window on a spring morning.

Grandioso is as favourite a word with Dvořák as *nobilmente* with Elgar, and sure enough it is written over the first climax in the first movement as well as making an appearance in the scherzo and finale. We share the composer's pleasure in these outbursts of healthy sound, but the really arresting thing in the first movement is not any outburst, but the soft start of the development. The repeat must be taken if this passage is to have its due effect. The 'first-time' fourteen bars then give place to this bare and mysterious music which is almost without parallel in the composer's work:

The movement is so rich in material that it is difficult to resist numerous quotations—but all a book of this kind can hope to do is to send the reader to the score. It must suffice to say that Dvořák, diffuse as he may often be, has here complete command of his richness of invention and organizes his themes with exquisite art.

Dvořák's awareness of his classical heritage shows again at the beginning of his slow movement. The youth who rushed out of a concert in Prague where the ninth Symphony was being given, crying 'I must write like that,' remembers how Beethoven began the slow movement of that work—and modestly emulates him:

There is a simple and sincere man singing for sheer happiness—and how characteristic is the little scurry of notes at the end of the tune! The rustic note which comes more prominently into the G major Symphony, Op. 88, closes the first section of the movement. Then, at some length, but not too long for the captivated listener, Dvořák sets down his various and romantically lovely thoughts in dreamlike orchestration.

Beethoven's opening bars were a gateway, Dvořák's—as you see when you follow through the movement—were a foundation-stone, for the sequence of notes which bind the whole movement together, as in the slow movement of the F major Symphony, continually suggest themselves in new forms.

The scherzo, here styled *Furiant,* is not very typical of that dance. Its exhilarating measures give place, in the trio, to the humours of the piccolo. Beethoven's bassoon in the 'Pastoral' Symphony may have suggested this charming little trio, but Dvořák's player is much more ambitious.

How satisfactory it must be for a composer to write a completely successful last movement—something as rare as the completely successful last act of a play. The final movement of this Symphony, as Tovey says, 'is admirably endowed with the quality that is rarest of all in post-classical finales, the power of movement.'

The circumstances which brought the seventh Symphony, in D minor, Op. 70, to birth in 1884–5, have been related elsewhere. There seems to be no doubt that Dvořák was now aiming at the conquest of the musical world.

The friend of Brahms would show his kind patron, his enthusiastic English public and the more critical audiences of Berlin and Vienna, that he, with the minimum of appeal to national sentiment, could give the world a symphony on the largest scale. He had given them a parallel to Brahms's No. 2, but now he would give them a Brahms No. 3—and even more than that. Whether or not he wholly succeeded in this vaulting ambition, the D minor Symphony is undoubtedly a great work. To ambition, to artistic mastery, were added the last expression of the inner spiritual conflict and grief which had already appeared in the F minor piano Trio, Op. 65.

It can be argued that some impurity of style, at one moment a suggestion of Brahms in the second subject of the first movement, at another, of Wagner in the *Tristan* episode of the slow movement, is a flaw in this Symphony, but if so it is, taken by itself, little more than a surface one. Dvořák can be, consciously or otherwise, reminiscent without losing his individuality.

To compare the opening of the early D minor Symphony and its use of diminished sevenths with the same things in this later work is to look on the apprentice and then on the master. The notes will speak better than words:

and

This stormy movement, as austere and gloomy in its orchestration as it is tragic in its thoughts, gives place to Dvořák's loveliest slow movement—which means one of the loveliest in the whole of music. It is perhaps not too much to say that no one since Beethoven had written music of such absolute classical purity as the opening bars of the movement:

Dvořák could not continue like that—he soon becomes his most romantic self—but it is wonderful that he could write four such bars. Not long after the start of the movement comes the deepest sigh yet uttered by Dvořák in his music, and eloquent of the trials he had borne:

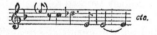

That sigh will be heard once more, with greater intensity, in the slow movement of his penultimate quartet.

The long coda is not only of entrancing beauty, but it begins with a stroke of genius, the return, on the cellos, not of the opening bars of the first theme, but of its second limb.

The bucolic gaiety of the scherzo in the D major Symphony finds no place here. Instead Dvořák gives us a movement—except in the short but restless trio—of intense nervous energy. There is a double theme; and it is worth noting that though the counterpoint is in no way remarkable the composer gives such rhythmic individualization to his two tunes that the result is very effective.

The tragic note is maintained in the grand gesture with which the final movement begins, but this movement just fails to reach the heights of the preceding ones. This may well be because it lacks the rhythmic variety of the corresponding movement of the D major Symphony and is somewhat square in treatment.

Five more years elapsed before the appearance of the eighth Symphony, in G major, Op. 88, known as the 'English' Symphony, for no better reason than that it was published, after much haggling with Simrock, by Novello. It is actually by far the most national in flavour of all his symphonies, and in point of form, at least as regards the first two movements, the most original.

The essential point of the opening movement is the juxtaposition of the rather ecclesiastical-sounding theme—masked in the introductory bars:

and the flute theme which immediately precedes it:

The two themes are finely worked together; there is a good second theme and two subsidiaries, and the impression the movement gives is one of great virility with moments of extraordinary charm, due to the exquisite writing for the woodwind.

The path of the listener through the maze of so many tunes is made easy because both the development and the recapitulation have a full—in the second case very dramatic—statement of the introduction for a chapter-heading. In the recapitulation Dvořák omits any reference to the first example above.

The slow movement is completely original from start to finish. It could stand as a miniature tone-poem of Czech village life described by a highly sensitive man. There is a touch of pain in the opening harmonies that becomes pronounced later on. Of this the bird-calls on the flute and oboe are heedless, but these calls are given very different emphasis on the strings as if, as it were, they had passed into the mind of the composer, sitting in his garden, and been tinged with his sad thoughts. An exquisitely consolatory coda concludes this section. And then? Something no one could possibly have pre/ dicted. We are out on the village green on a festival day. The village band, cimbalom and all, is evidently on its toes, and presently along comes either the priest or the chief worthy. It is all childlike and enchanting. But how is Dvořák to return to the mood of his opening bars? The solution, when worked out, is simple. He uses the coda/phrases, puts in his bird/calls, and then the poignant phrases of the start. In fact he simply works in reverse. But this time there is a big and pain/laden climax. Back we go, by a very easy transition, to the revels on the village green and reach a coda which varies the previous solution in a masterly way. This movement, which derives its material entirely from the opening phrases, I take to be one of the considerable achievements of symphonic literature.

The scherzo is amiable rather than striking, but the waltz/trio has all Dvořák's unique melodic charm. For the finale he chooses theme/and/variation form, the theme being itself a variant of the second example opposite, but this somewhat noisy movement is not among his successes, and one is left with a feeling of disappointment that the expectations aroused by the first two movements have not been fulfilled in the last two.

That sense of disappointment is spread over all the movements of Dvořák's last Symphony, in E minor, Op. 95 ('From the New World'), composed in 1893, and his most popular symphonic work. To some criticism of so well/established a favourite may border on heresy, but it must be pointed out that its lucidity of exposition, its melodic fertility, its brilliant orchestration and undeniable surface charm hide undoubted weakness. Before trying to assess the causes of this weakness it may be well again to dispose of the controversy regarding the use of 'original American' (that is, Negro/spiritual) melodies. Dvořák very rarely quotes original tunes of any kind, and he did not consciously do so here. As he said himself in a letter to Nedbal—about to conduct the Symphony in Berlin in 1900—'Leave out that nonsense about my having made use of original American national melodies.' To Dvořák all the works of his American period were 'genuine Bohemian music.' At the same time he wanted to write for America music which would show his awareness of such melodies and their possible use as a basis of a national art, and also give expression to his great sympathy for the oppressed coloured people.

In an interview given to the *New York Herald* Dvořák said, with exaggerated enthusiasm:

> In the Negro melodies of America I find all that is needed for a great and noble school of music. They are pathetic, tender, passionate, melancholy, bold, merry, gay or what you will. There is nothing in the whole range of composition which cannot be supplied from this source. . . . I am satisfied that the future music of this country must be founded on what are called the Negro melodies.

His note-books show an early form of the slow introduction to the E minor Symphony, and also contain one, at least, of the themes of the slow movement. Internal evidence would seem to show that Dvořák depended rather too much on these note-books. The music has not the inner compulsion of the three great symphonies that preceded it. The slow movement, for example, does not create its own form, its elements are not integrated, as in the corresponding movement of the G major Symphony. The famous series of chords that lead from the final E minor chord of the first movement to the remote key of the *Largo*—D flat major—are indeed a stroke of genius, but the two tunes following the lovely lament, a homesick cry on the English horn, sound—beautiful as they are—like an easy substitution for a process of continuous thought.

The juxtaposition of the two 'limbs' of the first subject of the first movement again strikes one as slightly mechanical, and the second limb sounds manufactured.

More serious is the pronounced reliance on sequential treatment and repetition in the first and last movements (and repetition in the third movement). The music gives an impression of vitality—and, of course, it *has* vitality—but examined closely it is often more busy, even fussy, than vital. It may be said, perhaps, that the nature of the material requires all the phrase-repetition that so bothers one, but such an explanation is not very convincing.

A 'Fabricated' Work

There remains the question of quotation, in each of the movements after the first, of themes from the preceding ones. It is ingeniously done, particularly in the scherzo, in which the quotations are much more subtly introduced than in the other two movements. But dramatic justification, present certainly in the slow movement, seems lacking in the later pages of the finale. Dvořák presents all his main themes in various disguises, and then makes them take their bow before the curtain. The effect is to draw attention to the cleverness of the dramatist by letting us leave the theatre with an unnecessary reminder of the *dramatis personae*. It is depressing to contemplate this work from the heights of the D minor and D major Symphonies, but such depression is not likely to be widespread. The discerning critic can see that Dvořák broke away from classical symphonic form in the G major Symphony with results that are, on the whole, successful. But the E minor Symphony, on a close analysis, reveals itself as no new solution of the problem but as, in Constant Lambert's words, a 'fabricated' work. Even so good a friend of Dvořák's as Sir Henry Hadow calls it 'opportunist.'

CHAPTER XIX

CHAMBER MUSIC

If we include some small pieces for various combinations, Dvořák's chamber works amount to thirty-six. Since Professor Šourek's article appeared in Cobbett's *Cyclopedic Survey of Chamber Music* a hitherto unpublished string Quartet in F minor (originally Op. 9) was published in 1929 by Breitkopf & Härtel, and the same firm also issued a *Capriccio* (*Concert Piece,* originally Op. 49) for violin and piano, arranged by Günther Raphael, in that year.

As Dvořák's considerable output of large chamber-music works is spaced out fairly evenly throughout his life it seems best to follow it through in chronological order.

The unpublished works consist of four string Quartets, a string Quintet and a piano Quintet.

The manuscript of the string Quintet in A minor, with two violas, Dvořák's actual Op. 1 (with the exception of two polkas and a galop), is dated 1861, and signed Leopold Antonín Dvořák. It is in three movements, there is no scherzo, and the music, influenced by Mozart and Beethoven, is said to be of a melancholy character. Stefan's most interesting comment on the work concerns the finale, in which Dvořák, as so often in later works, quotes, or at least hints at, a theme used in the slow movement.

Even at this early stage his sense of construction seems to have been mature, and as a practical instrumentalist he knows how to produce sonorous sound; but there is as yet no national note. The next work, a string Quartet in A major (1862), does contain a scherzo which, though influenced still by Beethoven, points 'to Dvořák's later use of Bohemian folk-dance motives.' This Quartet is said to be a happier work, freer and more spontaneous in invention and altogether more mature. At the end of the manuscript appear the words 'Thank God,' and these, or 'Finished with God's help,' are to be seen on all his subsequent manuscripts.

Both this work and the next two string Quartets, in D major and E minor (1870), were only preserved by chance, since Dvořák had determined on their destruction and only copies in the hands of friends saved them from being a total loss. But he thought the first half of a section of the E minor Quartet worth building up into the *Nocturne* in B major for strings, Op. 40, which is described in the chapter on miscellaneous orchestral works. In view of the Wagnerian character of this *Nocturne* it would be particularly interesting to see this one-movement Quartet. It falls into five sections. Dvořák's attraction to Wagner—strong at this time—colours also the second Quartet, in D major, but as a prophylactic he quotes in the scherzo the Czech song *Hej Slované*. The Quartet contains Dvořák's first rondo. There is no scherzo in the piano Quintet in A major of 1872, which sees Dvořák regaining his balance after the Wagnerian crisis. One can well believe on the evidence of the early piano works and songs that the writing for the piano in this Quintet is ineffective. Stefan says that 'the pathos of the first and last movements is long drawn out,' and that it takes the composer 'a hundred and forty bars to state a single theme of the finale.' That Dvořák was often diffuse we all know, but this must be the longest theme in existence!

In one of the two Quartets of 1873, the one in A minor (originally Op. 12), Dvořák repeats the one-movement experiment of the earlier Quartet in E minor, but this time 'he has merely joined together four clearly defined movements.' The composer evidently felt this was only a mechanical proceeding, since he later separated the movements; but the lack of several pages at the end of the first movement has denied the Quartet performance or publication.

We now come to the published works. The first of these, the Quartet in F minor, 1873, is an extraordinarily interesting work to study, for if, as Stefan says, it is autobiographical in the manner of Smetana's *From my Life*, it gives a clue to Dvořák's emotional state at the time; and in any case it remains, with the Symphony in E flat major, the only evidence we have in print, except for a few songs, of what sort of music he was writing in this year.

The work is very frequently orchestral in feeling and lay-out, and the mixtures of styles most curious. What Gerald Abraham calls 'undissolved particles'[1] are abundant. The first movement is of

[1] Chapter on 'Dvořák's Musical Personality' in *Antonín Dvořák: his Achievement*, edited by Viktor Fischl (London, 1943).

prodigious length, but somehow Dvořák manages to keep it going, and there is something very appealing in this outburst of sound and fury set out with youthful pride in the use of various technical devices, learnt in long hours of study of great models. The second movement is a Mendelssohnian *canzona* which became, later, a *Romance* for violin and orchestra, and for the scherzo, *tempo di valse,* Dvořák turns to Chopin for model. Then, feeling the need of contrast, he changes the time to 2–4 and becomes much more himself in a rather Schumannesque dance-measure. *Sturm und Drang* might well be the motto of the sultry finale, generously provided with *tremolandi*, double-stopping and octave whirlwinds—a genuine storm in a tea-cup. But here again a primitive Slavonic dance peeps out when the tempest momentarily subsides (cue-letter G).

So far Dvořák has passed through three periods, one of fidelity to classical models, the second of following the red light of Wagner and the less pervasive lure of Liszt, and the third of trying to reconcile the opposing claims of classicism and romanticism. But now it is Smetana who beckons to him, and shows him the new, safe and profitable road of nationalism.

But Dvořák cannot yet—or for some time—express himself freely in this new way. He had spent hard years learning the ways of polite classical form, to which he had brought a natural instinct for logical construction. He had ventured into deep and alien waters and now was safely washed up on the bank again. He saw his country, but he had not lost sight of Beethoven. The result of these two strong influences makes the A minor Quartet, Op. 16, of 1874 one of great interest. The subject-matter of the first two movements is the most individual we have yet had from him in his chamber music. There are characteristic fingerprints at the end of the six bars of the first theme (quoted below) in the opening movement, and in the rising fourth of the second theme, but the working out of these themes is rather cramped and anxious.

Allegro, ma non troppo

The great sigh in the slow movements of the D minor Symphony, Op. 70 (page 167), and the G major Quartet, Op. 106, is clearly foreshadowed in the main theme of the slow movement of this Quartet, and indeed forms its chief interest. It is even given the *acciaccatura* which is written into its repetition in the Symphony. This is how it appears in the Quartet:

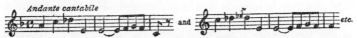

Another very characteristic touch is the development of the semiquavers at the end of the main theme rather than the essence of the theme itself. The scherzo seems to be an echo of Brahms's song *Der Schmied,* but its little trio is more original. Beethoven frowns at us from the finale, and one has reason, not for the first time, to wish he could have taken out copyright in the opening notes of the fifth Symphony. This overdriven movement offends against the canons of good quartet writing. It becomes almost symphonic in style. As for the next work, the Quintet in G major for two violins, viola, cello and double bass (1875), outrageously altered by Simrock from Op. 18 to Op. 77, its first and last movements, transcribed for orchestra, would serve excellently as operatic overtures. They remind one of Lortzing. The high spirits of the scherzo are irresistible even though one realizes how undistinguished the material is. That criticism applies also to the slow movement. Dvořák opens simply enough, but in his second theme becomes tortuous and dull. He has yet to win real freedom of lyrical expression, and his style is far from becoming as saturated with nationalism as was afterwards the case. The Quintet must indeed have been a shock as Op. 77, much more so than the string Quartet which Simrock calmly numbered Op. 80 instead of Op. 27. This Quintet was published in 1888. Two piano Trios—Dvořák often composed in pairs—were written in 1875 and 1876, and a piano Quartet in 1875.

The first of the Trios, the one in B flat major, Op. 21, limps painfully after Schubert in its first movement and—considering all that Dvořák had written up to now—is sometimes most inept in its modulations. The harping on the dominant is almost comic. Few movements by any composer say the same thing so persistently over and over again, and in spite of all the apparent vitality and bustle one arrives at the slow movement in a somewhat exhausted state. It proves lyrically refreshing though in no way outstanding melodically, but it is interesting to notice that the opening tune, in G minor, returns in F sharp minor (the home key being reserved for the coda) in a less elaborate shape. It forms the centre of the middle section. The composer's hand is learning cunning. His ability to write effective counter-melodies is shown in the rather charming scherzo which, incidentally, is burdened with a very artificial trio. It sounds as if Dvořák had thought he was being too frivolous, and had re-pented at length. The finale nearly succeeds in beguiling one, but it is too long, and Dvořák cannot yet write a free bass part for the piano.

This is evident also in the piano Quartet in D major, Op. 23, of this same year. One seems to hear the piano only in the treble register. The music is pleasant, but in no way remarkable. The first movement is too long for its subject-matter, which does not grow by repetition. For the second time in his published works Dvořák writes some variations on a theme, and again for a slow movement. The theme is tinged with a wistful melancholy, but in the first two variations the constant use of imitation jolts the listener into irritation, especially if repeats are used.

A modulatory passage, skilfully worked into the next variation, leads us into the remote key of E flat major—the music has so far been in B minor-D major—but the *salon* tinkle is still there and one begins to long for some thoughts of greater weight. There is a little deepening of emotion in Variation 5, but it is only in the coda that a note of true passion appears—too late to save the movement from triviality. Scherzo and finale are combined in the last movement, with the finale coming off second-best, owing to the conventional nature of its theme as contrasted with the attractive dance measure devised for the scherzo.

The G minor piano Trio, Op. 26 (1876), is a much more charac-teristic work than the Trio in B flat major of the year before. The first movement, too long by far, shows Dvořák clinging, indeed, to a little semiquaver phrase, derived from his first subject, like an in-experienced swimmer to a pair of water-wings; but the method, here in embryo, is that of most of the later works. In the pleasant slow movement—in shape like the main tune of the parallel movement in the E major Quartet—Dvořák uses only one theme, but he was not yet ready for the practice of such economy, so that the repetitions grow wearisome. The best music comes in the lively and rhythmically varied scherzo and the worst in the finale. This is a thoroughly bad movement: the piano writing is amateurish, the use of the melodic material fussy, and the last two pages would qualify for the adjective usually applied to Dvořák better than anything else of his that I know!

The string Quartet in E major, Op. 80, was begun on the day the piano Trio in G minor was finished. Like that work, it carries marks of the composer's recent bereavement. It is the tonality of the Quartet which betrays the grief Dvořák was feeling. In the opening movement, for which he has invented a peculiarly fruitful and expressive opening theme,

he continually sheers away from the major key; the slow movement is in A minor, the scherzo again looks away from the tonic key and its trio is in C sharp minor. This is also the key of the final movement, except for its closing bars, which run into E major as do the points at which Dvořák harks back to his original opening theme. The construction of the Quartet shows a great advance on that of the A minor, Op. 16, but Dvořák is still speaking with two voices, the voice of the pupil who has been reading the classics and the natural unaffected voice of the peasant. The opening theme could have been signed by Bach—it would make a wonderful fugue subject, and he has in fact used one very much like it—and other passages by Beethoven; but the dotted quaver figure in the second subject, which we shall soon meet with again—and in many other places in the A major Sextet —is pure Dvořák. The manner of its introduction is worth noting.

It comes along with the main stream, and one assumes it to be an outcrop of the first subject. Some new phrases appear, then the first subject again. But at cueletter B behold this outcropping, now not in D flat major as before, but in C sharp minor, and quite clearly the second subject. The movement has a very luminous and beautiful conclusion. Any one who knows the slow movement of the F major Symphony will recognize the affinity between it and that of the present Quartet. This A minor movement is, in my opinion, one of the gems of Dvořák's chamber music. It is beautifully scored, its two themes are most happily combined at the coda (cue-letter H), and the passage (cue-letter I) in which the first violin leads the music into a very soft chordal treatment of the second tune in A major—the one place where the sun breaks through the clouds—is exquisite. The off-the-beat scherzo continues the prevailing melancholy—the strong dynamic contrasts in the trio need to be carefully studied—and in the finale, liberally sprinkled with Schubert's triplets, the best music comes with the unexpected reappearance of the first movement's opening theme.

The Quartet in D minor, Op. 34, composed a few months after the *Symphonic Variations*, is dedicated to Brahms, but contains little flattery of Dvořák's new-found friend. The first movement reminds one rather of Schubert than Brahms and might, from its general tone of melancholy, have taken as its motto the opening lines of *Margaret at the Spinning-Wheel*: 'Meine Ruh ist hin, mein Herz ist schwer.' An interesting point is the thematic relationship between the two subjects of this first movement and the main subject of the slow movement. The two last bars of the opening theme:

are used for the beginning of the second subject; they influence the main theme of the slow movement, and are obviously quoted in the coda. Unlike the forced procedure in the 'New World' Symphony, the relationship here is really organic. The scoring in the deeply expressive slow movement is perhaps rather orchestral—there is a certain amount of five- and six-part harmony—but the rich effect on the muted strings is beautiful. It is Schubert again who seems to be the model for the elaborate detail which accompanies the high violin solo in the middle section. The scherzo is a delightful polka, with a trio in the style of a *sousedská*,[1] and the finale makes up in energy for what it lacks in distinction.

[1] The *sousedská* is a slow dance, rather similar to a waltz, and like it, in triple time.

String Sextet

Some of the happiness Dvořák must have felt at the success of his first set of *Slavonic Dances* seems to colour the delightful little work, *Bagatelles,* Op. 47, for two violins, cello and harmonium, which he wrote for the home music-making of his friend Srb-Debrnov in 1878. There are five short movements of which the first [1] and third are thematically related. The second movement is a minuet which uses a dotted quaver figure somewhere in every one of its hundred and nine bars. This looks intimidating on paper, but in performance the cunningly placed smooth harmonies of the other parts work a magic spell and the ear is not exacerbated. The other movements are a charmingly plaintive canon and a jolly polka in which Dvořák, in a way now becoming very familiar, recalls the very tuneful theme of the opening movement. We should be given a chance of hearing this lovely little work more often, even if it means hiring a harmonium. (That instrument is really needed—a piano cannot effectively render its part.)

The fresh and spontaneous invention found in the *Bagatelles* over-flows into the larger spaces of the Sextet in A major, Op. 48, which Dvořák began two days after completing the smaller work. The Sextet has the effect of a brightly coloured travel poster advertising Czechoslovakia. Šourek assures us that 'each theme pulses with strong Slavonic blood,' but to the outsider the three themes of the opening movement have an attractively Schubertian lilt, so that we seem to approach Dvořák's country through Austria. He is delightfully at ease in developing these themes in the course of the movement—at cue-letter N, *molto tranquillo,* in the coda, they are all on the most affectionate terms—and his practice of generating ideas from a phrase of his main theme is most happily in evidence in the opening pages of the move-ment where this phrase turns into a characteristic dotted quaver figure:

As in the E major Quartet, Op. 80, the sonnet-sequence of the later *Dumky* Trio is again foreshadowed in the slow movement,

---

[1] Dvořák quotes part of the folk tune *Hraly dudy* in his first theme.

marked *Dumka*,[1] of the Sextet. The lovely five-bar tune which forms the first section gives place to a slow rhapsodic gypsy music and this to a tender lullaby. The movement ends with a return to the opening section, considerably shortened: the gypsies have the last word in the coda. More local colour appears in the scherzo, which is styled *Furiant*, though it does not conform to the rhythmic rules of the type.[2] But it is clearly a peasant dance and the most vigorous movement of the kind that has appeared so far. As if to say that he owed his new-found freedom—for at one time Dvořák seemed to be shy of writing scherzos—to the *Slavonic Dances* we hear in the trio an echo of the A major section of the first *Slavonic Dance*. For the last movement there is a theme and five variations followed by a *stretto* (really another variation) and a *presto*; Dvořák, when happy, loves to prolong his leave-taking. The tonality of the theme wavers between B minor and A major, but the promise of the rather attractive tune is not entirely fulfilled. The variations have not the spontaneity of the earlier movements, and one or two of them sound 'worked.'

With the E flat major Quartet, Op. 51, of 1879, Dvořák reaches maturity in his chamber music. He feels able to let go of the hand of his masters, gaze unmoved upon his seducers, and write music that is completely and unmistakably his; music, too, which, like the Sextet, reflects his general contentment with life. The beautiful richness of tone, of which he had long had the secret, is here perfectly controlled, and the wealth of detail in all the movements marshalled with the hand of a master. One example of this: the counter-melody to the second subject in polka rhythm which goes on right up to the end of the exposition and which the little semiquaver figure in the opening subject may well have suggested to Dvořák. Here is a most happy marriage between the national dance and the composer's own intimate thoughts. His contrasts are very well planned—that hymn-like section in the first movement is a necessary moment of repose in all this flow of sound. The second movement, labelled *Dumka*,

---

[1] Dvořák defines this Russian term in his own way. Movements so entitled contain strongly contrasted sections, grave and melancholy, and occasionally gay.

[2] The *furiant* is a quick dance in often changing rhythm. Some of Dvořák's movements in this form keep, however, a regular rhythm.

again shows a big advance over the similar movement in the Sextet. In retrospect that seems like a sketch for what is now a real and novel art-form. Instead of three quite distinct tunes Dvořák uses only one with two contrasted 'limbs.' A change of time (2–4 to 3–8) and speed turns this two-part tune into a *furiant*, and so in alternating sections the movement is worked out. A genuine slow movement is provided by the *Romance*, a beautiful bit of writing, but marred—if you let it worry you—by a rather disturbing reminiscence of 'He shall feed his flock,' and the Quartet ends with a gay *skočná*[1] contrasted with a meditative tune, and finally brought into close relationship with it.

It might have been expected that after a patently Slavonic work like this, the *Czech Suite* for orchestra, of 1879, and the *Gypsy Songs* of 1880, Dvořák would have continued to exploit so happy a vein and one so obviously his own; but except for the jolly polka in the over-long final movement—one of his best tunes—the violin Sonata in F major, Op. 57, composed only two months later than the *Gypsy Songs*, is a sad disappointment. Its first two movements are indifferent Brahms.

A year later—and after the composition of the splendid Symphony in D major—comes another string Quartet, Op. 61, in C major. Dvořák again changes direction, or rather goes into reverse—back to Beethoven and Schubert. This is the Quartet which was announced for performance by Hellmesberger, to whom it was dedicated, before it was composed. Perhaps Dvořák's heart was not in it and he chose to exercise his craftsmanship rather than compel inspiration, or perhaps he wanted to demonstrate to Vienna that he need not rely on home produce. Whatever the reason, the result is unsatisfactory. Dvořák had far too great a knowledge of himself and reverence for Beethoven to attempt to challenge him on his own ground, but the nature of the writing in this Quartet compels the listener to measure the disciple against the master. Much lovely and luminous sound is here, but it has a conscience; and that is the last thing lovely sound should have. The conquering hero of a first theme in the opening movement:

[1] The *skočná* is a reel.

with which, one can imagine, Beethoven would have done so much, makes in fact little territorial conquest, and an unconscious reminis- cence of the second subject (cue-letter O) in the first movement of the previous Quartet in E flat only serves to remind us of the loss of the spontaneity and freshness which bubble out so freely there. It is the same with the very carefully laid-out slow movement, in which, in addition, the mixture of styles is disturbing. Beethoven and Schubert are joined by Chopin (the second tune); and how willingly would one sacrifice the elaborate detail displayed here for the *Dumka* of the E flat Quartet! The scherzo, even, is inhibited—it is thematicaly related to the theme above, and though the trio begins more hopefully, it ends with a display of ingenuity in the matter of harmonics. Alone in the finale, in which there is a feeling of relief and release, do we seem to hear the voice of the Dvořák we know and love. For the C major Quartet one can have admiration, but not love.

As every one knows, the F minor pianoforte Trio, Op. 65, is the first of a group of works which belong to the peak period of Dvořák's creative life. Temptation to write an opera in German, and so com- mand the attention of the operatic world at large, and the death of his mother, caused a painful emotional state in the composer, and the first fruits of this appear in the questioning opening theme. This Trio is very generally admired, and indeed there is much in it to compel admiration; but at the risk of being in a minority of one I am bound to say that Dvořák does not seem entirely to have struck off the fetters which bound him in the C major Quartet of a little more than a year before. (The only big work composed during the interim period was *Dimitri*.) Or rather it would be more true to say that he has put on new fetters stamped with the name of Brahms. The shape of the themes, the writing for the piano and the general feeling of the music 'continually do cry' Brahms. But Dvořák has attained his highest point, so far, of actual thinking in music, though the line of thought may not be wholly his own. And so this first movement is enormously interesting and stirring, and there are in it some finely dramatic strokes. Examine, for instance, the recapitulation at cue-letter I, particularly the point at which the music darkens and stills, and the questioning phrase is answered by a mysterious swirl of semiquavers. This powerful movement is followed by a scherzo in which the piano has an unusually important and effective share. The best thing in the singularly arid trio is the way in which Dvořák re-establishes the rhythm of the scherzo. I must confess to remaining unmoved by the slow movement. It is obviously deeply felt and sincerely written, but if one does, perhaps mistakenly, smell the lamp-oil, then it is impossible to be convinced by it. The finale is really another and larger scherzo in the manner of a *furiant* and with a trio of much, though short-lived, melodic charm, recalling the first waltz of Op. 54. There is splendid urgency and dramatic power in the movement and, when the final bars are reached, a sense of conflict resolved.

Most composers think twice, if at all, about writing a trio for strings only, but Dvořák, taking a holiday from big works, chose to write, in 1887, a string trio with an additional problem of balance in the use of two violins and viola rather than the more usual, but still rare, combination of violin, viola and cello. It appears that he intended his *Terzetto*, Op. 74, for the use of amateurs, but coming to realize it would prove too difficult, compensated them with the *Four Romantic Pieces* for violin and piano, Op. 75, for which he used his original sketches for the trio with delightful results. The *Terzetto* itself is a most charming and intimate little work. Its first and second movements have great sweetness of sound, which in the *Larghetto* sends one's mind back to the Mendelssohn organ sonatas. There is an eerie feeling in the passages of the vigorous little scherzo where the first violin and viola play *sul ponticello*, and the trio which follows takes the form of an enchanting *Ländler*. One lovely little point of craftsmanship: the descending scale passages for second violin and viola on the return to the waltz tune. There is considerable originality in the theme and variations which conclude the little work. The theme, springing from the first phrase of the opening movement, is rich in suggestion, mournful in tone, and the developments are surprising. The range and sudden contrasts of dynamics keep one on the alert, and in the first and longest variation there are both drama and pathos. Drama becomes intensified in the two short variations marked *moderato* (*quasi recit.*) and *moderato risoluto*, and these are followed by two quick variations of somewhat defiant rejoicing.

Two more works belong to 1887, the arrangement (or, possibly, revision of an arrangement) of twelve of the *Cypresses* songs, five of which, under the title of *Evening Songs*, were played at a popular concert a year later. Simrock three times refused this work and ten of the arrangements were eventually published by Hudební Matice. A note at the end of the score gives the history of the work under the following heading: 'The trifling compositions for string-quartetto are arisen as following'! They are, of course, miniature pieces, too intimate for the concert-hall and too little varied to be played right through; but they are ideal for home music-making, being within the scope of reasonably accomplished amateurs. Gramophone companies should take note of them, for, recorded, these small lyrics would prove invaluable when an awkward few minutes have to be filled up on the air. They would enchant the listener.

The other work is the pianoforte Quintet in A major, Op. 81. It is possible to assess the value of this Quintet without resorting to comparisons with similar works by Schubert, Schumann and Brahms. It is simply one of the most perfect chamber-music works in existence: perfect in that it accomplishes perfectly what it sets out to do, perfect as a whole and in all its parts. Here there is not a note too many—and there are plenty of notes!—the melodies are of the greatest beauty and freshness, and a joyous springtime happiness flows through the music. As a revelation of Dvořák's Czech soul it has its moments of sadness, but they are soon replaced by his native optimism and cheerfulness. The student of the score will find in these pages a turn of melody, harmonies, a point of form, used by the composer before, but never with this spontaneous rightness. The workmanship is that of a master—and one who has completely overcome a disability which so far has been hampering him; for Dvořák now uses the piano, in combination with strings, easily and effectively.

It is at last his friend, and he gives it music that is native to its genius and individual to him. Perhaps the two middle movements give the best evidence of this. Note the lay-out of the opening page of the *Dumka*, the tune for the high treble register of the piano while the strings' counter-melody (viola and first violin) is placed low down. The marriage of the two tunes, at the second *Tempo I*, is exquisitely contrived. This *Dumka* consists really of four variations on the opening theme with a twice-heard tune of contrast. Dvořák rarely wrote so ravishing a tune as this, and well-known though it is, it must be quoted here. Its fifth and sixth bars derive from (a) below.

The variants of the opening theme which steal into the delicious scherzo-waltz (a *furiant* in name rather than in fact) are another point of inspired craftsmanship. It will be seen that the cello phrase (*c*) is the second-violin phrase in augmentation (*b*) while both are diminutions of the original opening phrase (*a*):

Such is a cold analysis of lovely sound and sense. Another superb moment is the gradual approach to the recapitulation in the opening movement when the music, hushed to double *piano*, gradually grows in power and emotional intensity, modulating freely, until the main theme bursts out full-throatedly in piano and strings. But beautiful things greet us on every page of this 'sweet-scented manuscript,' the most lovable portrait of Dvořák and his country that the world possesses.

Nearly two years later—after the composition of *The Jacobin*—came the pianoforte Quartet in E flat major, Op. 87, a form not used by Dvořák since the D major work of 1875.

Up to cue-letter D, almost the end of the exposition in the first movement, there is excellent fare. The confident tune which the strings give out in unison at the start of the movement swings along grandly when the piano joins in, and the second tune, ingeniously introduced, has all Dvořák's pervasive lyrical charm; but the sudden tremolo for strings at cue-letter D gives cause for forebodings that are unfortunately justified. Dvořák decides to forget good chamber-music manners and to write a number of passages that are disagreeably melodramatic. These are blots on what should have been a fine movement. Occasionally the underlining is justified by the result. Piano and strings hammer out the opening theme in B flat minor, and jerk it abruptly into B minor in a way Beethoven would have applauded. Then, while the first violin very sweetly sings the second subject in B major, one hears that the cello is steadily urging it out of that key and in a moment we have reached the recapitulation, which starts, as in the first movement of the cello Concerto, not with the main tune, but with this same second subject in the tonic key. Why, after so fine a bit of craftsmanship as this, Dvořák chose to lapse again into melodrama in his coda he alone could tell. The striking modulations for the piano are blurred by 'ghostly' string *tremolandi,* and the end is unpleasantly flashy. A similar decline and fall occurs in the slow movement. The lyrical cello tune is heart-easing, but no true emotional intensity is achieved by the outburst of chromatic octaves with which the piano draws its companions into the C sharp minor section of contrast. This happens twice, and with a stifling elaboration of detail the second time. It is a relief to get to the charming waltz in the third movement with its 'oriental' second tune—a sort of slow mazurka—but the all-too-familiar rhythm and lay-out of the trio seem an unhappy solution of the problem of contrast. The last movement is full of a bucolic energy which carries one off one's feet—though there are some passages of quiet beauty—and to the final page only a full orchestra could do justice.

In the *Dumky* Trio of some months later—it was completed in February 1891—Dvořák recovers fully the integrity of style he had achieved in the A major pianoforte Quintet. The licence he gives himself here is of quite another and a creative order, and the emotional intensity of the music is reached by wholly legitimate means. By extending the *dumka* scheme in the Quintet he liberates himself from the conventional bonds of sonata form and composes what has been well called a sonnet-sequence of movements. Full enjoyment of the work depends on the acceptance of the slight monotony which a somewhat similar method of treatment—alternation of slow and fast —in each of the six movements involves. That done, and easily done, one can surrender oneself to the magical richness and variety of sound, the poetry and passion, contained in these musical sonnets. The opening number stands out for its challenging start and its brilliant combination of tunes in the *allegro*: but it is hard to particularize when every movement has its own individual appeal. Special mention must, however, be made of the exquisite third movement, *Lohengrin*-like in its introductory harmonies, but passing at once to a wistful reminiscence of the *larghetto* in Dvořák's own Serenade for strings. Of these first three movements each ends with the direction to go straight on: they are evidently to be regarded as directly connected. Thenceforward a short pause is indicated. Dvořák never surpassed the brilliance of the piano writing in this Trio and, perhaps with Hanuš Wihan in mind, he has given the cellist, as well as the violinist, a magnificent part.

Three years passed before Dvořák turned again to chamber music, and when he did so it was to record his happiness at finding himself among his own countrymen in their settlement at Spillville, Iowa, his delight at the beauty of the countryside, and at being away from the exciting but noisy life of New York. The F major string Quartet, Op. 96, has one of the loveliest beginnings in the whole range of chamber music. The most rigid purist could not take exception to the gentle movement set up by the *tremolandi* for the violins as a background, like rustling leaves in the wind, for the quiet entry of the main theme. This charming movement tempts one to poetic description, and though such temptation needs to be resisted one must point out the programmatic nature of the Quartet. Dvořák talks over some of his American experiences of an evening at the inn at Spillville, and evidently says something about the 'New World' Symphony—if one can judge from a few thematic resemblances. Inevitably his thoughts turn to home, and the poignant tune of the slow movement is full of the nostalgia of the exile. Dvořák rarely achieved so deep an intensity of emotional expression as in the great soaring phrases of this movement, with the cello, in its highest register, or the second violin, singing a passionate duet with the first violin; while throughout the rocking figure of accompaniment is maintained. And how different is the whispered ending—viola *tremolando*—to the passage with which we had to quarrel in the coda of the first movement of the E flat piano Quartet.

The scherzo, like the slow movement, is all spun out of one theme. It is the most humorous movement Dvořák has written. There was a 'damned bird (red, only with black wings)' that kept singing, but, however irritating, it provided the composer with an excellent idea of which he has made delightful use:

Once one knows the little programme the effect (to adapt the famous description of a funeral march in *The Promenade Ticket*) of the alternating sections is 'Damn that bird'—'But it's a rather pretty bird'—'Nevertheless damn it.'

There is, according to Šourek, a little bit of programme in the lively final movement. He says that the short imitation of a chorale 'such as might be improvised softly on the organ' is undoubtedly a reminiscence of the church at Spillville. The composition of the

Quartet occupied Dvořák only fifteen days.[1]   At the end of the score
he wrote: 'Thank God! I am content: it has gone very quickly.'
Perhaps it went a little too quickly here and there, but on the whole
this delightfully spontaneous work well deserves its success.

The string Quintet, Op. 97, was begun three days later and finished
in a month.   Elsewhere in this book is described Dvořák's interest
in the Iroquois Indians who were visiting Spillville at this time, and
it is their music, instead of a 'damned bird,' that gave him the drum
rhythms of the first movement and the scherzo as well as the melodies
that go with them.   Both these and the nature of the harmonies lend
an exotic atmosphere to the Quintet, which is very different from the
pure country air of the preceding Quartet and might, if one heard the
work too often, become somewhat oppressive.   The whole technical
apparatus is more complex, though sometimes the thematic material,
or its treatment, borders on the trivial.

One feels this in the opening theme and its immediate section of
contrast (both subject to repeats) so that the next tune, of folksong
character, brings some fresh air into this rather hectic merrymaking.
The end of the Quintet with its ponderous descending bass—which
cries out for the brass—and orgy of triplets and dotted quavers is
perhaps the worst bit of chamber-music writing Dvořák ever
perpetrated.

There are compensations elsewhere.   The lovely first viola solo—so
reminiscent of the third tune in the slow movement of the 'New
World' Symphony—which forms the trio of the scherzo—an excellent
movement altogether, and the striking slow movement.   In the latter
Dvořák drops the Red Indians, with their songs and dances, and
goes to church.   The tone of the movement—a theme and five variations—is deeply devotional.   The first strain of the theme, in A flat
minor, suggests Dvořák praying to Beethoven, for the answer in the
major key that follows is unmistakably related to the composer of the
pianoforte Sonata, with variations, in A flat.   In the coda, which
consists only of the second strain, the effect of Beethoven gazing out
of the score is almost startling.   In the fifth variation devotion gives

[1] It is often said Dvořák completed the Quartet in three days, but according to Stefan it was only the sketches that were ready in this short space
of time.

way to a frolic on the village green: which is just as it should be. The detail in this movement is exceedingly elaborate, the sweetness occa-sionally too penetrating, but the variations, repeating in every case the opposed tonalities of the theme, hold a curious fascination. There are signs in this work that Dvořák was beginning to exhaust his American sources of inspiration, and the little Sonatina in G major for violin and piano, his hundredth opus, is little more than chips from his workshop lovingly fashioned into a gift for his children. It would appear from the first movement that Dvořák had heard *Clementine*—she makes an effective entrance! The little slow move-ment, the gem of the work, is based on a theme noted down by Dvořák when he saw the Minnehaha Falls: the melancholy of this tune gives place to a delicate little mandolin serenade.

A little over a year later, while still in America, Dvořák began work on another string Quartet (the one in A flat major, Op. 105), but composed only a few pages. Both the last Quartets therefore can be considered as having been composed at home. Dvořák, in these two Quartets, casts aside all traces of the slippered ease which we find, at some points, in the American works, and it is moving to find him still seeking new solutions of formal problems in the last period of his creative career. Symphonies lay behind him, the symphonic poems before—he felt that sonata form, according to classic models, was exhausted, and yet he still had something to say in the medium in which his first large-scale music had been written.

The G major Quartet, Op. 106, if unequal, is by far the greater work of the two: indeed it contains Dvořák's two greatest quartet movements. The carefree nature of the opening theme of the first movement—a Bohemian and not an American bird's song—scarcely prepares one for the powerful structure built up on it; but its rising sixth becomes one of the pillars of the movement:

If the second subject expresses Dvořák's joy in being in his own countryside again, he could not have found a more fragrant and lovely

melody than this, or introduced it with greater subtlety. The grand slow movement contains a phrase:

which carries our minds back to the inner conflict and sorrow that find expression in the D minor Symphony, and more particuarly to that great sigh in the slow movement (page 167).

As Dvořák seems to be reliving old battles and griefs, the emotional fervour and the dramatic tension grow until there comes a triumphant outburst in C major, a tremendous affirmation of patriotic and spiritual faith. The workmanship in this movement is consummate. The opening theme, out of which the whole movement grows, is treated with infinite variety and richness of detail and when, after that great climax, the recapitulation begins, the composer is not content with mere repetition but embellishes and newly develops his theme. If he failed in dramatic concentration in his operas, being bound by words, he here achieves it to perfection, and the work-up to the peak climax, unforgettable in performance, is one of the great pages of quartet literature.

To follow so sublime a movement can have been no easy task, but the rough gestures of the scherzo are surely exactly right. Šourek says it has no power to move us, but we do not want to be moved after the great emotional experience the previous movement brings. We want to be rudely shaken up—and we are. The rhythms are unusually well varied, and the trio provides a well-planned and not at all a 'sweet' contrast. Then Dvořák has to face the problem of his last movement. It is experimental and it is a worthy failure. The main idea is the antithesis between the dreamy opening and its quick, almost Haydnesque variant. In the very centre of the Quartet this leads to the unexpected entry of the second subject from the first movement, followed by an allusion to the opening subject of that movement. This technique was used, or abused, in the 'New

World' Symphony, but here it is subtilized and made really meaningful. It is the Beethovenian episode, with the only example of exotic
harmony in the Quartet, which somehow disturbs the balance and
prevents the movement from reaching complete success. But this is
of course only a matter of opinion. As in the D minor Symphony,
Dvořák here aimed at the stars, and there are not many who do that
with so impressive a measure of success.

The A flat major Quartet, Op. 105, if unadventurous, is happy
and springlike music, which shows the same careful workmanship
and gives us, by common consent, Dvořák's finest scherzo. Once
again the final movement could with advantage have been shortened.
It is to be hoped that this fine pair of works may be more frequently
heard, for in this kind Dvořák never did anything better.

For the sake of completeness there should be mentioned here a
Ballade for violin and piano, Op. 15 (1885), which is romantically
pleasing but suffers rather from lack of contrast, and the charming
and rarely played Rondo for cello and piano (later orchestrated),
Op. 94 (1891), which Dvořák composed some time before he left for
America. Without opus number there are the *Capriccio* for violin
and piano (originally Op. 49) arranged by Günther Raphael and
published only in 1929; the *Polonaise* in A minor of 1879, which is
the companion piece to the *Polonaise* in E flat major for orchestra;
and a *Gavotte* for three violins in G minor composed in 1890.

APPENDICES

APPENDIX A

CALENDAR

(Figures in brackets denote the age reached by the person mentioned during the year in question.)

Year	Age	Life	Contemporary Musicians
1841		Antonin Dvořák born, Sept. 8, at Nelahozeves near Prague, son of František Dvořák, an innkeeper and butcher.	Chabrier born, Jan. 18; Pedrell born, Feb. 19. Adam aged 38; Auber 59; Balakirev 5; Balfe 33; Bendl 3; Berlioz 38; Bishop 55; Bizet 3; Borodin 7; Brahms 8; Bruch 3; Bruckner 17; Cherubini 81; Chopin 31; Cui 6; Dargomizhsky 28; Delibes 5; Donizetti 44; Franck 19; Gade 24; Glinka 38; Goldmark 11; Gounod 23; Gyrowetz 78; Heller 26; Křižkovský 21; Lalo 18; Liszt 30; Lortzing 38; Macfarren 28; Marschner 46; Mendelssohn 32; Mercadante 46; Meyerbeer 50; Mussorgsky 2; Offenbach 22; Ponchielli 7; Raff 19; Rheinberger 2; Roskošny 8; Rossini 49; Rubinstein 11; Saint-Saëns 6; Schumann 31; Serov 21; Škroup 40; Smetana 17; Spohr 57; Spontini 67; Stainer 1; Strauss (J. ii) 16; Svendsen 1; Tchaikovsky 1; Tomášek 67; Verdi 28; Wagner 28; Wallace 29.
1842	1		Boito born, Feb. 24; Cherubini (82) dies, March 15; Massenet born, May 12; Sullivan born, May 13.

Year	Age	Life	Contemporary Musicians
1843	2		Grieg born, June 15.
1844	3		Rimsky - Korsakov born, March 18.
1845	4		Fauré born, May 13.
1846	5		
1847	6		Mackenzie born, Aug. 22; Mendelssohn (38) dies, Nov. 4.
1848	7	Listens with delight to the itinerant musicians who play at his father's inn and begs the village schoolmaster to teach him the violin and singing.	Donizetti (51) dies, April 8; Duparc born, Jan. 21; Parry born, Feb. 27.
1849	8	Becomes a chorister in the village church.	Chopin (40) dies, Oct. 17.
1850	9	Plays the violin in a little band conducted by his father in an amateurish way, also at festivals and pilgrimages.	Fibich born, Dec. 21; Gyrowetz (87) dies, March 22; Tomašek (76) dies, April 3.
1851	10	Makes rapid progress on the violin.	d'Indy born, March 27; Lortzing (48) dies, Jan. 21; Spontini (77) dies, Jan. 14.
1852	11	His violin playing and singing in church develop his precocious musical gifts in a natural way.	Stanford born, Sept. 30.
1853	12	Is sent to the neighbouring town of Zlonice, where he lives with an uncle and begins to take lessons in the elements of musical theory from his schoolmaster, Antonín Liehmann, who is also an organist and conducts a small band.	
1854	13	Learns to improvise and play from a figured bass.	Humperdinck born, Sept. 11; Janáček born, July 14.
1855	14	The family has now moved to Zlonice and D. is sent to	Chausson born, Jan. 21; Liadov born, May 11.

Year	Age	Life	Contemporary Musicians
		Kamenice, where he is to learn German, and is taught music by the organist Hancke.	
1856	15	D. is called home from Kamenice to help in his father's butchery, his father being too poor to continue with his education; but Liehmann, firmly believing in D.'s future, again teaches him.	Martucci born, Jan. 6; Schumann (46) dies, July 29; Taneiev born, Nov. 25.
1857	16	Liehmann having persuaded D.'s father that the butcher's trade is not for him, he is allowed to go to Prague for further study, Oct. He enters the Organ School of the Society for Church Music in Bohemia, learning the organ under Josef Foerster, sen., theory under František Blažek and singing under Josef Zvonař.	Bruneau born, March 1; Elgar born, June 2; Glinka (54) dies, Feb. 15.
1858	17	Becomes familiar with the musical classics. He plays the violin in the orchestra of the Society of St. Cecilia, conducted by Antonín Apt, who introduces many romantic works.	Leoncavallo born, March 8; Puccini born, June 22.
1859	18	His uncle discontinuing his small allowance, he is obliged to leave the Organ School. He joins the orchestra conducted by Komsák as viola player.	Foerster born, Dec. 30; Spohr (75) dies, Oct. 22.
1860	19	His salary being very small, he is obliged to augment his income by teaching. Polka for piano composed.	Albeniz born, May 29; Charpentier born, June 25; Mahler born, July 7; Wolf born, March 13.

Year	Age	Life	Contemporary Musicians
1861	20	He is not in a position to make himself known as a composer, and only a few intimate friends know of his creative activities. String Quintet in A minor (Op. 1) composed (unpublished).	MacDowell born, Dec. 18; Marschner (66) dies, Dec. 14.
1862	21	Opening of the Czech National Theatre, where Komsák's band is occasionally employed. Later, when the theatre becomes more firmly established, D. and other members of the band are drawn into the permanent theatre orchestra conducted by J. N. Mayr. String Quartet in A major composed (unpublished).	Debussy born, Aug. 22; Delius born, Jan 29; Kovařovic born, Dec. 9.
1863	22		Mascagni born, Dec. 7.
1864	23		Meyerbeer (73) dies, May 2; Strauss (R.) born, June 11.
1865	24	Friendship with Bendl (27), who becomes conductor of the Hlahol choral society and makes D. acquainted with the world's great music by lending him scores and giving him the use of his piano, D. having been too poor to have one of his own. Symphonies in C minor and B flat major. Cello Concerto in A major composed. 4 songs (Op. 2).	Dukas born, Oct. 1; Glazunov born, Aug. 10; Sibelius born, Dec. 8.
1866	25	Smetana (42) is appointed chief conductor at the Czech National Theatre, where D. still plays the viola.	Busoni born, April 1.

Year	Age	Life	Contemporary Musicians
1867	26	Comes under the beneficial influence of Smetana (43).	Granados born, July 29.
1868	27		Bantock born, Aug. 7; Rossini (76) dies, Nov. 13.
1869	28		Berlioz (66) dies, March 8; Dargomizhsky (56) dies, Jan.; Pfitzner born, May 5; Roussel born, April 5.
1870	29	Tragic opera, *Alfred*. String Quartets in D major and E minor (unpublished) composed.	Balfe (62) dies, Oct. 20; Mercadante (75) dies, Dec. 17; Novák born, Dec. 5; Schmitt born, Sept. 28.
1871	30	Some of D.'s smaller works begin at last to be heard at concerts. *The Orphan*, ballad for voice and piano (Op. 5), and first version of *King and Collier* composed.	Auber (89) dies, May 12; Serov (51) dies, Feb. 1.
1872	31	*Hymnus* from Vítěszlav Hálek's poem *The Heirs of the White Mountain* (Op. 30), 4 Serbian and 6 Bohemian Songs (Opp. 6 and 7) and piano Quintet in A major (originally Op. 5)	Scriabin born, Jan. 6; Vaughan Williams born, Oct. 12.
1873	32	Performance of the *Hymnus*, with which D. for the first time makes a great impression. He leaves the Czech National Theatre orchestra and becomes organist at St. Adalbert's Church, a post that leaves him time for composition and teaching. Marriage to Anna Čermáková, a contralto in the chorus of the National Theatre. *Romance* for violin and orchestra (Op. 11); Symphony in E	Rakhmaninov born, April 1; Reger born, March 19.

Year	Age	Life	Contemporary Musicians

flat major; string Quartet in F minor; string Quartet in A minor.

1874   **33**   Comic operas, *The Pig-headed Peasants* and revision of *King and Collier*, modelled on Smetana's (50) folk operas, composed. The latter is produced. *Rhapsody* for orchestra (originally Op. 15) and Symphony in D minor (originally Op. 13). Scherzo from the latter and E flat major Symphony performed with considerable success.

Holst born, Sept. 21; Schoenberg born, Sept. 13; Suk born, Jan. 4.

1875   **34**   Brahms (42) and Eduard Hanslick (50), as adjudicators for a commission appointed to award government gratuities to poor 'Austrian' musicians, become acquainted with D.'s work and are much impressed by it. Opera, *Vanda*, composed, also Serenade for strings in E major (Op. 22); piano Trio in B flat major (Op. 21); piano Quartet in D major (Op. 23); Symphony in F major (Op. 76); string Quintet in G major (Op. 77).

Bizet (37) dies, June 3; Ravel born, March 7.

1876   **35**   *Vanda* produced in Prague. On the recommendation of Brahms (43) D. receives the grant offered by the Austrian Ministry of Culture. Death of the eldest of D.'s three

Falla born, Nov. 23; Wolf-Ferrari born, Jan. 12.

Year	Age	Life	Contemporary Musicians
		children, after which he begins the composition of the *Stabat Mater* (Op. 58). Piano Trio, G minor (Op. 26); string Quartet, E major (Op. 80); *Moravian Duets* (Opp. 20 and 32); songs (Opp. 3 and 31); piano Concerto, G minor (Op. 33); *Dumka* and Variations for piano (Opp. 35 and 36).	
1877	36	*Stabat Mater* (Op. 58) finished. Comic opera, *The Peasant a Rogue*; string Quartet in D minor (Op. 34) and *Symphonic Variations* for orchestra (Op. 78, originally Op. 40).	Dohnányi born, July 27.
1878	37	Brahms (45) induces Simrock to publish the *Moravian Duets,* which are so successful that the publisher asks for more works. *The Peasant a Rogue* produced in Prague. *Slavonic Dances,* set I (Op. 46) written at Simrock's request, first for piano duet and concurrently scored for orchestra. Serenade, D minor, for wind instruments (Op. 44); 3 *Slavonic Rhapsodies* for orchestra (Op. 45); *Bagatelles* for harmonium, 2 violins and cello (Op. 47); string Sextet, A major (Op. 48).	
1879	38	The *Slavonic Dances* become enormously popular in Germany and England. Violin Concerto in A minor (Op.	Bridge (Frank) born, Feb. 26; Ireland born, Aug. 13; Medtner born, Dec. 4; Ostrčil born, Feb. 25; Respighi born,

Year	Age	Life	Contemporary Musicians
		53) begun. Suite in D major for orchestra (Op. 39); string Quartet, E flat major (Op. 51); Psalm 149 for chorus and orchestra (Op. 79).	July 7; Scott (Cyril) born, Sept. 27.
1880	39	Violin Concerto (Op. 53) finished. Sonata in F major for violin and piano (Op. 57); Symphony in D major (Op. 60).	Bloch born, July 24; Offenbach (61) dies, Oct. 4; Pizzetti born, Sept. 20.
1881	40	Comic opera, *The Pig-headed Peasants* (*see* 1874), produced in Prague. *Legends* for piano duet (Op. 59); string Quartet, C major (Op. 61).	Bartók born, March 25; Miaskovsky born, April 20; Mussorgsky (42) dies, March 28.
1882	41	Opera, *Dimitri*, composed and produced in Prague. Visit to Dresden for the production of *The Peasant a Rogue* in German (*Der Bauer ein Schelm*).	Kodály born, Dec. 16; Křička born, Aug. 27; Malipiero born, March 18; Pick-Mangiagalli born, July 10; Raff (60) dies, June 24–5; Stravinsky born, June 17; Vycpálek born, Feb. 23.
1883	42	Is invited to visit London the following year. He receives tempting offers to settle in Vienna, including the guarantee of the production of a German opera from his pen. He hesitates and finally rejects the offer, wishing to remain true to his nationality. Visit to Hamburg for a production of *The Peasant a Rogue*. Piano Trio in F minor (Op. 65); *Scherzo capriccioso* for orchestra (Op. 66), Dramatic Overture, *Husitská* (Op. 67).	Bax born, Nov. 6; Casella born, July 25; Szymanowski born, Sept. 21; Wagner (70) dies, Feb. 13; Webern born, Dec. 3; Zandonai born, May 28.
1884	43	Visits England for the first time. Conducts the *Stabat*	Smetana (60) dies, May 12.

Year	Age	Life	Contemporary Musicians

Mater in London, at the Albert Hall, also various orchestral works at the Philharmonic Society's concerts and the Crystal Palace, March. He is invited to appear at the Worcester Festival in the autumn. Between these two visits he buys a small property called Vysoká near Příbram, where in future he spends much of his time. At Worcester he conducts the *Stabat Mater* and the second Symphony. He is invited to appear at the Birmingham Festival the next year and to write a new work specially for it. On returning home he sets to work on the cantata, *The Spectre's Bride* (Op. 69), the words of which, by K. J. Erben, are to be translated into English.

1885 44 Symphony in D minor (Op. 70) finished. Third visit to England; he conducts the new Symphony at a Philharmonic concert in London, April. On his return to Prague he finishes *The Spectre's Bride* and goes to Birmingham for its production at the Musical Festival, Aug. The work is published by Novello & Co. Visit to Vienna for the production of *The Peasant a Rogue*.

Berg born, Feb. 7; Křižkovský (65) dies, May 8.

1886 45 Composition of the oratorio, *St. Ludmilla* (Op. 71), for the

Liszt (75) dies, July 31; Ponchielli (52) dies, Jan. 16.

Year	*Age*	*Life*	*Contemporary Musicians*
		Leeds Festival, where he conducts it on his fifth visit to England, autumn. The work is also given three performances in London. *Slavonic Dances*, set II (Op. 72), composed.	
1887	46	*Terzetto* for 2 violins and viola (Op. 74); piano Quintet in A major (Op. 81); Mass in D major (Op. 86).	Borodin (53) dies, Feb. 28; Vomáčka born, June 28.
1888	47	Makes friends with Tchaikovsky (48), who is on a visit to Prague, Feb. Composition of the opera, *The Jacobin*, finished.	
1889	48	*The Jacobin* produced in Prague. Piano Quartet in E flat major (Op. 87); Symphony in G major (Op. 88).	
1890	49	The fourth Symphony produced at a Philharmonic concert in London during his sixth visit to England. He also makes a tour in Germany and visits Russia. The University of Prague confers the honorary degree of Doctor of Philosophy on him; he is also elected a member of the Czech Academy of Art and Science and receives the Austrian Order of the Iron Crown of the third class. Composition of the Requiem for solo voices, chorus and orchestra (Op. 89).	Franck (68) dies, Nov. 8; Gade (73) dies, Dec. 21.
1891	50	Appointed professor of composition, orchestration and form at the Prague Conservatory, spring. Seventh visit to	Bliss born, Aug. 2; Delibes (55) dies, Jan. 16; Jirák born, Jan. 28; Prokofiev born, April 23.

Year	Age	Life	Contemporary Musicians
		England to receive the honorary degree of Mus.Doc. at Cambridge. Eighth visit for the production of the Requiem at the Birmingham Festival.	
1892	51	Composition of the *Te Deum* for solo voices, chorus and orchestra (Op. 103). D. is invited to act as director of the newly opened National Conservatory in New York. He obtains leave from the Prague Conservatory and sails for the U.S.A. He has a great success as teacher and as conductor of his own works. The Negro singer, Henry Thacker Burleigh (26), makes him acquainted with the songs of his race.	Honegger born, March 10; Lalo (69) dies, April 22; Milhaud born, Sept. 4.
1893	52	Symphony in E minor, 'From the New World' (Op. 95), composed. Summer holiday spent among the Czech colony at Spillville, Iowa, where he writes the string Quartet in F major (Op. 96) and the string Quintet in E flat major (Op. 97). First performance of the Symphony, by the New York Philharmonic Society, under Anton Seidl (43), Dec. Sonatina in G major for violin and piano (Op. 100); cantata, *The American Flag* (Op. 102).	Gounod (75) dies, Oct. 18; Hába born, June 21; Tchaikovsky (53) dies, Nov. 6.
1894	53	Summer again spent at Spillville. Suite for piano (Op. 98), afterwards orchestrated; *Biblical Songs* (Op. 99); *Humoresques*	Chabrier (53) dies, Sept. 13; Rubinstein (64) dies, Nov. 20; Schulhoff born, June 8.

Year	*Age*	*Life*	*Contemporary Musicians*
		for piano (Op. 101).	
1895	54	Cello Concerto in B minor (Op. 104) and string Quartet in A flat (Op. 105) begun in New York. D. returns to Prague and resumes his professorial duties at the Conservatory.	Castelnuovo-Tedesco born, April 13; Hindemith born, Nov. 16.
1896	55	Ninth visit to London, where the cello Concerto is heard for the first time, March. Symphonic poems for orchestra, *The Water-Goblin, The Noonday Witch, The Golden Spinning-Wheel, The Wood Dove* and *Hero's Song* (Opp. 107–11). String Quartet in A flat finished; String Quartet in G (Op. 106).	Bruckner (72) dies, Oct. 11.
1897	56		Bendl (59) dies, Sept. 20; Brahms (64), dies, April 3.
1898	57	Composition of the comic opera, *The Devil and Kate*, begun.	
1899	58	*The Devil and Kate* finished and produced in Prague.	Poulenc born, Jan. 7; Strauss (J. ii) (74) dies, June 3.
1900	59	Composition of the opera, *Rusalka,* and the *Festival Song* for chorus and orchestra (Op. 113).	Fibich (50) dies, Oct. 15; Křenek born, Aug. 23; Sullivan (58) dies, Nov. 22.
1901	60	Continues to teach at the Conservatory, of which he is now appointed director.	Rheinberger (62) dies, Nov. 25; Stainer (61) dies, March 31; Verdi (88) dies, Jan. 27.
1902	61		Walton born, March 29.
1903	62	Opera, *Armida*, based on Tasso's *Gerusalemme liberata.*	Wolf (43) dies, Feb. 22.
1904	63	Dvořák dies in Prague, May 1.	Albeniz aged 44; Balakirev 68; Bantock 36; Bartók 23; Bax 21; Berg 19; Bliss 13;

Year Age   Life   Contemporary Musicians

Bloch 24; Boito 62; Bruch 66; Bruneau 47; Busoni 38; Casella 21; Castelnuovo-Tedesco 9; Charpentier 44; Cui 69; Debussy 42; Delius 42; Dohnányi 27; Dukas 39; Duparc 56; Elgar 47; Falla 28; Foerster 45; Glazunov 39; Goldmark 74; Granados 37; Grieg 60; Hába 11; Hindemith 9; Holst 30; Honegger 12; Humperdinck 50; d'Indy 53; Ireland 25; Janáček 50; Jirák 13; Kodály 22; Kovařovic 42; Křenek 4; Křička 22; Leoncavallo 46; Liadov 49; Mackenzie 57; Mahler 44; Malipiero 22; Martucci 48; Mascagni 41; Massenet 62; Medtner 25; Miaskovsky 23; Milhaud 12; Novák 34; Ostrčil 25; Parry 56; Pedrell 63; Pfitzner 35; Pick-Mangiagalli 22; Pizzetti 24; Poulenc 5; Prokofiev 13; Puccini 46; Rakhmaninov 31; Ravel 29; Reger 31; Respighi 24; Rimsky-Korsakov 60; Roskošný 71; Roussel 35; Saint-Saëns 71; Schmitt 34; Schoenberg 30; Schulhoff 10; Scott (Cyril) 25; Scriabin 32; Sibelius 39; Stanford 52; Strauss (R.) 40; Stravinsky 22; Suk 30; Svendsen 64; Szymanowski 21; Taneeiv 48; Vaughan Williams 32; Vomáčka 17; Vycpálek 22; Webern 21; Wolf-Ferrari 28; Zandonai 21.

APPENDIX B

THE fiftieth anniversary of Dvořák's death, 1st May 1954, fittingly provided the occasion for undertaking the publication of a complete edition of the composer's works. The Czechoslovak Ministry of Culture, in agreement with the Antonín Dvořák Society in Prague, had already appointed, in 1951, a special Board, under the chairmanship of Otakar Šourek—the foremost authority in this field—with authority to prepare a new and critical edition of Dvořák's compositions, the first fruits of which appeared in January 1955. Sixteen publishers had before shared in the publication of Dvořák's compositions; opus numbers and dates were in a state of confusion, and there were many deviations from the original manuscripts. This highly important and difficult editorial work has been spread over a number of years. At the present time perhaps the most valuable feature of this great undertaking has been the publication of all the composer's symphonies and symphonic poems. Many miniature scores have also been issued, and many works made available outside the complete edition.

For these the latest catalogue of Artia, Prague, should be consulted. Previous editions, in many cases, are of course still available; but it is the complete edition to which the student of Dvořák's compositions should turn.

DRAMATIC WORKS

Op.

Alfred the Great. Heroic Opera in three acts. Book by Theodor Körner. 1870. (Only the *Tragic Overture* has been published: see Orchestral Works: Overtures.)

14. *King and Collier (Král a uhlíř).* Book by B. Guldener. First version 1871; rewritten 1874; revised 1887.

17. *The Pig-headed Peasants (Tvrdé Palice).* Comic Opera in one act. Book by Josef Štolba. 1874.

Vanda. Tragic Opera in five acts. Book by Zakrejs and Beneš-Šumavský. 1875. (Only the overture has been published: see Orchestral Works: Overtures.)

37. *The Peasant a Rogue (Šelma Sedlák).* Comic opera in two acts. Book by J. O. Veselý. 1877.

64. *Dimitri.* Opera in five acts. Book by M. Červinková-Riegrová. 1881-2; revised 1883 and 1894.

84. *The Jacobin.* Opera in three acts. Book by M. Červinková-Riegrová. 1887-8; revised 1897.

Appendix B—Catalogue of Works

Op.
112. *The Devil and Kate* (*Čert a Káča*). Opera in three acts. Book by
A. Wenig. 1898–9. U. 1908.
114. *Rusalka.* Opera in three acts. Book by Jaroslav Kvapil. 1900.
115. *Armida.* Opera in four acts. Book by Jaroslav Vrchlický. 1902–3.

INCIDENTAL MUSIC
62. Incidental music to the play *Josef Kajetan Tyl*, by F. F. Šamberk.
1881–2.

Date of   CHORAL WORKS
Composition
1872. *The Heirs of the White Mountain* (Vít. Hálek). Patriotic Hymn for
chorus and orchestra, Op. 30. 1872. Revised 1880.
1876. Four Songs for chorus, Op. 29.
      1. Evening's Blessing ⎫ Heyduk
      2. Cradle Song ⎭
      3. I do not say it ⎫ Folk Poems
      4. The Forsaken One ⎭
1877. Eight Choral Songs for Male Voices, Heyduk and Moravian folk
poems.
      1. The Ferryman
      2. The Beloved as Poison-mixer
      3. I am a fiddler (Guslar)
      4. The Guelder-Rose
      5. The Betrayed Shepherd
      6. The Sweetheart's Resolve
      7. The Czech Diogenes
      8. The song of a Czech
1877. Three Slovakian Folksongs for male chorus and piano duet, Op. 43.
      1. Grief
      2. The Magic Well
      3. The Maiden in the Forest
1876–7. *Stabat Mater* for solo voices chorus and orchestra, Op. 58.
1878. Five Choruses for Male Voices (Lithuanian Folksongs).
      1. Village Gossip
      2. Dwellers by the Sea
      3. The Love-Promise
      4. The Lost Lamb
      5. The Sparrows' Party

Date of
Composition

1879. The 149th Psalm for male chorus and orchestra (1879) and mixed
choir (1887) (originally Op. 52), Op. 79.

1882. *Amid Nature* (Vít. Hálek). Five choruses for Mixed Voices,
Op. 63.
1. A song went to my heart
2. Evening bells in the grove
3. Golden fields
4. Birch-tree by the verdant slope
5. This is in truth a day of joy

1884. *The Spectre's Bride* (K. J. Erben). Dramatic Cantata for solo voices,
chorus and orchestra, Op. 69.

1885. *Hymn of the Czech Peasants* (K. Pippich) for chorus and orchestra,
Op. 28.

1886. *St. Ludmilla* (Jaroslav Vrchlický), Op. 71. Oratorio for solo
voices, chorus and orchestra.

1887. Mass in D major, for solo voices, chorus and orchestra, Op. 86.
Orchestral version 1892.

1890. Requiem Mass for solo voices, chorus and orchestra, Op. 89.

1892–3. *Te Deum* for soprano and bass solo, chorus and orchestra, Op. 103.
(There is a version with English text by R. Vaughan Williams:
Lengnick.)

1893. *The American Flag* (Rodman Drake). Cantata for alto, tenor and
bass solo, chorus and orchestra, Op. 102.

1900. *Festival Song* (Jaroslav Vrchlický) for chorus and orchestra, Op. 113.

VOCAL DUETS

1875. Four Duets for soprano and tenor (after Moravian national songs),
Op. 20.
1. Destination
2. The Farewell
3. The Silk Ribbon
4. The Last Wish

1876. *Moravian Duets* (after Moravian folksongs). 13 duets for soprano and
contralto, Op. 32.
1. Watch, love
2. Speed thee, swallow
3. An my scythe were whetted sharp and keen
4. Ere we part, love, kiss me
5. Small our hamlet

      6. The Forsaken Lassie
      7. Brooklet and Tears
      8. The Modest Lassie
      9. Ringlet and Wreathlet
   10. Show thy verdure
   11. The Captured Bride
   12. Consolation
   13. The Pleading Rose

1876. *The Soldier's Farewell.* Duet for soprano and contralto (from Duets, Op. 32).

1877. Four Duets (after Moravian folk poems), Op. 38.
      1. The False Hope
      2. Never parted
      3. The Harvesters
      4. Death in Autumn

1879. Duet for contralto and baritone with organ, Op. 19.
      O Sanctissima

1881. Duet for soprano and contralto. *There on our roof* (Moravian folk poem).

SONGS

1865. *Evening Songs* ('Cypresses'). Op. 2. G. Pfleger-Moravsky (revised 1882) (see also Op. 83).
      1. Go forth my song, delay not
      5. 'Twas wondrous sweet that dream of ours
   11. Nought to my heart can bring relief
   13. Rest in the valley

1871. Op. 5. K. J. Erben.
      The Orphan

1872. Op. 6. Serbian Folk Poems.
      1. The maiden and the grass.
      2. Warning
      3. Flowery Omens
      4. No escape

   Op. 7. Königinhof Manuscripts.[1]
      1. The Nosegay

---

[1] Some of these songs date from 1871, but which there is no available evidence to tell. Op. 9 is also given to the early string Quartets (*see* page 212)

 2. The Rose
 3. The Cuckoo
 4. The Lark
 5. The Forsaken
 6. The Strawberries

Op. 3. *Evening Songs*. Vít. Hálek.

 1. The stars upon the firmament
 2. I dreamt that you had died
 3. I am the knight of fairy-tale
 4. May the Lord delight

1876. Op. 9.[1] E. Krašnohorská.

 1. Therefore
 2. Consideration
 Vít. Hálek.
 3. Quiet is the leaves' evening song
 4. Spring flew hither from afar

Op. 31. *Evening Songs*. Vít. Hálek.

 5. Visions of heaven I fondly paint
 6. This would I ask each tiny bird
 7. Like to a linden tree am I
 8. All ye that labour come to Me
 9. All through the night a bird will sing

1878. Posthumous work, *Hymnus ad Laudes in festo Sanctae Trinitatis*
(voice and organ).

Op. 50. Nebeský.

 1. Koljas
 2. Naiads
 3. Lament for a City

1880. Op. 55. Heyduk.

 1. I chant my lay
 2. Hark how my triangle
 3. Silent Woods
 4. Songs my mother taught me
 5. Tune thy strings, O gypsy
 6. Freer is the gypsy
 7. The cloudy heights of Tatra

---

[1] Some of these songs date from 1871, but which there is no available evidence to tell. Op. 9 is also given to the early string Quartets (*see* page 212).

Date of
Composition

1885. Posthumous work.   Czech Folk Poems.
    1. Lullaby
    2. Disturbed Devotion

1886. Op. 73.   Czech Folk Poems.
    1. Good night
    2. The Mower
    3. The Maiden's Lament
    4. And mine 's the horse named Falka

1887. Op. 82.   Malybrok-Stieler.
    1. Leave me alone
    2. Over her Embroidery
    3. Springtide
    4. At the Brook

1888. Op. 83.   Pfleger-Moravský (revisions of *Cypresses*, 1865).
    2. When thy sweet glances on me fall
    3. Death reigns in many a human breast
    4. Thou only dear one
    6. I know that on my love to thee
    8. Never will love lead us
    9. I wander oft past yonder house
    14. In deepest forest glade I stand
    17. Nature lies peaceful

1894. Op. 99.   Biblical Texts (for sources see page 101).
    1. Clouds and darkness
    2. Lord, Thou art my refuge and my shield
    3. Hear my prayer
    4. The Lord is my shepherd
    5. I will sing new songs of gladness
    6. Hear my prayer
    7. By the waters of Babylon
    8. Turn Thee to me
    9. I will lift mine eyes up to the mountains
    10. O, sing unto the Lord

1895.   F. L. Jelinek.
Lullaby

1901.   Svatopluk Čech.
The Smith of Lešetin

Dvořák

CHAMBER MUSIC
Trios

1875. Piano Trio in B flat major. Op. 21.
1876. Piano Trio in G minor, Op. 26.
1883. Piano Trio in F minor, Op. 65.
1887. *Terzetto* in C major for two violins and viola, Op. 74.
1891. *Dumky* Trio for piano, violin and cello, Op. 90.

Quartets

1862. String Quartet in A major (originally Op. 2).
1870. String Quartet in D major (originally Op. 9).
1870. String Quartet in E minor, Op. 10 (completed and edited by
  G. Raphael).
1873. String Quartet in F minor (originally Op. 9).
1873. String Quartet in A minor (originally Op. 12).
1874. String Quartet in A minor, Op. 16.
1875. Piano Quartet in D major, Op. 23.
1876. String Quartet in E major (originally Op. 27), Op. 80.
1877. String Quartet in D minor, Op. 34.
1879. String Quartet in E flat major, Op. 51.
1881. String Quartet in C major, Op. 61.
1887. *Evening Songs* ('Cypresses'), originally for voice and piano, 1865,
  Songs Op. 2 and Op. 83.
1889. Piano Quartet in E flat major, Op. 87.
1893. String Quartet in F major, Op. 96 ('American' Quartet).
1895. String Quartet in A flat major, Op. 105.
1895. String Quartet in G major, Op. 106.

Quintets

1861. Quintet in A minor for 2 violins, 2 violas and cello, Op. 1.
1872. Quintet in A major for piano, 2 violins, viola and cello, (originally
  Op. 5).
1875. Quintet in G major for 2 violins, viola, cello and double bass
  (originally Op. 18), Op. 77.
1887. Quintet in A major, for piano, 2 violins, viola and cello, Op. 81.
1893. Quintet in E flat major for 2 violins, 2 violas and cello, Op. 97.

Sextet

1878. Sextet in A major for 2 violins, 2 violas, and 2 cellos, Op. 48.

Appendix B—Catalogue of Works

Violin and Piano

1873. *Romance* in F major, Op. 11 (see Orchestral Works: Concertos and Concert Pieces).

1878. *Capriccio* (originally Op. 49).

1879. *Mazurka,* Op. 49 (see Orchestral Works: Concertos and Concert Pieces).

1880. Sonata in F major, Op. 57.

1885. *Ballade* in D minor, Op. 15.

1887. *Four Romantic Pieces,* Op. 75.

        1. *Allegro moderato*

        2. *Allegro maestoso*

        3. *Allegro appassionato*

        4. *Larghetto*

1893. Sonatina in G major, Op. 100.

Cello and Piano

1865. Concerto in A major for cello and piano (see Concertos).

1879. Polonaise in A minor.

1891. *Silent Woods* (see Orchestral Works).

1891. Rondo in G minor, Op. 94 (see Orchestral Works: Concertos and Concert Pieces).

Miscellaneous

1878. *Bagatelles* for 2 violins, cello and harmonium (or piano), Op. 47.

1880. Waltzes for string quartet. No. 1 in A major; No. 4 in D flat major, from piano Waltzes, Op. 54.

1890. *Gavotte* in G minor for 3 violins.

ORCHESTRAL WORKS
Symphonies

1865. Symphony in C minor (*The Bells of Zlonice*) (originally Op. 3). Unpublished.

1865. Symphony in B flat major (originally Op. 4). Unpublished.

1873. Symphony in E flat major (originally Op. 10).

1874. Symphony in D minor (originally Op. 13).

1875. Symphony in F major, 'No. 3' (originally Op. 24); revised 1887, Op. 76.

1880. Symphony in D major, 'No. 1,' Op. 60.

Date of
Composition

1886. *Slavonic Dances*, Second Series (orchestral version of piano duets, Op. 72), Op. 72.

Miscellaneous

1870. *Nocturne* in B major for string orchestra, Op. 40.

1875. *Serenade* in E major for string orchestra, Op. 22.

1877. *Symphonic Variations on an Original Theme* (originally Op. 40), Op. 78.

1878. *Serenade* in D minor for 2 oboes, 2 clarinets, 2 bassoons, double bassoon, 3 horns, cello and double bass, Op. 44.

1879. *Suite* in D major (*Czech Suite*), Op. 39.

1879. *Festival March* in C major, Op. 54.

1879. *Polonaise* in E flat major.

1881. *Legends* (10) (orchestral version of piano duets, Op. 59), Op. 59.

1883. *Scherzo capriccioso* in E minor, Op. 66.

1895. *Suite* (Orchestral version of piano Suite, Op. 98), Op. 98.

PIANO MUSIC
Piano Solos

1860. *Polka*, E major.

1862. *Polka* in B flat major and *Galop* in E major, Op. 53.

1876. *Two Minuets* in A flat major and F major, Op. 28.

1876. *Dumka* (*Elegy*) in D minor, Op. 35.

1876. *Theme with Variations* in A flat major, Op. 36.

1877. *Scotch dances*, Op. 41.

1877. *Two Furiants*, Op. 42.

1879. *Silhouettes*. Twelve piano pieces, Op. 8.

> 1. E major; 2. D flat major; 3. D flat major; 4. F sharp minor; 5. F. sharp minor; 6. B flat major; 7. D major; 8. B minor; 9. C sharp minor; 10. G major; 11. A major; 12. C sharp minor.

1880. Four Piano Pieces, Op. 52.

> 1. Impromptu; 2. Intermezzo; 3. Gigue; 4. Eclogue.

1880. *Eight Waltzes*, Op. 54.

> 1. A major; 2. A minor; 3. E. major; 4. D flat major; 5. B flat major; 6. F major; 7. D minor; 8. E flat major.

1880. *Waltz* in D major.

1880. *Six Mazurkas*, Op. 56.

> 1. A flat major; 2. B flat major; 3. D minor; 4. D major; 5. F major; 6. B minor.

Date of
Composition

1880. *Four Eclogues.*

1880. *Two Impromptus.*

1881. *Three Album Leaves.*

1882. *Impromptu* in D minor.

1884 (?). *Humoresque* in F sharp minor.

1884. *Dumka* and *Furiant* in C minor, Op. 12.

1887. *Two Pearls: Round* (F major) and *Grandfather's Dance with Grand-mother* (G minor).

1889. *Poetic Pictures:* Thirteen piano pieces, Op. 85.

　　1. *Twilight Way.* 2. *Toying.* 3. *In the Old Castle.* 4. *Spring Song.* 5. *Peasants' Ballad.* 6. *Sorrowful Reverie.* 7. *A Dance.* 8. *Goblins' Dance.* 9. *Serenade.* 10. *Bacchanalian.* 11. *Tittle-tattle.* 12. *At the Hero's Grave.* 13. *On the Holy Mount.*

1894. *American Suite* in A major, Op. 98.

1894. *Eight Humoresques,* Op. 101.

　　1. E flat minor; 2. B major; 3. A flat major; 4. F major; 5. A minor; 6. B major; 7. G flat major; 8. B flat minor.

1894. Two Piano Pieces (*Berceuse*—G major, and *Capriccio*—G minor).

Piano Duets

1877. *Scottish Dances* in D minor, Op. 41.

1878. *Slavonic Dances* (First Series 1–8), Op. 46.

　　1. C major; 2. E minor; 3. D major; 4. F major; 5. A major; 6. A flat major; 7. C minor; 8. G minor.[1]

1881. *Legends* (10), Op. 59.

　　1. D minor; 2. G major; 3. G minor; 4. C major; 5. A flat major; 6. C sharp minor; 7. A major; 8. F. major; 9. D major; 10. D flat major.[1]

1884. *From the Bohemian Woods* (Six Character Pieces) (No. 5 arranged for cello and piano, 1891; for cello and orchestra, 1893), Op. 68.

　　1. *In the Spinning-room*
　　2. *On the Dark Lake*
　　3. *Witches' Sabbath*
　　4. *On the Watch*
　　5. *Silent Woods*
　　6. *In Troublous Times*

---

[1] These pieces were orchestrated by the composer. See under Orchestral Works: Miscellaneous.

Date of
Composition
1886. *Slavonic Dances* (Second Series, 9–16), Op. 72.
        9. B major; 10. E minor; 11. F major; 12. D flat major; 13. B
flat minor; 14. B flat major; 15. A major; 16. A flat major.[1]

---

[1] This piece was orchestrated by the composer. See under Orchestral
Works: Miscellaneous.

APPENDIX C

Albani, Emma (1852–1930), Canadian soprano singer. Studied with Duprez in Paris and Lamperti at Milan. Made her first stage appearance at Messina in 1870, and first in London, at Covent Garden, in 1872; lived and taught there, but toured widely. D.B.E., 1925.

Barnby, Joseph (1838–96), English conductor, composer and organist. Held various organ appointments in London and gave annual Bach performances at St. Anne's, Soho. Precentor at Eton College, 1875–92, then principal of the Guildhall School of Music. Distinguished as choral conductor. He was knighted in 1892.

Bartoš, František (1837–1906), Moravian musicologist. Edited three collections of Moravian folk music.

Becker, Jan (1833–84), German violinist, settled at Florence from 1866, where he established the Florentine String Quartet.

Bendl, Karel (1838–97), Czech composer, who spent some of his life in France, Belgium and Italy, but was a nationalist of the school of Smetana. He wrote operas, choral and orchestral works, church and chamber music.

Bennevic, Antonín (Anton Bennewitz) (1833–1926), Czech violinist and teacher. Studied in Prague, was concert master at the Mozarteum at Salzburg, later at Stuttgart. Taught at the Prague Conservatory from 1866 and was its director from 1882 to 1901.

Bennett, Joseph (1831–1911), English music critic and author. Wrote programme notes for the Philharmonic Society's concerts and was for many years critic of the *Daily Telegraph*.

Blažek, František (1815–1900), Bohemian theorist. Taught at the Organ School of Prague, where Dvořák was his pupil.

Bouhy, Jacques Joseph André (1848–1929), Belgian baritone singer. Studied at Liége and Paris, where he made his first appearance at the Opéra in 1872. Director of the New York Conservatory, 1885–9. Lived and taught in Paris from 1907.

Brüll, Ignaz (1846–1907), Austrian composer and pianist. Studied in Vienna and toured as concert pianist. His best-known work is the opera, *Das goldene Kreuz* (*The Golden Cross*).

Buck, Dudley (1839–1909), American composer and organist. Studied at his native place, Hartford, Conn., at Leipzig and Dresden. Held many organ posts until 1903 and wrote a large variety of music as well as some books on the art.

Bülow, Hans von (1830–94), German pianist and conductor, first husband of Cosima Wagner. At first wholly devoted to Wagner's cause, but later equally enthusiastic for Brahms and Dvořák.

Černohorský, Bohuslav Matěj (1684–1742), Bohemian friar, composer and theorist. He held church appointments at Padua and Assisi, where Tartini was his pupil. From about 1735 he was director of music at St. James's Church in Prague.

Chézy, Wilhelmine (or *Helmina*) *von, née von Klencke* (1783–?), German dramatist and novelist. Wrote the libretto of Weber's *Euryanthe* and the play *Rosamunde* for which Schubert provided incidental music.

Cowen, Frederic (1852–1935), British composer and conductor. Studied in London, Leipzig and Berlin. Conductor by turns of the London Philharmonic Society, at Liverpool and at Manchester. Composed symphonies, operas, oratorios and many miscellaneous works.

Damrosch, Walter (born 1862), American conductor and composer of German descent. Studied in Germany and settled in U.S.A. in 1871. He became conductor of the New York Oratorio and Symphony Societies in 1885.

Door, Anton (1833–1919), Austrian pianist, pupil of Czerny and Sechter. He toured widely in Europe and taught at the Imperial Institute in Moscow and the Vienna Conservatorium.

Dussek, Jan Ladislav (*Dušek*) (1761–1812), Bohemian pianist and composer. He worked abroad in London and Paris, and as a composer was an important forerunner of the later great writers for the piano, many of whose characteristics he anticipated.

Ehlert, Louis (or *Ludwig*) (1825–84), German pianist, composer and critic. He was a pupil of Mendelssohn at Leipzig and taught at various places, including Berlin and Florence.

Fibich, Zdeněk (1850–1900), Czech composer. Very precociously gifted, he studied at Leipzig, Paris and Mannheim, but later became a musical nationalist to some extent. He wrote more than 600 works of various kinds, including operas, symphonies, chamber music, etc.

Finck, Henry Theophilus (1854–1926), American music critic and author. Musical editor of the New York *Evening Post*, 1881–1934. Among his books are studies of Wagner, Grieg and Paderewski.

Foerster, Josef (1833–1907), Bohemian composer and organist. Wrote mainly church music and was organist at the cathedral of Prague from 1887 and professor at the Prague Conservatory.

Foerster, Josef Bohuslav (born 1859), Czech composer, son of the preceding. Studied at the Prague Organ School. From 1893 to 1903 he was music critic and teacher at Hamburg, his wife, Berta Lauterer, being engaged at the opera there. Until 1918 they were in Vienna doing similar work, then returned to Prague, where he was appointed professor at the Conservatory, and director in 1922. He wrote much music of various kinds, including four symphonies, operas and chamber music.

Gassmann, Florian Leopold (1723–74), Bohemian composer. Lived in Vienna, where he was appointed musical director to the court in 1772.

Gericke, Wilhelm (1845–1925), Austrian conductor. Worked at Linz and Vienna, then became conductor of the Boston Symphony Orchestra, 1884–9 and 1898–1906.

Gevaert, François Auguste (1828–1908), Belgian musical historian and composer. He studied at Ghent, worked as organist there and made his name as a composer. Later travelled in Spain, Italy and Germany. Director of music at the Paris Opéra, 1867–70, whereafter he devoted himself mainly to the writing of important historical and theoretical works; but he had produced a number of operas and other music before. Director of Brussels Conservatoire from 1871.

Hanslick, Eduard (1825–1904), Austrian music critic. Wrote for the *Neue freie Presse* in Vienna and was lecturer on music at the university. A fierce opponent of Wagner and ardent partisan of Brahms. Wrote the book *Vom musikalisch Schönen* (*Of the Beautiful in Music*).

Hellmesberger, Joseph (1829–93), Austrian violinist. Professor of his instrument at the Vienna Conservatorium and its director from 1851; conductor of the Gesellschaft der Musikfreunde in 1859; leader at the Imperial Opera from 1860.

Herbeck, Johann (1831–77), Austrian conductor. Lived in Vienna; appointed conductor to the Gesellschaft der Musikfreunde in 1859 and director of the Court Opera in 1871.

Herbert, Victor (1859–1924), Irish-American cellist, conductor and composer. Studied in Germany and toured Europe; settled in New York in 1886 and remained for the rest of his life, becoming a naturalized American citizen.

Herold, Jiří (1875–1934), Czech viola player. Member of the Bohemian String Quartet from 1906 and professor at the Prague Conservatory from 1922.

Hoffmann, Karel (1872–1936), Czech violinist, pupil of Bennevic (q.v.) at the Prague Conservatory; founder of the Czech String Quartet in 1892 and professor at the Conservatory from 1922.

Holmes, Edward (1797–1859), English pianist, teacher and music critic. Worked in London at first but settled in New York in 1849. He wrote the earliest English biography of Mozart.

Janáček, Leoš (1854–1928), Czech (Moravian) composer, son of a poor schoolmaster, became a boy chorister at the monastery of the Austin Friars at Brno, later earned his living as music teacher and went to the Organ School in Prague for study. Conducted various choral societies, made some desultory studies at Leipzig and Vienna, and in 1881 returned to Brno to found an Organ School there. He taught there until it was taken over by the State in 1920, when he became professor of a master class at the Prague Conservatory. Made close studies of folk-song and speech. Wrote nearly a dozen works for the stage, orchestral, chamber and choral music, etc.

Joachim, Joseph (1831–1907), Hungarian (Germanized) violinist and composer. Lived successively at Leipzig, Weimar, Hanover and Berlin; frequent visitor to England; founder of the Joachim Quartet, 1869, and head of one of the musical departments of the Royal Academy of Arts in Berlin.

Kaan-Albest, Heinrich von (1852–1926), Galician composer. Taught at the Prague Conservatory, 1890–1907. He wrote two operas, a ballet and various other works.

Kneisel, Franz (1865–1926), Rumanian violinist. Studied in Bucharest and Vienna. Went to U.S.A. in 1885 and founded the Kneisel Quartet that year.

Knittl, Karel (1853–1907), Czech conductor. He became administrative director of the Prague Conservatory in 1901, Dvořák being the nominal director.

Krejčí, Josef (1822–81), Czech organist and composer. Became director of the Organ School in Prague, 1858, and of the Conservatory, 1865.

Kretzschmar, Hermann (1848–1924), German writer on music, teacher and conductor. He succeeded Joachim as head of the Berlin Hochschule in 1909. His chief literary work is a *Führer durch den Konzertsaal* (*Guide through the Concert-Room*), containing analytical notes on many classical works.

Lloyd, Edward (1845–1927), English tenor singer. Choirboy at Westminster Abbey in London until 1860 and Gentleman of the Chapel Royal from 1869. He made his first important public appearance at the Gloucester Festival in 1871.

Mackenzie, Alexander Campbell (1847–1935), Scottish composer. Studied in Germany and at the Royal Academy of Music in London, of which, after fourteen years as violinist and teacher at Edinburgh and some years at Florence, he became principal in 1888. He was knighted in 1895. His works include operas, oratorios and many orchestral, vocal and chamber compositions.

Mandyczewski, Eusebius (1857–1929), Austrian musicologist. Studied at the Vienna Conservatorium. In 1880 he became keeper of the archives of the Gesellschaft der Musikfreunde and in 1897 professor at the Conservatorium. Editor of the complete Schubert edition and of that of Haydn's works now abandoned.

Manns, August (1825–1907), German conductor. At first a clarinettist and violinist in various bands and orchestras in Germany, Later a bandmaster. He went to London as sub-conductor at the Crystal Palace, 1854, and became full conductor the following year, when he enlarged the orchestra. He began popular Saturday concerts in 1856 and conducted the Handel Festival, 1883–1900. Knighted in 1904.

Margulies, Adele (born 1863), Austrian pianist. Studied at the Vienna Conservatorium and settled in the U.S.A. in 1881.

Mason, Daniel Gregory (born 1873), American composer and writer on music, grandson of Lowell Mason, composer of 'Nearer, my God, to Thee,' and son of a member of the firm of piano makers, Mason & Hamlin. He graduated from Harvard and studied music in New York, later with d'Indy in France. Composed a variety of works and wrote a number of books on music.

Mühlfeld, Richard (1856–1907), German clarinet player. In the grand ducal orchestra at Meiningen from 1873. Brahms wrote his four late chamber works with clarinet parts, Opp. 114, 115, 120 (1 and 2), for him.

Mysliveček, Josef (1737–81), Bohemian composer. Wrote mainly Italian operas, with which he had a great success in Italy, Munich, Vienna and elsewhere.

Nedbal, Oskar (1874–1930), Czech conductor, viola player and composer. Pupil of Dvořák, member of the Bohemian String Quartet and from 1896 conductor of the Czech Philharmonic Society in Prague.

Nejedlý, Zdeněk (born 1878), Czech musicologist. Lecturer at Prague University and professor from 1905. His books include a history of music in Bohemia, works on Fibich, Mahler, Foerster, Novák and Smetana, on Beethoven's quartets and on Wagner.

Newmarch, Rosa (neé Jeaffreson) (1857–1940), English writer on music. Wrote programme notes for the Queen's Hall orchestral concerts, 1908–1927. She specialized in Russian and later Czech music and wrote several books on these subjects.

Nikisch, Artur (1855–1922), Hungarian-German conductor. Studied in Vienna and made his first appearance there in 1874. He held important appointments at Leipzig, Boston, Budapest and Berlin, and toured widely in Europe and America.

Novák, Vítězslav (born 1870), Czech composer. Studied law and philosophy in Prague and music with Dvořák. Held important teaching appointments there from 1909 to 1922, most of the prominent younger Czech composers having been his pupils. He has written large quantities of music of all kinds.

Ondříček, František (1859–1922), Czech violinist. Pupil of his father and at the Prague and Paris Conservatories. Made his first appearance in Paris in 1882 and then went on tour. Professor at the Vienna Conservatory, 1911–19, and then at that of Prague.

Parker, Horatio William (1863–1919), American composer and church musician. Studied at Boston and Munich, where he was a pupil of Rheinberger. He held various church appointments in New York, where he taught counterpoint at the National Conservatory under Dvořák's direction, and at Boston, and wrote much music of various kinds, large choral works being particularly numerous. The most important is the oratorio *Hora novissima*.

Procházka, Ludovic (1837–88), Czech musical propagandist who did much work on behalf of Smetana and published a collection of Slavonic folksongs.

Reinecke, Carl Heinrich Carsten (1824–1910), German pianist, conductor and composer. Settled at Leipzig from 1843; conductor of the Gewandhaus concerts there and professor of composition at the Conservatorium from 1860.

Richter, Hans (1843–1916), Austro-Hungarian conductor. Studied in Vienna, where he played the horn at the Kärntnertor Theatre, 1862–6. Assistant to Wagner, opera conductor at Budapest and Vienna. He was the first to conduct Wagner's *Ring* at Bayreuth in 1876. Conducted much in London between 1877 and 1910, and was conductor of the Hallé concerts in Manchester, 1900–11.

Rummel, Franz (1853–1901), German pianist born in London. Studied at the Brussels Conservatoire and later taught there, 1872–6. He toured widely in Europe and America and taught for some years at Stern's Conservatorium in Berlin.

Seidl, Anton (1850–98), German conductor born in Budapest. He studied at the Leipzig Conservatorium from 1870 and two years later went to Bayreuth as Wagner's assistant. Conductor at the Leipzig Opera,

1879–82, afterwards toured and conducted German opera at the Metro-politan in New York intermittently from 1885 to his death.

Šourek, Otakar (born 1883), Czech critic and musicologist. Dvořák's chief biographer and author of various works on him, including a thematic catalogue.

Stamitz, Johann Wenzel Anton (1717–57), Bohemian composer. Member of the Mannheim school of early symphonists.

Suk, Josef (1874–1935), Czech composer and viola player. Studied under Dvořák at the Prague Conservatory and in 1898 became his son-in-law. Second violin in the Czech String Quartet from 1892. In 1922 he was appointed professor of composition at the Prague Conservatory and became its director in 1930. His works are almost wholly instru-mental, though they include a Mass; his output in orchestral, chamber and piano music was equally large.

Thomas, Theodore (1835–1905), American conductor of German descent. Was taken to U.S.A. in 1845; appeared in New York with an orchestra formed by himself in 1862; organized the Cincinnati Musical Festival in 1873 and became conductor of the New York Philharmonic Society in 1877 and of the Chicago Symphony Orchestra in 1891.

Weinberger, Jaromír (born 1896), Czech composer. Studied with Hofmeister and Křička in Prague and with Reger in Germany. Professor of com-position at the Conservatory of Ithaca, New York, 1922–6, but returned to Europe to conduct and teach in various places. His best-known works are the opera, *Švanda the Bagpiper*, and the orchestral variations on *Under the spreading chestnut-tree*.

Wihan, Hanuš (1855–1920), Czech cellist. Studied at the Prague Con-servatory and made his first appearance in Berlin in 1876. Solo cellist in the Munich court orchestra, 1880, and professor at the Prague Con-servatory, 1887. Founded the Czech String Quartet in 1892. Dvořák dedicated his cello Concerto to him.

Zach, Jan (1699–1773), Bohemian composer. Conductor of the archduke's orchestra at Mainz. Wrote church and instrumental music.

Zvonař, Josef Leopold (1824–65), Bohemian theorist, writer on music and composer. Student at the Organ School in Prague, of which he later became director. One of the founders of the choral society Hlahol, (1861) and of the Umělecká Beseda (Society of Arts). He wrote the first Czech treatise on harmony (1861) and *Monuments of Early Czech Music* (1860–4).

BIBLIOGRAPHY

Bartoš, Josef, 'Antonín Dvořák.' (Prague, 1913.)

Carner, Mosco, 'Dvořák.' (Biographies of Great Musicians.) (Novello, London, 1941.)

Clapham, John, 'Dvořák and the Impact of America.' (*Musical Review,* Vol. XV, 1954, p. 203.)

——, 'Dvořák and the Philharmonic Society.' (*Music & Letters,* Vol. XXXIX, 1958, p. 123.)

——, 'Dvořák's First Cello Concerto.' (*Music & Letters,* Vol. XXXVII, 1956, p. 350.)

——, 'The Evolution of Dvořák's Symphony "From the New World."' (*Musical Quarterly,* Vol. XLIV, April 1958, p. 167.)

Fischl, Viktor (editor), 'Antonín Dvořák: his achievement.' (Lindsay Drummond, London, 1942.)

Hoffmeister, Karel, 'Antonín Dvořák.' (Prague, 1924.) Edited and translated by Rosa Newmarch. (John Lane, London, 1928.)

Horejs, 'Antonín Dvořák: Life and Work in Pictures.' (Artia, 1960.)

Šourek, Otakar, 'Antonín Dvořák: Life and Works.'

—— 'Dvořák: Letters and Reminiscences,' edited by O. Šourek.

—— 'Musical analyses of Dvořák's Works.' Vol. I, Orchestral Works; Vol. II, Chamber Music.

    (Translated by R. Finlayson-Samsour and all published by Artia, Prague, 1954.)

Stefan, Paul, 'Antonín Dvořák.' (New York, 1941.)

MISCELLANEOUS WORKS

Altmann, Wilhelm, 'Antonín Dvořák im Verkehr mit Fritz Simrock.' (*Simrock Year Book,* Vol. II, Berlin, 1929.)

Anderson, W. R., 'Dvořák.' *Lives of the Great Composers,* ed. by A. L. Bacharach. (London, 1935.)

Bráfová, Libuše, 'Rieger-Smetana-Dvořák' (in Czech). (Prague, 1913.)

Hadow, W. H., 'Antonín Dvořák.' *Studies in Modern Music,* Vol. II. (London, 1926.)

Hudební Matice Umělecké Besedy (published by). Collection of articles by various Czech writers. (Prague, 1912.)

Mason, Daniel Gregory, 'From Grieg to Brahms.' (New York, 1927.)

Newmarch, Rosa, 'The Music of Czechoslovakia.' (Oxford and London, 1942.)

Dvořák

Šourek, Otakar, Article in Cobbett's *Cyclopedic Survey of Chamber Music*. (Oxford and London, 1929.)
—— 'Anton Dvořáks Kammermusik' (*Simrock Year Book*, Vol. II, Berlin, 1929.)
—— 'Anton Dvořáks Orchesterwerke.' (*Simrock Year Book*, Vol. III, Berlin, 1930.)

REVIEWS AND MAGAZINES

Dvořák, Antonín, 'Music in America,' in collaboration with Edwin Emerson. (*Harper's Magazine*, New York, 1895.)
— 'Schubert,' in collaboration with Henry T. Finck. (*Century Magazine*, New York, 1894.)
Emde, H. von, 'Amerikanische Neger-Musik.' (*Die Musik*, Berlin, 1905.)
Evans, Ramona, 'Dvořák at Spillville.' (*The Palimpsest*, State Historical Society of Iowa, 1930.)
Hely-Hutchinson, Victor, 'Dvořák the Craftsman.' (*Music & Letters*, Vol. XXII, No. 4, London, 1941.)
Hollander, H., 'Dvořák the Czech.' (*Music & Letters*, Vol. XXII, No. 4, London, 1941.)
Hopkins, Harry Patterson, 'Student Days with Dvořák.' (*The Etude*, Philadelphia, 1913.)
Lockspeiser, Edward, 'The Dvořák Centenary.' (*Music & Letters*, Vol. XXII, No. 4, London, 1941.)
Kinsella, H. G., 'Dvořák at Spillville.' (*Musical America*, New York, 1933.)
Krehbiel, Henry E., 'Dvořák.' (*Century Magazine*, New York, 1892.)
Löwenbach, Jan, 'Dvořák in America.' (*Hudební Review*, Prague, 1911, one of two Dvořák numbers issued that year.) (In Czech.)
Nejedlý, Zdeněk, 'Smetana und Dvořák.' (*Prager Rundschau*, Prague, 1934.)
Pellegrini, H., 'Personal Memories of Dvořák' (in German). (*Neue Musikzeitung*, Stuttgart, 1914.)
Shelley, Harry Rowe (and others), 'Dvořák as I knew him.' (*The Etude*, Philadelphia, 1913.)
Stefan, Paul, 'Dvořák once more in America' (hitherto unpublished letters). (*Musical America*, New York, 1938.)
Thurber, Jeanette M., 'Dvořák as I knew him.' (*The Etude*, Philadelphia, 1919.)

INDEX

Index